CATHERINE BOOTH

Also by Roger J Green
  War on Two Fronts: The Redemptive Theology
    of William Booth

Catherine Booth

*A Biography of the Co-founder
of The Salvation Army*

ROGER J GREEN

THE SALVATION ARMY

MONARCH
Crowborough

British Library Cataloguing Data
A catalogue record for this book is available
from the British Library

Co-published with The Salvation Army
101 Queen Victoria Street, London EC4P 4EP.

*Cover portrait painting of Catherine Booth
by Lt Col Peter Dalziel.*

ISBN 1 85424 380 2

Designed and produced by Bookprint Creative Services
P.O. Box 827, BN21 3YJ, England for
MONARCH PUBLICATIONS
Broadway House, The Broadway
Crowborough, East Sussex TN6 1HQ
Printed in Great Britain

Reproduced from the original text by arrangement
with Baker Books

If the presence of women is to be felt to the degree that Catherine passionately wished, particularly within the church, a call to action is in order. This biography of Catherine Booth as presented by Dr. Roger J. Green is just that. . . . The legacy entrusted to us by this beautiful life is seen in the record of shared ministry, women and men together, which has been the hallmark of Salvation Army service across the years. It is a legacy to be cherished and acted upon in every generation.

Dr. Kay F. Rader, Mrs. General
The Salvation Army International Headquarters
London

An up-to-date and insightful examination of the life of Catherine Booth, the "Army mother." It's a theologically sensitive analysis of Catherine Booth's impact on Army mission and methods, avoiding both the extremes of hagiography and unfair critique. It contains a wealth of primary source material, appropriately contextualized and interpreted in a clear and cogent narrative style.

Dr. R. David Rightmire
Professor of Bible and Theology
Asbury College
Wilmore, Kentucky

Roger J. Green's comprehensive biography of Catherine Booth . . . genuinely captures the soul and spirit of a true heroine—one of the most renowned women in the history of the church. . . . As cofounder with her husband of The Salvation Army, she became the consummate wife, mother, friend, advocate, theologian, and preacher. This book is a treasure trove of inspiration, insight, and instruction that belongs on the bookshelf of every pastor, student of church history, and, indeed, every Christian.

Lt. Colonel William W. Francis
Principal
The Salvation Army School for Officer Training
Suffern, New York

This book is dedicated to the countless women soldiers and officers of The Salvation Army who have steadfastly followed in the work of Catherine Booth, but especially to one—my mother, Mrs. Brigadier Dorothy B. Green, gentle warrior of the Lord.

Contents

Foreword

"The twentieth century will not close without the presence of women being felt," declared a former United States congresswoman. A woman before her time, nineteenth-century co-founder of The Salvation Army, Catherine Mumford Booth, can almost be heard to say, "Could it have taken so long?" Indeed as early as 1860 she declared, "Whether the Church will allow women to speak in her assemblies can only be a matter of time." In 1930 her illustrious daughter, Evangeline Booth, first woman General of The Salvation Army, said, "The forces of prejudice, of selfishness, of ignorance, which have arrested the progress and curtailed the influence of womankind for centuries are receding from the foreground of the future."

Now, facing the end of the twentieth century, time is of the essence. If the presence of women is to be felt to the degree that Catherine passionately wished, particularly within the church, a call to action is in order. This biography of Catherine Booth as presented by Dr. Roger J. Green is just that.

He writes of things past from the perspective of the future. His language, style, and presentation of this extraordinary nineteenth-century woman are twentieth-century "reader-friendly." The fascination with which he has painstakingly pursued his study of Catherine Booth's life has enabled Dr. Green to present a striking portrait that begs response.

The reader is at once enthralled by her life and inspired by her example, though her achievements may seem to be beyond the reach of all but the most gifted.

Catherine Booth was constrained by her compassion for the lost. She was possessed of a measure of charisma that matched the strength of her "settled views." Yet when thrust into public ministry by an inescapable sense of calling, she found herself as journalist W. T. Stead put it, "drawn forward against her own strong natural opposition."

Even Catherine Booth was not always strong. And Roger Green has been faithful to show her for the woman she was. In presenting each stage of her life, he has combined admiration with honesty. The result is a delightfully captivating and revealing account of her remarkable life.

Catherine Booth was living proof of God's unlimited gifts. Although it is as preacher that she should be most notably remembered, her achievements in other areas of service were equally impressive. While mother of eight lively children, she established herself as a credible author, teacher, minister to the poor, preacher to the prosperous, advocate for the powerless, and a full participant in the development and leadership of the Movement.

The legacy entrusted to us by this beautiful life is seen in the record of shared ministry, women and men together, which has been the hallmark of Salvation Army service across the years. It is a legacy to be cherished and acted upon in every generation. Dr. Green is of the conviction that had it not been for Catherine Booth there would have been no Christian Mission, nor Salvation Army. Were her legacy to be lost, the Army of today—and tomorrow—would surely be less than she desired and God intended.

Kay F. Rader, D.D.
Mrs. General
International Headquarters
London, England

Acknowledgments

This has been a work in progress for many years, and I am indebted to several people. I will attempt to mention here the most important and ask forgiveness of those whose names I have omitted. First is my wife Karen. She has not only been accepting of the time spent on this work but has encouraged me all along the way. I owe her my continued thanks.

I am grateful also to Gordon College for their assistance in this work. The visionary Faculty Development Plan, which has supported me with needed finances and sabbaticals for this project, is much appreciated. I am especially grateful to one member of my Faculty Development Plan, Dr. Marvin R. Wilson, Harold J. Ockenga Professor of Biblical and Theological Studies at Gordon College and a friend of many years. His help in choosing a publisher as well as his assistance in many of the details of putting a project like this together have been considerable.

Of the endorsements that have been given to this work, two have come from close friends—one from Lt. Colonel William W. Francis, presently the principal of The Salvation Army's College for Officer Training in Suffern, New York, and the second from Dr. R. David Rightmire, professor of Bible and theology at Asbury College. Both of these gentlemen are students of Salvation Army history and theology.

I am grateful, also, to my friend Mrs. General Kay F. Rader of The Salvation Army for agreeing to write the foreword to this book. In spite of an extremely busy and demanding schedule of international engagements, she readily undertook this responsibility and, by doing so, affirmed our common interest in the life and ministry of Catherine Booth.

The research for this work was conducted in many different places, but my thanks are especially extended to the staffs of three institutions. First, the staff of the British Library were constantly helpful. Also, Susan Mitchem, the archivist/supervisor of The Salvation Army Archives and Research Center at The Salvation Army National Headquarters in Alexandria, Virginia, and her staff were always willing to lend assistance, answer my questions, and share the pictures of Catherine Booth used in this biography. And finally, of inestimable assistance were Lt. Colonel Jenty Fairbank and Gordon Taylor of The Salvation Army International Heritage Centre in London, England. It is beyond all doubt that I could not have completed this work without their constant assistance through these many years. They and their staff have been extremely generous in their time and resources, and the many informal conversations with them were often as illuminating and helpful in my research as were the hours spent in my research at the center. I look forward to many more years of work with these dedicated people.

The staff at Baker Book House has been helpful, but I thank especially Dan Van't Kerkhoff. His constant acknowledgment of my work and his continued advice have been invaluable.

In spite of the assistance and encouragement of these as well as many others, the work that follows is entirely my own. I offer it to the reader, accepting the credit for what may be of value as well as the blame for any failure.

Introduction

꧁꧂

Catherine Booth began her public speaking in 1860, and years later, after the conclusion of one of her addresses in Exeter Hall in London, a gentleman exclaimed, "If ever I am charged with a crime, don't bother to engage any of the great lawyers to defend me; get that woman!" Such was often the effect of the diminutive and frail Catherine Mumford Booth on many of those who heard her. Her preaching was sometimes likened to that of a lawyer: mastering her facts, arguing her case, and pressing home her claims in the minds and hearts of her audience. This was not always the case. Catherine was reared in a strict Methodist home and, except for the occasional female class meeting leader, saw few women in places of responsibility and fewer still preaching the gospel. She entered public life reluctantly but responded in earnest to what she perceived to be the calling of God.

Even as a child she was deeply convicted about spiritual matters. She grew into both a knowledge and an assurance that she was a child of God by grace, which was confirmed in later life with an experience of sanctification. Although her careful religious rearing as well as her fear of being influenced by the world led her throughout her lifetime to live a strict personal life (there were no cards, novels, frivolous clothing, or alcohol allowed in the Booth home), it would be false to conclude that the religious life was for her a dull habit. The opposite was the case. She regarded religion joyfully, centered on a living and vital relationship with Jesus Christ and manifested by a life of consecrated service for Christ and his kingdom. This was biblical blessedness for Catherine Booth, and she reveled in the wedding feast of the kingdom of God.

Catherine was a woman of clear convictions and she was both single-minded and consistent in those convictions throughout her lifetime. She often referred to her "settled views," sharing them and trying to convince others of their correctness and of the righteousness of her causes. Such views were the substance of her writing, her teaching, and, above all, her preaching. Her friend W. T. Stead wrote of her, "She preached out of the fullness of her heart. As she had lived so she preached."[1]

To the several vocations of her life—wife, mother, friend, advocate, and preacher—Catherine consecrated herself completely. However, by her own admission, she felt most at home on the platform of a place like Exeter Hall in London or in a Salvation Army corps preaching the gospel. That was the life she felt destined to, and it is as preacher that Catherine should be most notably remembered.

She moved people deeply with her verbal skills, her commitment to the ideas she espoused, and the passion of her delivery. She served her Christ and her generation well by founding, along with her husband William, a mission and an Army. She gave herself in utter abandonment to God and to his work as she perceived it. In spite of personal faults and physical frailties, she was unselfish in her devotion to God and his kingdom and perceived the work of The Salvation Army as of divine origin and initiative. It could never be said of Catherine Mumford Booth that she thought of herself before others or that preaching the gospel or defending her beloved Army were means toward fulfilling her own needs or stroking her own ego. Seriousness about her vocation and commitment to a cause and a life greater than herself prevented Catherine from the kind of egocentric ministry too often seen in our times.

This writer has researched many aspects of the life and ministry of Catherine Booth and has made every attempt to deal with them honestly and openly. Her faults have not been ignored, and her lack of good judgment on some matters will not be hidden from the eyes of the readers.

There are three primary biographies of Catherine Booth as well as many briefer biographies to which the present writer is indebted. W. T. Stead, already referred to in this introduction, wrote a glowing account of the woman he so admired. His is a brief biography but helpful in that it was written from the perspective of a contemporary of Catherine's outside The Salvation Army. Catherine's son-in-law, Frederick Booth-Tucker, wrote a laborious two-volume work titled *The Life of Catherine Booth, The Mother of The Salvation Army*. The strength of this source is the general reliability of the chronology of Catherine's life. The problems with the Booth-Tucker biography, however, are many—the two chief ones being his vision of his mother-in-law as virtue incarnate, with absolutely no problems, faults, or blemishes, and his often inaccurate and sometimes misleading quotations from original sources such as letters.

The third biography is by Catherine Booth's granddaughter and namesake, Catherine Bramwell-Booth. This biography is also problematic in not presenting a complete picture of the cofounder of The Salvation Army. Also the book is constructed in such a way that matters of chronology in Catherine Booth's life are very difficult to follow. Nevertheless, there is helpful material here, especially in the use of Catherine's correspondence.

While relying on these and other biographies, as well as a wealth of additional material, I have attempted to see Catherine as she was—faults and all. It is of no service trying to understand this great woman if her humanity does not shine clearly through the text. In order to accomplish this, I have attempted, perhaps in a more limited way than I would have liked, to place her in the context of her Victorian world as well as her Wesleyan framework. She was a woman immeasurably indebted to such a background and likewise a woman who contributed to the shaping of the culture in which she lived and labored. This was especially true of the evangelical Protestant culture of the nineteenth century.

Her greatest contribution there, of course, was that of liberating thousands of women from the constrictions of a fallen culture for service in the kingdom of God through the ministry of The Christian Mission and especially The Salvation Army. This was her greatest legacy, which she understood to be the fulfillment of the biblical promise that "your sons and your daughters shall prophesy" (Acts 2:17), the natural response to the glorious grace of God in Christ, and the joyous vocational following of the Savior's life, ministry, death, and resurrection. "Do you also follow Christ?" was Catherine's constant and pressing question to her listeners.

To the readers of this biography, I offer the following explanations. First, I have attempted to let Catherine speak for herself. In this regard, I trust that the quotations from Catherine—some of them rather long—are nevertheless illuminating and will give the reader a sense of this woman's passion for the things of God that mattered most to her.

Second, I have worked hard to steer a delicate middle course with this biography. I trust that this book will be helpful to the lay reader interested in the life and ministry of this great woman and in the history of The Salvation Army. However, for the serious scholar intent on pursuing further research on women in ministry, Victorian studies, or the history of Evangelicalism, I would like to think that the text as well as the notes and the bibliographic references will be of assistance. I repeat here what I wrote in a previous work—this is a beginning and not an ending. I gladly refrain from the bane of contemporary scholarship in which members of the academy think that their word is the last and final one on every matter under the sun. I look forward to my own continued research of Catherine Booth as well as to the writings of others who find in this subject a genuine fascination beyond a general interest.

In the meantime I offer here what I pray is a new and fresh look at this woman, this cofounder of The Salvation Army, Catherine Mumford Booth. And I trust that the time spent in reading this book will prove to be beneficial to everyone.

1

Beginnings

࿐

Life from 1829 to 1851

Catherine Booth preached her last sermon on Thursday, June 21, 1888, at the City Temple in London, nearly thirty years after the beginning of her public ministry. Dr. Joseph Parker, one of "the most famous preachers in England,"[1] had invited the cofounder of The Salvation Army to preach in his magnificent Congregational church, built only fourteen years earlier. Preaching was a remarkable accomplishment for a woman who, by this time in her life, was seriously debilitated from cancer, yet she took this occasion once again to preach the gospel. She was so incapacitated from the strain of her preaching that she had to sit quietly on the platform for almost an hour before she could be removed to the cab and taken home.

She preached for about an hour, as was her custom, and was determined that her illness was not going to deter her from this opportunity. After all, "The area and a good part of the gallery of the City Temple were filled with an audience consisting, for the most part, of business gentlemen and outside friends who had come to hear Mrs. Booth preach."[2] A longtime friend and supporter, T. A. Denny, had read passages from both 1 and 2 Corinthians, which provided the texts for the sermon. Catherine chose in this last sermon to preach on the missionary task of the church and on the possibility of converting the entire world to Jesus Christ. With her sure understanding of the Bible to encourage her, she delivered in a straightforward manner her sermon as a series of facts "regarding which there can be no dispute" and "no division of opinion."[3] She set out to convince her congregation of professing Christians of both the truth of the doctrine of holiness and the subsequent empowerment of a holy people to win the world for Jesus.

Defending the teachings of her Salvation Army, especially that of holiness of heart and life, she proclaimed:

> Perhaps on no point has The Salvation Army suffered persecution more than on this one point of its teaching—that it teaches a Saviour not only willing to pardon but who does pardon absolutely, and who communicates a sense of that pardon by His Holy Spirit to the hearts of those who truly repent and sincerely believe, with a living faith, in Him, and not only washes their past sins away but has the power to keep them from their sins, and will, if they trust in Him, enable them to live in righteousness and holiness all their lives, walking in obedience to His commands, keeping that inner law of which we have just heard—the law of Christ—which is the most perfect law and fulfills all others—loving the Lord thy God with all thy heart, mind, soul and strength, and thy neighbour as thyself.[4]

Catherine was certain she understood the Bible rightly on this and many other doctrines of the Christian faith, including doctrines of sin and salvation. She also made a clear distinction between Christian ethics and civilized morals. But because this was intended to be a missionary address, she prepared a sermon appropriate to the hour and concentrated primarily on a missionary challenge. After reviewing the missionary and evangelistic enterprise of the church to date, she confessed, "For my own part, my soul blushes with shame, and if I did not believe that we were inaugurating a higher standard of devotion, and a greater and more comprehensive idea of self-abandonment and labour for God, I should die of grief. I believe God is stirring a few real people all over the world, and giving them to see the effects of the past."[5]

By this time in her life and ministry, Catherine had expanded her vision of Christianity's reason for existence. She firmly believed that salvation encompassed not only the soul of the individual but a fallen cosmos and that Christ's Christianity would bring about "peace, purity, good-will, beneficence, truth, and justice which always follow in the wake of true Christianity."[6] In characteristic opinionated and forthright language, she continued, "And I say if these results do not follow it is a bastard Christianity; its fruits prove it to be so."[7] A just order would include the emancipation of slaves, the rescue of downtrodden women, and the care of helpless children. The care of the disenfranchised follows from a correct understanding of the Christian gospel, so preached Catherine Booth. She pressed the truth of the gospel on her listeners that day and left no middle ground for compromise, comfort, or security. Speaking of that gospel, she said, "If it is not true, be done with it; if it is true, act upon it!"[8]

There was no lack of strength or conviction in either the words or the manner of this woman of only fifty-nine years of age and of rapidly failing health. She did not merely or even politely occupy the pulpit of City Temple that day—she dominated it and commanded likewise the attention of her congregation as she drove home her message. An American in her audience that morning, Dr. Parkes Cadman, recorded many years later, "I have not heard since, anything which moved me more deeply."[9] This had been her style for nearly thirty years of her public ministry, and thousands of people in England had become accustomed to both the words and the presence of this preacher.

How Catherine Booth came to this high point in her life and ministry is a story worth telling afresh, and it begins on the day of her birth, as Catherine Mumford, January 17, 1829, at Ashbourne in Derbyshire, England.

The background and beginnings for Catherine Mumford were, to say the least, commonplace and uninspiring. Her mother, Sarah—whose maiden name was Milward—grew up in a loveless environment. Her mother had died when she was young, and her father and an aunt reared her. Before Sarah's marriage to John Mumford, she had had at least one unhappy relationship with a gentleman to whom she became engaged. But the wedding was called off, presumably because she learned that appearances are sometimes deceiving, and he was not the kind of man she could have loved had she known more about his true self. It was during a time of severe depression, brought about when she learned that this gentleman had gone mad, that this Church of England woman came to full consciousness of some facts about herself and her God. She realized that she was a sinner in rebellion against God; that God had made the provision of salvation through his Son's life, death, and resurrection; and that she needed to respond to God's grace by faith.

Although her *Book of Common Prayer* provided some consolation to her at this decisive time in her life, especially when she contemplated the words, "I believe in the forgiveness of sins," it was through the ministry of the local Methodist preacher that she repented and trusted by faith in Christ to save her. She thereupon joined the Methodists. She not only affirmed the Methodist doctrines such as holiness but strived to live the pious and rather ascetic life customary of many nineteenth-century Methodists with whom she entered into fellowship. There was for her a necessary renunciation of certain activities that she now considered "worldly"—such as cardplaying, dancing, or attending the theater. There was also a conscious attempt at plainness of dress, hairstyle, and manner, which she associated with Methodist piety. No frivolities, extravagances, or glitter and gold for her. All this renunciation gave pause to her father and aunt. They were decidedly condescending toward Sarah for her newfound religious experience and for her religious eccentricities.

Sarah Milward's life was about to change, however. An itinerant Methodist lay preacher by the name of John Mumford came to Ashbourne to conduct religious services. Sarah Milward and

John Mumford met, became engaged, and, although the father and aunt protested, were married. Very little is known of John Mumford's background. He was a carriage builder by trade, committed to total abstinence, and interested in politics. But there was a sort of sadness about him, which increasingly came to light during Catherine's lifetime. When Catherine was still a child, her father gave up his lay preaching and grew increasingly diffident toward religious matters.

His troubles increased. Often penniless, he turned his back on total abstinence and evidenced a drinking problem and eventually renounced religion outright. The following entry appears in Catherine's diary, written when she was eighteen:

> I sometimes get into an agony of feeling while praying for my dear father. O my Lord, answer prayer and bring him back to Thyself! Never let that tongue, which once delighted in praising Thee and in showing others Thy willingness to save, be engaged in uttering the lamentations of the lost. O awful thought! Lord have mercy! Save, oh save him in any way Thou seest best, though it be ever so painful. If by removing me Thou canst do this, cut short Thy work and take me home.[10]

There were times in Catherine's adult life when she had to support her father financially, and often things seemed desperate. Happily, in 1861 John Mumford was led back to the Lord and the church by his daughter and even attended some of her public meetings.

At the time of Catherine's birth, though, there was stability in the Mumford home, with her father both practicing his trade and preaching the gospel. Catherine was the only daughter. There were four sons, but only John survived past infancy. Very little is known about John, and after his move to America at the age of sixteen, he plays no significant part in his sister's life. Catherine recounted the earliest recollection of her life as

> that of being taken into a room by my mother, to see the body of a little brother who had just died. I must have been very young at the

time, scarcely more than two years old. But I can remember, to this day, the feelings of awe and solemnity with which the sight of death impressed my babymind. Indeed, the effect produced on that occasion has lasted to this very hour. I am sure that many parents enormously under-estimate the capacity of children to *retain* impressions made upon them in early days.[11]

Catherine Mumford—or Kate, as she was called—was close to her mother, and that companionship was nourished and cherished by both mother and daughter until Mrs. Mumford's death on December 16, 1869. Sarah Mumford was, to say the least, a strong-willed woman with definite ideas on many subjects. However, she had no stronger or more forthright opinions on any matter than that of rearing, nurturing, educating, and training children in the home. She had an unnatural dread of her son and daughter being infected by relationships with other children outside the home and in the schools. She "shrank from permitting her daughter to suffer the contaminating influence of badly brought up children."[12] She positively dreaded the thought of teachers somehow instilling rebellion against parents and of inculcating false values and cheap morals. Public education, she was convinced, endangered the soul. There would be no such pitfalls for Sarah Mumford's children. Catherine herself reflected such attitudes in later years.[13]

Given Sarah Mumford's many prejudices against public schooling, it is rather remarkable that she decided finally to place Catherine, at the age of twelve, in school from 1841 to 1843. She was convinced by a mutual friend in the Boston chapel that the teachers in this particular school were of one mind with Mrs. Mumford on the education and training of children within a religious environment, where serious study was promoted and where discipline kept the children on the straight and narrow path. Catherine's educational sights were raised with this two-year experience as she studied history, geography, English composition, and mathematics. Her formal education outside of the home was ended abruptly, unfortunately, by a problem with her spine. She spent the next few months in bed, and her education continued as it had begun—in the home under the watchful eye of her mother.

In later years she saw this misfortune as providential because she turned her attention to the study of church history and theology. Her reading included works by Butler, Wesley, Finney, Fletcher, Moshein, and Neander, a diverse and unfocused smattering but nonetheless obviously attractive to Catherine. It would be Finney especially whom she would learn to appreciate.

Other than her brother, John, young Kate had no childhood friends and very few passing acquaintances. Her education in the home was an isolating experience, but that she did not react to it adversely is witnessed by the fact that she educated her own eight children in precisely the same way. She saw virtue in such an educational experiment in spite of the fact that the environment created in the home was an artificial one, and certainly the children must at times have missed the pleasures of both learning and playing with other children of their own ages and interests. Also, her own children had educational opportunities later in their lives that she did not have. Her granddaughter noted, "As she grew older she felt increasingly the intellectual limitations of her immediate circle and quite guilelessly remarked on finding herself 'different.'"[14] Indeed, later in life Catherine herself stated, "I have often repined and murmured at the permissions of Providence with reference to my education and *bitterly wept* for the loss of advantages, but I thank God for what no education could have given me, and for what thousands who have possessed all its advantages *have not*."[15]

What took place in the Mumford home under the tutelage of Sarah Mumford may best be described as a school for training and learning. W. T. Stead rightly noted, "The austere but tender mother was all the world to her daughter: her companion, her confidante, her spiritual directress, her teacher."[16] The school for training involved the training of the soul and the shaping of the character. Sarah Mumford taught not only the precepts of the Bible, the importance of prayer, the fear of the Lord, and the necessity of holy, principled living; she also instilled in Kate the need for constantly examining her conscience to determine if there were sins that were unconfessed or faults that needed to be corrected. Constant and vigilant introspection, coupled with Mrs. Mumford's priestly assurance of complete forgiveness by the Lord, was the key to this school of character. Kate yearned after God and wanted to be found pleasing in his eyes. Again, what Kate learned she gladly taught, because what has been described became a model for the rearing of the eight Booth children in later years.

The home was also an educational institution. The principal learning experience centered around a command of the English language through constant reading and writing. Young Catherine learned to read by reading religious books, but it comes as no surprise that the focus of her reading was the Bible. She read long passages from Scripture, pronouncing difficult words and names until she got them right to the satisfaction of her mother. Before the age of twelve, Kate had read through the entire Bible eight times, and such familiarity with the Bible, begun at that young age, continued throughout her lifetime and formed a biblical foundation for her later preaching and teaching.

Two things Sarah Mumford did not introduce into the curriculum, primarily because of her own notion of what was worldly and of the devil. First, there would be no novels or works of fiction. She refused to have Catherine "waste her time or sympathies upon anything of an imaginary character, however excellent the moral intended to be drawn."[17] Second—and here Mrs. Mumford reflected plain prejudice—French would not be studied in the Mumford household. It was, she reasoned, the language of infidels, renegades, and godless heathens. She had more than just a distaste for the French language and all the literature the French produced—she was positively horrified by it. In this decision Catherine disagreed with her mother, although not at the time. She wrote in later life:

> I cannot but think that on this point my dear mother was mistaken, and that she might have allowed me the opportunity of acquiring the language, while guarding me from the evils she so dreaded. I have

found this to be possible in the case of my own children, having taken every care that they should read no French books concerning the purity and safety of which I was not perfectly satisfied. At the same time I believe that thousands have indirectly been ruined, both for this world and the next, owing to the use in schools and academies of the works of Voltaire, and other brilliant but ungodly French writers.[18]

Catherine was a child of delicate health, and one must ask what influence her physical health had on a rather reclusive childhood. Or did her confinement to home and family accentuate her childhood ailments, making them worse in her own mind than they actually were? In any case, during her childhood, she and her mother were constantly concerned about matters of her health, and an almost unnatural preoccupation with health problems would be characteristic of Catherine throughout her entire life.

In 1834 the Mumford family moved from Ashbourne to Boston in Lincolnshire where Catherine's father continued his trade as a carriage maker. By this time preaching was no longer an avocation with him, but he was still much involved in the temperance movement. The only gospel he now preached was that of temperance, by which he meant total abstinence.

During the middle thirties a growing movement for temperance turned towards teetotalism. The word *teetotal* was invented by a Lancashire working man in 1834. For it was quickly discovered that a demand for temperance was morally weak compared with a demand for total abstention. And so began the bands of hope, pledges, processions which reached national influence and even the Irish people in the campaigns of Father Mathew. In England they were usually led by Methodists or old dissenters. . . . By 1842 there was a group of about six hundred separated from Conference and organized as the Teetotal Wesleyan Methodists.[19]

Temperance meetings were conducted in the Mumford household, and Catherine began to realize at that early age what issues were at stake in this social cause. There were indelible impressions made on her young mind, and throughout her adult life few causes would be more important than that of total abstinence. So critical was this matter to her that many years after 1834, while drawing up a list of qualifications that any future husband must possess, Catherine determined that he must be a total abstainer.[20] She spoke about this conviction with William Booth when she met him. At the time he drank moderately.[21]

It is beyond doubt that Catherine's critical faculties after the move to Boston when she was only five years old are highly exaggerated by some of her biographers. She could not possibly as yet have had a full awareness of the social, political, religious, and economic ramifications of the arguments of the temperance leaders whom she heard in the Mumford household. It can be said, however, that her interest in the movement did increase— by the time she was twelve, she was the secretary of a Juvenile Temperance Society.

Another social issue that was taking shape in the heart and mind of young Catherine was that of the treatment of animals. She suffered extremely, both physically and emotionally, when she saw animals mistreated; and she often interceded personally to prevent a horse from being beaten or a donkey from being harshly prodded. In later years her knowledge of the slaughter of animals caused her to become a strict vegetarian, a position shared by William Booth. The eight Booth children were reared in a vegetarian home. Likewise, vegetarianism was encouraged in the followers of Catherine and William Booth in their religious societies.[22] The proper treatment of animals was also one of the stipulations for membership.[23] Catherine herself took a stand against the barbaric sport of foxhunting practiced among the gentility.[24] She once wrote, "My childish heart rejoiced greatly in the speculations of Wesley and Butler with regard to the possibility of a future life for animals, in which God might make up to them for the suffering and pain inflicted on them here."[25]

One poignant incident in her childhood was so dramatic and, as she believed, so utterly cruel that she recalled it years later with great sadness. The Mumford family owned a retriever named Waterford, and Catherine recounts a special bond between her and that dog, stating that they were "inseparable companions."[26] Catherine visited her father one day at his place of business, leaving the dog outside while she went in to speak with her father. She evidently stumbled after entering the building and cried out. Waterford, ever protective of his mistress, crashed through the large plate glass window, causing, so Mr. Mumford thought, needless damage to his business establishment. Mr. Mumford was so incensed by this that he had the animal immediately destroyed. Catherine was inconsolable.

This incident is instructive not only because it partially explains Catherine's continuing sensitivity for all suffering creatures, but it also helps to explain why she was close to her mother, who was the stable and steady influence in her life. From all indications, John Mumford was impetuous, perhaps moody, and definitely given to emotional peaks and valleys, as his joining of various causes demonstrates. He was sometimes religious, sometimes not. At one time all consumed with the temperance movement, at another time an alcoholic himself. Occasionally thoroughly immersed in his work, but many times likely to be out of work. He gave people around him reason not to trust him. And there were undoubtedly times when Catherine and her mother also doubted his stability, justifiably so.

There appears to be a loneliness in Catherine's young life, resulting from the way she was reared. When she wrote many years later about the incident surrounding her dog's death, she ended her account with this insightful but sad sentence: "The fact that I had no childhood companions doubtless made me miss my speechless one the more."[27]

Catherine's home was certainly a religious one—after the religion of the Wesleyan Methodists. She was reared in that tradition and was used to attending the Wesleyan chapel in Boston. In fact, from all accounts, even as a young girl she enjoyed going to the meetings of the Wesleyans, hearing the often dramatic preaching, and at times writing her own outlines of the sermons. Her religious training in both home and chapel emphasized holiness of heart, holy living manifested in a life of self-denial, and the evangelistic work of the church in both home and foreign missions. It is worth noting that such characteristics, along with the primacy of preaching, would later become central to the life of The Christian Mission and The Salvation Army.

When Catherine was fifteen, the family made a move that would prove fortuitous for Catherine's future. They left the secure life they enjoyed in Boston and moved to London, settling in Brixton. Catherine had never visited London and could not have known that much of the remainder of her life would be lived out in this great but frightening city. At this time, only her mother joined the Wesleyan church in Brixton. Catherine regularly accompanied her mother, was attentive to the sermons, and continued to enjoy Methodist singing. She also joined the weekly Methodist class meeting led by a Mrs. Keay. These meetings, formulated by John Wesley, were considered by Wesley himself to be the strength of Methodism and the source of its spiritual power and influence. The class meeting provided an opportunity for the members to study Scripture, confess sins, receive assurance of pardon, witness to lives of holiness, and otherwise support and strengthen the sisters and brothers of the movement. Membership in these classes would usually number about a dozen people, and the class meeting leaders were laypeople. Henry Rack wrote, "The class meeting became so vital and integral a part of the Methodist polity and seemed so clearly to express its values of a mixture of individual and collective piety and 'fellowship' that it achieved an almost mythical status as a picture of true Methodism. An early preacher found that the Methodists in class 'lived as the Christians of old, having all things in common.'"[28]

[Neither Catherine nor her mother were completely pleased with life in that Methodist church. In contrast to the Boston church, the members of this community appeared to be "in a much more cold, worldly, and backslidden condition than those at Boston."[29] The Mumfords had distinct views about separation from the world in terms of dress, total abstinence, and attitude and found few Methodists in Brixton who shared such an outlook. Furthermore, while they were encouraged by the preaching, they were discouraged by a lack of energy in the prayer meetings that followed the sermon. This was the time, so they had learned in Boston and so Catherine had read in Finney, for reaping the harvest of the sermon, which had awakened the consciences of the people, pointed out their sin and need for forgiveness, and reminded them of the judgment of God as well as his love. In brief, this was the time for getting people saved—helping them cross the river into the promised land of God's kingdom and the full assurance of his pardon. Too little of this was being done at Brixton to suit the taste of Sarah Mumford and her daughter.[30]

The class meeting Catherine attended was likewise a source of disappointment. While she appreciated the leader (though disapproving of the worldly life of her daughter), she felt that the meeting lacked the seriousness and decisiveness originally designed by Wesley. She found the meetings innocuous, the testimonies demonstrating no power, and the exhortations long on comfort but short on challenge to live the life of the disciple of Christ, following him, if need be, to the cross. Catherine later wrote:

> There can be no doubt that the class meeting, as originally intended by Wesley, was an excellent arrangement, but the mere asking of empty questions as to how a person is getting on, and the leaving them to answer by the platitudes usual on such occasions, is to daub them with untempered mortar, and to lead them forth in the way of hollow profession and uncertainty. Pointed questions should be put, such as: Have you enjoyed private prayer during the week? How far have you been enabled to obey the precepts of Jesus Christ in dealing with your family or your business? Have you maintained a conscience void of offense toward men as well as toward God in these matters? Have you faithfully made use of your opportunities for doing good? How many have you spoken to about their souls? Have you succeeded in leading anybody to decision for salvation or consecration? Have you practiced any self-denial in order to extend the Kingdom of Christ?
>
> Such questions pressed home with the aid of the Holy Spirit would compel confession, and involve a repentance and reconsecration pro-

ductive of real results. But of course questions of this kind presuppose that those who ask them are themselves living up to the standard which they set before others, and this, alas, is too often not the case![31]

The discontent Catherine felt with the Brixton Methodists is probably best explained by understanding her own spiritual pilgrimage up to this point in her life. She had been raised in a tradition that stressed the salvation of the soul from a life of worldliness here on earth and from perdition and separation from God in the life to come. But that was not enough. One had to have the full assurance of salvation. In the Johannine sense, one had to know that he or she was a child of God. Such was a struggle not unfamiliar to John Wesley. Assurance of salvation was a central doctrine in the Methodism of Catherine's youth, and such Christian assurance was found by listening to the preaching of the church; searching one's heart, mind, and soul in the class meetings; and privately reading the Bible and praying for full assurance. This assurance "was given partly by simple observation of the facts that the fruits of the Spirit were being shown, but in addition that there was the 'Spirit witnessing with our spirit' that we are the children of God."[32] It is altogether possible that Catherine had read Wesley's two sermons titled "The Witness of the Spirit," the first published originally in 1746 and the second in 1767.

She was "truly and savingly converted"[33] at the age of sixteen, which meant she was assured both rationally and experientially that she was a child of God. She speaks of this time in her life as passing through "a great controversy of soul."[34] On the one hand, she confessed that she had lived a blameless life as far as outward appearance was concerned, was undaunted in her zeal for the gospel, and had gladly used the means of grace of the church. On the other hand, she still knew herself as a sinner, filled with self-doubts and occasionally demonstrating an angry temper. She lacked all assurance that she was definitely a child of God by his grace mediated through the Holy Spirit. Her experience at sixteen, encouraged, no doubt, by her mother, was one of searching for that assurance. Later reflecting on this time, Catherine said, "It seemed to me unreasonable to suppose that I could be saved and yet not know it."[35]

She testified that one morning during that time of struggle her eyes fell on these words from one of Charles Wesley's hymns with which she was quite familiar: "My God, I am Thine, What a comfort Divine, What a blessing to know that my Jesus is mine!" She then related her experience in this way:

> Scores of times I had read and sung these words, but now they came home to my inmost soul with a force and illumination they had never before possessed. It was as impossible for me to doubt as it had been before for me to exercize faith. Previously not all the promises in the Bible could induce me to believe: now not all the devils in hell could persuade me to doubt. I no longer hoped that I was saved, I was certain of it. The assurances of my salvation seemed to flood and fill my soul. I jumped out of bed, and without waiting to dress, ran into my mother's room and told her what had happened.
>
> Till then I had been very backward in speaking even to her upon spiritual matters. I could pray before her, and yet could not open my heart to her about my salvation. It is a terrible disadvantage to people that they are ashamed to speak freely to one another upon so vital a subject. Owing to this, thousands are kept in bondage for years, when they might easily step into immediate liberty and joy. I have myself met hundreds of persons who have confessed to me that they had been church members for many years without knowing what a change of heart really was, and without having been able to escape from this miserable condition of doubt and uncertainty to one of assurance and consequent satisfaction. For the next six months I was so happy that I felt as if I was walking on air. I used to tremble, and even long to die, lest I should backslide, or lose the consciousness of God's smile or favor.[36]

Her salvation assured, she decided to join the Wesleyan Church in Brixton.

Unfortunately, some illness seemed ever present in Catherine's life, and in the fall of 1846 she developed symptoms of consumption. For about six months she was confined to her room for rest and treatment. She was, however, able to travel in the spring of 1847 and went to Brighton, where she commenced writing a diary on May 12. This exercise would not last long, and the last entry is dated March 24, 1848. (She never kept a diary again.) The diary makes frequent references to her sickness, and she continued to be obsessed for the remainder of her life with her illnesses. Granted, she was not physically well much of the time, but she dwelt too frequently on her own illnesses and the sicknesses within her family.

Nevertheless, the diary also speaks of her spiritual health—her desire to give herself fully to the Lord, suffer for his sake, and adorn the doctrines of the gospel. With her Methodist inclination for introspection, self-examination, watchfulness and prayer, and careful scrutiny of one's life lest one become deceived by the devil and conform to the world, it comes as no surprise that both the diary and her correspondence, which Stead labels as "slightly priggish letters to her mother,"[37] reflect her spiritual preoccupations. She was perhaps learning the lesson of a carefully balanced spirituality so that her introspections produced a healthy Christian and did not deteriorate into a self-satisfied commendation of herself and a condemnation of all others who did not understand the Christian life in precisely the same way. Catherine Bramwell-Booth wrote,

> Between the paper covers of this penny exercise book may be found the confirmation of her son Bramwell's verdict that she was "by nature an unbeliever"; may be found, too, that the emphasis in her battle for faith centered in the strength of the soul to submit to the will of God. This for her was of the very essence of Christianity. Throughout her life her love to God grew and with it the determination to please the Beloved which love engendered. Such living is only possible by faith. Faith then, continued to the end of her life, as it was in the beginning, the essential victory.[38]

It is obvious that Catherine, by the age of eighteen, was thinking theologically. Her writings during this time demonstrate a grappling with theological issues as well as a knowledge of basic theological concerns and the language that both reflects and controls such concerns. She was especially interested in subjects such as election and other "Calvinistic doctrines,"[39] the atonement, and another of Methodism's emphases—Christian perfection. She spoke of sin as "an evil heart of unbelief, an impetuous will, and a momentary loss of common sense."[40] She prayed often for the salvation and restoration of her father. She also continued in experimenting in living the disciplined life of the Methodist, drawing up a set of rules for the new year 1848, and trying times of fasting. She was interested in ecclesiological matters and followed the debates of various reform movements within Methodism.

Some word concerning the development of Methodism will assist in understanding Catherine's interests in Methodism at this time. John Wesley, in the previous century, although living and dying as an Anglican priest, was the founder of Methodism as a renewal movement within Anglicanism. Wesley was decidedly not in favor of forming another denomination and was upset on learning that American Methodism, under the leadership of Francis Asbury and Thomas Coke, was leaning in that direction. John Wesley kept autocratic control of the movement; but a democratic impulse began to shape the future of Methodism when, in 1783, a Deed Poll was established, an annual conference was commenced, and a group of one hundred ministers, appointed for life, were convened to assist Wesley in the administration of Methodism. Wesley died in 1791, and the democratic movement within Methodism gained ascendancy.

New denominations were formed in England, following the lead of American Methodists. Among the Wesleyan Methodists of England, however, it appeared that there was an entrenched bureaucracy, and a group of agitators or reformers—depending on one's point of view—were calling for a democratization of Methodism as well as for other reforms. The *Wesleyan Times,* begun January 8, 1849, heralded the cause of the reformers, while the *Watchman* guarded business as usual. The battle for Methodism's soul in England, begun among the clergy, was taken to the local churches and to the laity. Everyone entered into the debate and wanted some voice in the future of the Methodism in which they had grown up and which they cherished.

The conflict between the conservative and reformed parties sharpened during a dispute over the American Methodist evangelist and holiness teacher, James Caughey, a person destined to have profound influence on Catherine and William Booth. In the spirit of trans-Atlantic revivalism, which was conducted in the nineteenth century and would be continued by such notable American preachers as Charles Grandison Finney and Dwight L. Moody, Caughey made four trips to England during his ministry to hold revivals, the first one being an extended visit, lasting from 1841 to 1847. One author describes Caughey in this way:

> He was a tall, thin, smooth-shaven, cadaverous person with dark hair. One who often saw him and well remembers him tells me that he wore a voluminous black cloak folded about him in a Byronic manner; his voice was subdued, he gave no sign of an excitable disposition, his preaching warmed slowly into heat and passion which communicated themselves with magnetic instantaneousness to his audiences.[41]

Despite his effectiveness, there was considerable dissension in the Wesleyan ranks over Caughey. His detractors did not argue over his theology, because he essentially believed and taught the same things they did. What they could not condone were his revivalistic techniques. Owen Chadwick describes these disputes within Methodism:

> From 1843 onwards there were long arguments over an itinerant evangelist from the American Methodists, James Caughey. American methods were organized like a machine, and Caughey had enemies. English preachers of Leeds and Sheffield and Birmingham testified that he wrought wonders in their parishes and had rare gifts of bringing the indecisive to decision. They protested that interference with Caughey would obstruct the work of God. Others could not bear his devices and dodges. They accused him of using decoy penitents to lead others forward to the communion rail, and of pretending to miraculous knowledge about individuals in his congre-

gations. He divided Methodists wherever he went. Conference of 1846 at last resolved to ask the Americans to recall him. It was not easy to persuade Methodists in York or Huddersfield to respect the ban.[42]

Caughey returned to America in 1847, not a moment too soon for some Methodists. Others, however, complained about the high-handed actions of the Conference.

The utmost stretch of charity could hardly invent any justifiable motive for their sudden banishment of the remarkable American evangelist Caughey, and this at a time when he was in the very zenith of his success. He was a Methodist minister, and his doctrines agreed in every particular with those of the Conference. Crowds flocked to his meetings from all the country-side, thousands of souls sought salvation, and the revival was at its floodtide, when the Conference compelled his withdrawal, causing wide-spread discontent among multitudes of the most loyal ministers and members of the Connexion, and exposing themselves to charges of envy and jealousy to which it was very difficult to reply.[43]

Richard Carwardine has expressed it this way:

Caughey's exclusion sent partisans rushing for their pens and produced waves of protest around the connection. Various circuits and special meetings issued testimonials to the revivalist's capabilities and good character; in pamphlets and journals, Conference came under fire. Caughey did not lack ministerial support, but most of his public defenders were incensed local preachers, leaders and trustees, and other prominent laymen ready to take matters into their own hands if their pastors would not act for them. The tone of their attack ranged from the mild to the vitriolic, but the argument in essence was always the same: Conference's inflexible standing by connectional discipline in a decade when denominational growth was low, relative to overall population and the increases of past decades, demonstrated that Conference's position was, "in effect, one of distinct opposition to revivals of religion and the salvation of souls." Church order was important, but was not an end in itself: "is there not reason to *fear* lest [Methodism] should become a mere compacted frame work of ecclesiastical guards and precautionary regulations . . . ?" Thrown on the defensive, Conference sympathizers tried to cast doubt on Caughey's revival figures and stooped on occasion to impugning the American's integrity on the slavery issue.[44]

Catherine sided with the Reformers for two reasons. First, although an admirer of Wesley, she supported a more democratic approach to church government, which was part of the Reformers' platform. They wanted to rescue Wesleyanism from what they perceived to be an autocratic group of ministers unsympathetic to the democratic impulses of the times and to the opinions of others in the denomination. For most of them, the actions taken against Caughey were arbitrary. Catherine's views would change dramatically in later life, but at this time she was in favor of a more congregational system of government. She was also on the side of the Reformers in longing for revivalism to sweep through Methodism. The Reformers, she reasoned, emphasized revival—the winning of souls for Christ—and holiness—purity of life and empowerment for ministry. These were the tenets of James Caughey, and his dismissal was generally lamented by the Reformers because his preaching continually brought these matters into focus for Methodism.

To show her support, Catherine attended several meetings of the Reformers and heard speeches and resolutions by ministers who had been expelled from the Conference for their supposed agitation within the ranks. She even attended a meeting at Exeter Hall in London. For her efforts, and for her sympathy, her membership in the local class meeting was not renewed after she had been warned not to show open support for the Reformers. Membership at that time was renewed quarterly, and not to be renewed meant expulsion. Catherine Mumford, by this action, had been summarily dismissed from the Wesleyan Methodist Church in which she had been reared and which she loved. She later wrote:

This was one of the first great troubles of my life, and cost me the keenest anguish. I was young. I had been nursed and cradled in Methodism, and loved it with a love which had gone altogether out of fashion among Protestants for their church. At the same time I was dissatisfied with the formality, worldliness, and defection from what I conceived Methodism ought to be, judging from its early literature and biographies as well as from Wesley's own writings and his brother's hymns. I believed that through the agitation something would arise which would be better, holier, and more thorough. Here were men who, in my simplicity, I supposed wanted to bring back the fervour and aggressiveness of by-gone days. In this hope and in sympathy with the wrongs that I believe the Reformers had suffered, I drifted away from the Wesleyan Church, apparently at the sacrifice of all that was dearest to me, and of nearly every personal friend.[45]

Both Catherine and her mother joined the Reformers, who rented a hall for religious services near their home. For three years, from 1852 to 1855, she taught a Sunday school class of fifteen girls whose ages ranged from twelve to nineteen. From all accounts, this was a successful class. Catherine was personally concerned for each of her charges and conducted the class much after the model of the Methodist class meeting. She enjoyed a tranquil and settled life at this time, living with her parents, teaching her class at the church, and participating in the shaping of Methodism through the Reform movement. However, her life was at a turning point that she could not possibly have imagined. It was during this time that she met another sympathizer with the Reformers—William Booth.

2

Providential Meeting

❦

Catherine Mumford and William Booth

William Booth was born the same year as Catherine, 1829, in Nottingham. Two and a half months younger than she, his birthday was April 10. He was the son of a saintly mother, Mary Moss Booth, and a nominally religious father, Samuel Booth. William was spiritually nurtured by his mother and probably developed some sense for organizational and business matters from his father, although the relationship between father and son was distant.

Because his father was a member of the Anglican Church, William was baptized on April 12, 1829, at St. Mary's in Nottingham and was reared in that Anglican community until his teenage years. By all accounts, William did not have a happy childhood and "says that he got no help, as regards school work, in his home. He says that no one told him anything about religion. He speaks of his early days as 'a season of mortification and misery.' He makes it clear that his childhood was dark and unhappy."[1] This is quite a contrast to Catherine's childhood and a bit difficult to understand given the affection he had for his mother. The misery he attributed to his home life was probably largely due to the presence of his father, because it was the father who dominated the family life.

Samuel Booth, though illiterate, had been involved in many business ventures, beginning as a nail manufacturer and moving into the building trade. The family was well-off at the time of William's birth, so much so that the entry of the parish register for William's baptism records Samuel Booth as "gentleman,"[2] which was, by the nineteenth century, a very imprecise designation. Fortunes fall, however, and the Booth family eventually came on difficult and even desperate times. England was not a caste society, and Booth's father moved up and down the social ladder either as his finances permitted or his difficulties dictated. The family often lived in poverty. One biographer noted, "For the whole of William Booth's childhood and youth, his family was desperately poor."[3] To help matters, at age thirteen William was apprenticed as a pawnbroker's assistant, a trade by which he would support his mother and his three sisters after the death of his father in September 1842.[4]

William was a boy of religious leanings, probably due to the influence of his mother, and he was taken one day by an elderly neighbor couple to the Broad Street Wesleyan Methodist Chapel. Following his father's death, William decided to leave the Anglican church and began attending that Wesleyan church more regularly. He was only a nominal Christian at the time and records that he was converted in 1844 at age fifteen, probably while under the influence of the preacher Isaac Marsden. As was evident in Catherine's life, conversion under Wesleyan guidance entailed a deliberate separation from the godless world and a complete turning to God. Such abandonment meant rejecting evil companionship, worldly amusements, games, recreations, and even giving up novels or anything else that did not directly edify one's Christian life.

One expression of William's new adventure in Christianity was that of conducting street meetings in Nottingham with his closest boyhood friend, Will Sansom. At first Booth was reluctant to preach in the open air, as was John Wesley before him when Whitefield suggested it, but he was soon persuaded to do so and quickly became the recognized leader of a rather zealous group of street evangelists. He came in contact with others in Nottingham who were suffering the effects of poverty in their lives, not only through his work as a pawnbroker's assistant but through his ministry on the streets of Nottingham and through cottage prayer meetings and the visitation of the sick and dying. He desired to alleviate the poverty he knew firsthand but he had no real means at his disposal then to do so.

In any case, he became increasingly aware that he was destined by God and prepared by temperament to be a preacher of the gospel. His preparation for such a calling at this time consisted of reading the Bible, Finney, Wesley, and Whitefield. He was entranced by the preaching and teaching of the American Methodist James Caughey and was nurtured by his pastor, the Reverend Samuel Dunn, a Wesleyan with sympathy for the Reformers. At seventeen Booth became a local preacher with the Wesleyans and, at the urging of Dunn, considered the ministry as a vocation. Nottingham would not be the place for the fulfillment of his ambitions, however, and at nineteen William was ready for a change from the dreary routine of life there. He had left the pawnbroker business and was unemployed for a year except that he occasionally was asked to preach for "a pitiful wage."[5] His best friend, Will Sansom, died, and life for his mother and sisters remaining at home was desperate. So William moved to London in 1849.

He found work in the trade he despised, earning a living and continuing to support his family back home by working in a pawnbroker's shop in Walworth. Nevertheless, preaching the gospel continued as his primary interest, and the obvious need for salvation that he witnessed on the streets of London strengthened his resolve to do just that. So desperate was he to preach that he even entertained the thought of offering himself as a chaplain on a convict ship to Australia. Perhaps, he thought, the pathway to entering the ministry would be easier in Australia than in England, and the numberless English who were being sent to Australia in the nineteenth century provided any budding preacher with potential converts. This was but a fleeting idea though. He did not want to be that far away from his mother or from the opportunities to preach in England, his home.

There is evidence that he began preaching at various Wesleyan chapels in London and quickly discovered that things were heating up in the ranks over the issue of the Wesleyan Reform movement. In 1851 the Reverend Samuel Dunn was expelled from the Wesleyan Connexion.[6] William attended some meetings of the Reformers in London but beyond that did not identify with the Reform movement, thus making the withholding of his membership by the circuit minister for supposed sympathy with the Reformers seem both ironic and blatantly unfair.

On going to London, William preached his first sermon at the Walworth Road Wesleyan Chapel. One of the persons who heard Booth preach that morning was Edward Harris Rabbits, a wealthy boot and shoe manufacturer, a friend of the Mumfords, and one of the sympathizers of the Reformers.[7] Catherine's granddaughter describes Rabbits: "He was an old-fashioned Methodist who liked to hear 'Amens' in chapel, a local preacher and a 'light' in the Reform party. He began business, it was said, on a borrowed half-crown, and by the time the Mumfords came to know him he owned several flourishing boot shops and was reputed to be a millionaire. A shrewd masterful person, he was full of energetic interest in his boot-making and in religion."[8]

Rabbits was impressed with William's fervent evangelical preaching and in June 1851 "persuaded him to work among the Reformers, and later on proceeded to settle the business of his entrance into the ministry."[9] In April 1852 Rabbits encouraged Booth's desire to become a minister by supporting him financially for the first three months of his ministry. This gave the fledgling preacher the freedom to leave the pawnbroking business forever, secure a room in Walworth for five shillings a week, buy some furniture, and begin preaching full-time. One of the Reformers' chapels was Binfield House, situated on Binfield Road, Clapham. Two of the members of this church were Sarah Mumford and her daughter Catherine, who led a Bible class here. As Providence would have it—for this is how both Catherine and William described the circumstances of their meeting—William Booth preached at Binfield House "some months after he had joined the Reformers."[10] Both Sarah and Catherine were present and heard Booth preach on the text, "This is indeed the Christ, the Saviour of the World." Catherine was impressed with the sermon and said so to her friend Rabbits. Catherine and William were to meet for the first time two weeks later in Rabbits's home. He had arranged an afternoon tea for some of the Reformers of the district. Catherine, her mother, and William Booth had all accepted Rabbits's invitation to attend.

During the course of the afternoon, the host persuaded William to recite an odd American temperance poem titled "The Grogseller's Dream," although few persons in the room were actually teetotalers, and certainly Booth was not at this point in his life—his mother having introduced him to drink at age thirteen for medicinal uses. Evidently Rabbits was as interested in Booth's dramatic oratory skills as he was in the poem and persevered on a reluctant preacher to show off to the crowd.

As a result of the recitation, a discussion arose over the virtue of total abstinence and the vice of mere temperance. The chief advocate present for total abstinence was, of course, Catherine Mumford; and she let her opinions be known, probably supporting them with quotations from her reading of Charles Grandison Finney, who was committed to the cause of temperance and many other social causes, as is well documented by Keith J. Hardman.[11]

Supper was announced, and the conversation turned to other matters. The importance of the occasion was not, however, in the conversation about total abstinence but in the meeting for the first time of Catherine Mumford and William Booth. They would meet again, by God's grace.

April 10, 1852, was one of the most important birthdays in William's life. It happened to be a Friday—Good Friday, in fact—and was memorable on two counts. It was the day he finally traded the business of pawnbroking for the business of ministry, supported initially by Rabbits. "I shook hands with my cold-hearted master and said Good-bye," Booth later recounted.[12] He also later recalled that "on that day I fell over head and ears in love with the precious woman who afterward became my wife."[13] A chance encounter with Rabbits that day caused Booth to go with him to a meeting of the Reformers in a schoolroom on Cowper Street, City Road. Having now joined the Reformers, Booth's interest in its principles was increasing, and he could now, without fear of intimidation, attend the Reformers' meetings. Catherine Mumford, whom he had first met in Rabbits's home in 1851 and whom he had met occasionally following that introduction, was also present, and William drove her home after the meeting. This is Catherine's recollection of that evening:

> That little journey will never be forgotten by either of us. It is true that nothing particular occurred, except that as W. afterwards expressed it, it seemed as if God flashed simultaneously into our hearts that affection which afterwards ripened into what has proved at least to be an exceptional union of heart and purpose and life, and which none of the changing vicissitudes with which our lives have been so crowded has been able to efface.
>
> He impressed me.
>
> I had been introduced to him as being in delicate health, and he took the situation in at a glance. His thought for me, although such a stranger, appeared most remarkable. The conveyance shook me; he regretted it. The talking exhausted me; he saw and forbade it. And then we struck in at once in such wonderful harmony of view and aim and feeling on varied matters that passed rapidly before us. It seemed as though we had intimately known and loved each other for years, and suddenly, after some temporary absence, had been brought together again, and before we reached my home we both suspected, nay, we felt as though we had been made for each other, and that henceforth the current of our lives must flow together.[14]

Catherine's and William's feelings for each other were sure, and they were certainly in love. But William's situation with the Reformers was not as steady as when he had been welcomed to that body by Rabbits; and as was often the case in his life, he was prone to bursts of enthusiasm marked with times of despondency, despair, and doubt. The Reformers were learning that their rebellion against an autocratic Wesleyanism did not prevent similar autocratic tendencies within their movement, especially among those who were empowered to lead. Likewise, the fervor for evangelism among the Reformers, while noble, did not deter jealousies from creeping into the movement among the pastors themselves. And finally, there was great divisiveness as early as 1852 among the Reformers—some wanting to return to the mother church, some wanting to align themselves with other Methodist denominations, while others stalwartly insisted on creating their own denomination. Begbie summarized Booth's attitude at this time toward the Reformers: "The more he saw of the Reformers the less he liked them."[15] The uncertainty of the future of the movement caused William grave concern for his own ministry and future. Added to this was his growing love and affection for Catherine. They were increasingly aware that they both wished to be engaged and married, in spite of their anxieties about a sufficient salary and a steady position in ministry—which were deemed necessary for a secure future together.

Catherine and William were often apart after their initial meetings, but a voluminous correspondence began during their separation that provides many insights into their lives from 1852 onward. In the letters of this period, Catherine is often seen consoling, counseling, encouraging, and comforting William. In the first extant letter from Catherine to William dated May 11, 1852, and addressed to "My Dear Friend," we see much sympathy from Catherine over William's present circumstances and his natural tendency to fret and worry. Her instruction, "Never mind who frowns, if God smiles," is followed after a couple of paragraphs by this friendly advice: "You have some true friends in the circuit and what is better than all you have a friend above whose love is as great as his <u>power</u>. He can easily open your way to another sphere of influence greater than you now conceive of."[16]

Catherine was willing to trust the future to Providence and she is clear in a letter of May 13, 1852, that such trust was extended to their engagement. The letter speaks profoundly of God's intervention in their lives in vocation, in engagement, and in marriage. On Saturday evening, May 15, 1852, Catherine and William were engaged.[17] Thus began, by all accounts, one of the great loves of the Victorian world, a steady and constant love that prevailed through the many trials that came during their hectic life together. Their love and friendship continued unabated and grew and developed until Catherine's death in 1890.

The correspondence following the engagement, especially that of Catherine to William, is a blend of rapturous and heavenly joy when reflecting on the engagement; purest bliss when thinking about each other, their growing love, and their anticipated marriage; and counsel and advice concerning all kinds of matters that would pertain to their life and ministry together. All through her life Catherine demonstrated "her tendency to decide what is right for others."[18]

Such an inclination was no less evident in her correspondence to the man she loved and whom she would eventually marry, and her advice to him on various matters was boundless—she wrote about preaching, family, the rearing of children, health matters, and even studying. "I am sorry to hear you talk," Catherine wrote to William in June 1852, "of '<u>trying</u> to be a student once more and if you fail giving it up forever.' Don't say I will <u>try</u>; but I <u>will</u> be one. At least you <u>can study</u> whether you make much out or not, be determined to stick to it, and what is to hinder you?"[19] Catherine, much more than William, knew the virtue of a life of study and realized its value both for the expansion of one's mind and for the sake of the gospel. She was a student and, both in Wesleyanism and in Congregationalism, was exposed to preachers and teachers who demonstrated the life of the mind. One of the persons she admired most, Charles Grandison Finney, although not formally trained, had become a student of the Bible and of theology. Catherine appreciated that and wanted William to develop the habits of a good student.

The chief issue to be decided during this time, however, was this: With what denomination would William choose to prepare for the ministry? In this, as in all other matters, he respected Catherine's opinions. William, at twenty-three, was going through serious theological turmoil that also affected his denominational allegiance. As has been mentioned, he was becoming increasingly disillusioned with the Reformers and perceived some of the leaders of that movement to be simply self-serving individuals, greedy for the power of leadership positions. The Reform movement was clearly unstable at this time and likewise unsettling to William Booth. He knew he would have to look elsewhere, and as usual, "Miss Mumford threw her whole heart into the question."[20] Also, to complicate matters, "They both agreed that the arrangement with Mr. Rabbits should come to an end when the three months were completed in July."[21]

Their eyes briefly turned toward Congregationalism as a possibility. About this time, and for uncertain reasons, Catherine began attending a Congregational church in Stockwell. The pastor was the Reverend David Thomas. It is difficult to say whether Catherine began attending the church because William showed some interest in Congregationalism as a place for ministry, or whether her introduction to Congregationalism stirred his interest. In any case, Catherine later recorded these reflections:

> It was at this time, when the way to the Ministry seemed totally closed in the Methodist direction, that W.'s attention was turned to the Congregational Church. I think this was my doing; indeed, I know it was; but, until he came to this dead stop, he would never hear of it, and even now his difficulties appeared almost insurmountable. To leave Methodism seemed an impossibility. His love for it at that time amounted almost to idolatry. . . .
>
> Although I could sympathize with all this, and had a fair share of love for the Church to which I also owed much and in which I had experienced a great deal of blessing, still, I had nothing like his blind attachment. For one reason, I had not been actively engaged. Mine

had been more the position of a spectator; and, moreover, I argued that, once settled in a Congregational pulpit, he could impart into his service and meetings all that was good and hearty and soul-saving in Methodism; at least, I thought he could, and consequently, I pressed him very strongly to seek an open door for the exercise of his Ministry among the Independents.

He was slow to accept my counsel. He had formed a very lofty notion of the intellectual and literary status of the Body, and was fearful that he was not equal in these respects to meet what would be required of him. But I was just as confident as he was fearful. I felt sure that all that was wanted by him was a sphere, and that once gained, I saw no difficulty in his being able to organize a church of workers, and make them into Methodists in spirit and practice, whether they were such in government or no.

Perhaps I was very simple in these notions; I had little or no experience at that time as to the difficulty of over-ruling the prejudices and changing the customs which had been handed down from generation to generation. However, I was young and sanguine, and already had come to have considerable faith in the enthusiastic energy and devotion of my beloved, and I thought if he could once get into the leadership anywhere, he could carry the people whithersoever he would.

With such reasonings as these, and seeing that there was no other way by which he could reach the sphere to which his soul believed God had called him, he gave in, and resolved to seek an open door for the preaching of Jesus Christ, and to bringing lost sinners to God amongst the Congregationalists.[22]

From July to October 1852 consideration of a ministry in Congregationalism continued. William had met an outstanding Congregational leader, preacher, and editor by the name of Reverend Dr. John Campbell, and that initial meeting proved to be encouraging. Campbell gave William cause to believe that he would have a successful ministry among the Congregationalists, for which Booth sincerely thanked him in a letter dated June 25, 1852. Booth interviewed with three other Congregational ministers, and the last of the three, the Reverend Dr. James William Massey of the Home Missionary Society of the Congregational Union, was as discouraging about Booth's intentions as Camp-

bell was encouraging. Massey's advice was to sit under the tutelage of an Independent minister for two years before considering the training involved for Congregationalism at the Training
Institution at Cotton End. Booth was discouraged. Had not God
called him to ministry, and had he not already proved to some
degree his ability to preach? How, he thought, could two years
of inactivity be useful to any degree?

Providentially, Dr. Campbell came to Booth's assistance, and
Booth was admitted to Cotton End. However, one doctrinal matter had to be settled in Booth's mind before entering the training
institution. He understood that Congregationalism taught Calvinist doctrines of election and limited atonement, which in the nineteenth century was to say that God had chosen those who were
to be saved and the atonement applied to them alone. This of
course had been the focus of the argument of John Wesley with
his friend George Whitefield in the previous century, dividing
Methodism. The debate continued into the nineteenth century.[23]

Booth's understanding of the Bible, combined with his immer-
sion in both the life of John Wesley and in Wesleyan Methodist
doctrine, would never allow him to believe, preach, or teach such
doctrines. He believed that Christ died on the cross for "the
whosoever" and believed likewise in the possibility of all people
being saved who trusted in Christ by faith. In that regard the
atonement was universal. Catherine's own antipathy to Calvinism had begun to take shape at age fourteen and she was well
aware of the theological issues involved, although she had not
grappled with the theological implications to the extent of John
Wesley or even of Charles Finney. Her expression of theological
matters was always simple and direct, if not always precisely
accurate, as the following statement demonstrates:

> We knew that the basis of the Congregational theology was Calvin-
> ism. We were both saturated, as it were, with the broadest, deepest,
> and highest opinions as to the extent of the love of God and the bene-
> fit flowing from the sacrifice of Jesus Christ. We were verily extrem-
> ists on this question. The idea of anything like the selection of one
> individual to enjoy the blessedness of the Divine favour for ever and

ever, and the reprobation of another to suffer all the pains and penalties of everlasting damnation, irrespective of any choice, conduct, or character on their part, seemed to us to be an outrage on all that was fair and righteous, to say nothing about benevolent. We not only thought this, but felt it. On this, at least, we were in perfect harmony.[24]

Much of the Calvinism of the nineteenth century was less precise about the doctrine of double election than Catherine describes in this paragraph. Also, the Wesleyan theology in which Catherine was reared, while allowing that free will and choice of God's grace insured salvation, was equally clear that neither conduct nor character, however noble or enlightened, was the basis for salvation.

She was less diplomatic in her reactions to Calvinism when many years later, writing to her eldest son, she referred to that particular theological perspective as "this bear of hell—Calvinism."[25] Her polemics, however, must be taken in context. After all, Catherine would later preach in Congregational churches, and she did not speak publicly, but only privately, against Calvinism. She was concerned with the pastoral implications of an entrenched and, what she considered to be, hardened Calvinist theology. She wanted to make the gospel available to all and invited all to accept by faith God's grace, manifested most surely by a universal atonement. Any doctrine of election and limited atonement suffocated the fullness of the biblical message as Catherine understood it. These had been Wesley's concerns also. "Wesley would have liked predestination to be an 'opinion,' not breaking communion, but could not gain agreement on this and indeed often treated it as a deadly poison not to be tolerated."[26]

What to do about Calvinism was their major problem with Congregationalism but not their only one. There was also the issue of how free Booth would be to teach and preach the views he believed to be soundly biblical, even if they departed from standard Congregational teaching.

In the end there were enough misgivings about Congregationalism that William finally declined Campbell's gracious offer of admittance into Cotton End and thereby, after six months' training, into the Independent ministry. The parting was congenial, and less than three years later Catherine and William would be married in a Congregational church by the Reverend Thomas, the minister of the church that Catherine continued to attend. Thirty-six years later Catherine would deliver her last public address in Dr. Joseph Parker's City Temple, a Congregational church. In the meantime, although not formally matriculated at a college, William was reading, probably on the advice of Catherine, who was more naturally disposed than William toward the training of the mind. On July 28, 1852, William wrote to Catherine, "I am reading Finney and Watson on election and final perseverance, and I see more than ever reason to cling to my own views of truth and righteousness."[27]

The question now remained, Where to go from here? However, that is not precisely how Catherine and William framed the question. For them, the more appropriate language for asking about these matters was this: Where is God, by his gracious providence, leading us?

The answer came surprisingly soon. William was invited to the Spalding circuit by a group of Reformers who were searching for someone to minister there. The Reformers were predominant among the Wesleyans in that country town, and the laity there were mostly Reformers. Word had come to them that William Booth was still searching for a pastorate and, although greatly disillusioned with the Reform movement generally, might be more receptive to an invitation to a country circuit far removed from the movement's political realities. Naturally, the major obstacle to accepting such an invitation was that Catherine and William would be separated. They had enjoyed, since their first meeting, their nearness to one another, which nurtured their love. A separation of this sort would be a trial for both of them. Added to that were Catherine's misgivings still about the Reformers and what future William could possibly have with this disjunctive movement. Catherine was sure that this move to Spalding might delay William's training and eventual ordination, but she was ready to submit to what she perceived to be the working of God in their lives and knew from previous experience that his ways were often mysterious. William moved to Spalding at the end of November 1852.

Booth was very pleased with his reception at the circuit. His letters to Catherine reveal his contentment with the ministry there. His preaching was well received, people were being saved, and the ministry flourished. Catherine expressed her delight at William's happiness coupled with the fine reception he was enjoying at Spalding. Though separated, the two kept in touch with frequent, lengthy letters.

Catherine's letters to William at Spalding are most interesting, because they reveal her theological proclivities as well as her considered advice on all sorts of matters, both of which she was always ready and willing—indeed eager—to share. She gives William sound advice on what to study, what to read, how to preach, and how to conduct his meetings. She wrote,

> Watch against mere animal excitement in your revival service. I don't use the term in the sense in which . . . revivalists would use it, but only in the sense in which Finney himself would use it; remember Caughey's silent soft, heavenly carriage; he did not shout; there was no necessity; he had a more potent weapon at command than noise; I never did like noise and confusion, only so far as I believed it to be the natural expression of deep anxiety—wrought by the Holy Ghost.[28]

She knew the history of Methodism and revivalism enough to be wary of the enthusiasts whose preaching and meetings sometimes went to the extremes Catherine feared.

She wrote about the spirit of prayer, life in Christ, and how profitable it is to read good biographies. And once she chided William for not writing as often as he should. "My dearest William, What can be the reason I have received no letter neither yesterday nor today, you said in your last you would write on Monday all well. I have passed two days of strange agitation, especially today which has made me quite poorly. You really must be punctual in writing for the sake of my health, if on no other account."[29] Aside from these issues, however, three concerns of Catherine's are worth noting, which are underscored by both the length of the letters and the passion of her expression when writing about these matters.

First, it became evident to Catherine that William was becoming a favorite son among the parishioners at Spalding. His preaching was well received, people responded readily to his evangelical fervor, and he was personable and well liked. Catherine, however, sensed a danger in such attention and influence, and that concerned her. In a letter dated December 5, 1852, Catherine had a friendly word of caution for her beloved: "My dearest love, beware how you indulge that dangerous element of character <u>ambition</u>."[30] Catherine was obviously ambivalent about William's growing popularity, because on the one hand she wished for denominational affiliation that would insure William a place where his leadership skills would be appreciated, but on the other hand she warned him against ambition, which is certainly needed to some extent if one is to become a leader.

The second issue, always critical to Catherine, was whether William was studying sufficiently. Her advice about the necessity of study, given in June 1852 shortly after their engagement, was reiterated especially now that William was involved in an active ministry of preaching the gospel. On December 12, 1852, she wrote:

Do assure me, my own dear William, that no lack of energy or effort on your part shall hinder the improvement of those talents God has intrusted to you, and which he holds you responsible to improve to the uttermost. Your duty to God, to His Church, to me, to yourself, demands as much. If you really see no <u>prospect of studying</u>, then I think, in the highest interests of the future, you ought not to stay.

I have been revolving in my mind all day which will be your wisest plan under present circumstances, and it appears to me that as you are obliged to preach nearly every evening and at places so wide apart, it will be better to do as the friends advise, and stop all night where you preach. Do not attempt to walk long distances after the meetings. With a little management and a good deal of determination, I think you might accomplish even more that way as to study, than by going home each night. Could you not provide yourself with a small leather bag or case, large enough to hold your Bible and any other book you might require—pens, ink, paper, and a <u>candle</u>? And presuming that you generally have a room to yourself, could you not rise by six o'clock every morning, and convert your bedroom into a <u>study</u> till breakfast time? After breakfast and family devotion could you not again retire to your room and determinedly apply yourself till dinner time? Then start on your journey to your evening's appointment, get there for a comfortable tea and do the same again! I hope, my dearest love, you will consider this plan, and adhere to it, if possible, as a <u>general practice</u>, admitting a few exceptions which circumstances may occasion. Don't let little difficulties prevent its adoption. I am aware you would labour under many disadvantages, but once get the habit of abstracting your mind from your surroundings and it will become easy. Do not be over-anxious about the future. Spalding <u>will not be your final destination</u>, if you <u>make the best of your ability</u>.[31]

Catherine wrote in a later letter, "I hope you are <u>studying</u>; you do not mention it. Be determined to make the most of every moment; <u>do not let trifles</u> interrupt your study hours and attention."[32]

Third, Catherine felt a special need to write William about the importance of being clear on temperance. Perhaps this became a particularly pressing issue since Catherine received a letter from William stating, "I had to have brandy twice; was real ill; thought much of you." He repeated in that same letter, "In the morning I had again to take Brandy twice." And still later in the letter he informed his dearest that a gentleman in the circuit advised that "I must take port wine, that he could tell by my voice and experience that it would do me good. My health is of first importance. What do you say my dearest?"[33] Well, in a letter from Catherine dated December 27, 1852, William would learn precisely what Catherine would have to say on this subject.

I need not say how willing, nay, how anxious, I am, that you should have anything and everything which would tend to promote your <u>health</u> and happiness. But so thoroughly am I convinced that port wine would do neither, that I should hear of your taking it with unfeigned grief. You must not listen, my love, to the advice of everyone claiming to be experienced. Persons really experienced and judicious in many things, not unfrequently entertain notions the most fallacious on this subject. I have had it recommended to me scores of times by these individuals. But such recommendations have always gone for nothing, because I have felt that, however much my superiors such persons might be in other respects, on this subject I was the best informed. I have even argued the point with Mr. Stevens [her doctor], and have, I am sure, completely set him fast for arguments to defend alcohol even as a medicine. I am fully and forever settled on the physical side of the question. I believe you are on the moral and religious, but I have not thought you were on the physical. Now my dearest it is absolutely necessary in order to save you from being influenced by other people's false notions, that you should have a settled, intelligent conviction on the subject. And in order that you may get this, I have been to the trouble of unpacking your box in order to send you a book, in which you will find several green marks and pencillings. I do hope you will read it, even if you sit up an hour later every night till you have done so, and I would not advise this for anything less important.

It is a subject on which I am most anxious you should be thorough. I abominate that hackneyed but monstrously inconsistent tale—a teetotaler in principle, but obliged to take a little for my "stomach's sake!" Such teetotalers aid the progress of intemperance more than all the drunkards in the land! And there are sadly too many of them among ministers. The fact is notorious, and doubtless the fault is chiefly with the people, who foolishly consider it a kindness to "put the bottle to their neighbor's mouth" as frequently as they will receive it! But my dear William will steadfastly resist such foolish advisers. I dare take the responsibility (and I have more reason to feel its weight than any other being). I have far more hope for your health, because you abstain from stimulating drinks, than I should if you took them. Flee the detestable thing as you would a serpent. Be a teetotaler in principle and practice.[34]

In the meantime, back home Catherine was preparing for their wedding and contemplating such issues as courtship, marriage, and the rearing of a family. She had decided views about the sacredness of engagement, strengthened perhaps by an unfortunate incident of a friend of hers whose engagement was broken off hastily by her suitor who found a woman from a wealthier family to marry. Catherine's friend was emotionally destroyed by this unhappy incident, and Catherine was incensed. Referring to the hapless suitor in a letter about the incident, she wrote, "He has resigned office and says he will emigrate. I should hope he will! He ought to be sent out of the country free of expense!"[35]

From her experience of a long courtship and engagement—more than three years, from 1852 to 1855—Catherine later cautioned young people against rushing into either engagement or marriage.

> Perhaps the greatest evil of all is hurry. Young people do not allow themselves time to know each other before an engagement is formed. They should take time and make opportunities for acquainting themselves with each other's character, disposition and peculiarities before coming to a decision. This is the great point. They should on no account commit themselves until they are fully satisfied in their own minds, assured that if they have a doubt beforehand it generally increases afterward. I am convinced that this is where thousands make shipwreck and mourn the consequences all their lives.
>
> Then again, every courtship ought to be based on certain definite principles. A fruitful cause of mistake and misery is that very few have a definite idea as to what they want in a partner, and hence they do not look for it. They simply go about the matter in a haphazard fashion, and jump into an alliance upon the first drawings of mere natural feeling regardless of the laws which govern such relationships.
>
> In the first place, each of the parties ought to be satisfied that there are to be found in the other such qualities as would make them friends if they were of the same sex. In other words there should be a congeniality and compatibility of temperament. And yet how many seek for a mere breadwinner, or a housekeeper, rather than for a friend, a counsellor and companion. Unhappy marriages are usually the consequences of a too great disparity of mind, age, temperament, training or antecedents.[36]

Catherine later in life claimed, "As quite a young girl I made up my mind to certain qualifications which I regarded as indispensable to the forming of any engagement."[37] There were four qualifications, all fortunately met by William, the first of which was a oneness of mind on religious matters. "In the first place, I was determined that his religious views must coincide with mine. He must be a sincere Christian, not a nominal one, or a mere church member, but truly converted to God."[38] Next, she resolved that the man she would marry would have to possess basic common sense and not be a fool. The third principle spoke to the biblical, theological, and cultural mandate that was most critical in Catherine's thinking and that provides a preview of her views on the equality of women and men. Catherine wrote:

> The third essential consisted of oneness of views and tastes, any idea of lordship or ownership being lost in love. There can be no doubt that Jesus Christ intended, by making love the law of marriage, to restore woman to the position God intended her to occupy; as also to destroy the curse of the Fall, which man by dint of his merely superior physical strength and advantageous position had magnified, if not really to a large extent manufactured. Of course there must and will be mutual yielding wherever there is proper love, because it is a pleasure and a joy to yield our own wills to those for whom we have real affection, whenever it can be done with an approving conscience. This is just as true with regard to man as to woman, and if we have never proved it individually during married life most of us have had abundant evidence of it at any rate during courting days.[39]

Finally, Catherine had resolved never to marry a man "who was not a total abstainer, and this from conviction, and not merely to gratify me."[40] As has been mentioned, Catherine was busy at work to convince William of the virtues of total abstinence. William eventually became convicted by the weight of her argument, and Catherine was delighted to marry a total abstainer.

Catherine, according to her own later reckonings, which certainly were rather selective at that point, also claimed that there were rules that she had formulated regarding the conduct of married life and these she also shared. It is evident that these rules had been in effect in her marriage for many years when she published them. She believed that a happy marriage demanded never keeping any secrets from her husband "in anything that affected our mutual relationship or the interests of the family."[41] She was also determined never to have a separate, secret purse apart from her husband's finances. The third and fourth principles were integrally related. She determined that

> in matters where there was any difference of opinion, I would show my husband my views and the reasons on which they were based, and try to convince in favour of my way of looking at the subject. This generally resulted either in his being converted to my views or in my being converted to his, either result securing unity of thought and action. My fourth rule was, in cases of difference of opinion, never to argue in the presence of the children. I thought it better even to submit at the time to what I might consider to be mistaken judgment, than to have a controversy before them. But of course when such occasion arose I took the first opportunity for arguing the matter out. My subsequent experience has abundantly proved to me the wisdom of this course.[42]

From all accounts of the earliest journal of William Booth, and as has already been noted, all was going well in Spalding. He felt that he was able to preach with great liberty and that as a result of his preaching people were being saved and sanctified. He recounted in his journal the many places in the Spalding district where he had preached, names of small towns such as Donnington, Swineshead Bridge, and Caistor. His greatest discouragement came as a result of occasional failing health due to his tiring schedule of preaching and visitation. He suffered from dyspepsia his entire adult life and also had periods of depression. Obviously his physical and emotional ailments fed on each other.

In spite of all apparent success, however, William felt unsettled for two reasons. He imagined he might have more freedom in his ministry by emigrating to America, perhaps stirred by accounts of Finney's or Caughey's ministries there. Two letters from Catherine allude to this prospect. In the first she wrote, "As to going to America, I should not think of letting mere fear of the water prevent such a step, if I thought it your path—I should say go if two Atlantics rolled between. But I do think our own country needs all our aid."[43] In the second, written on December 1, 1853, she wrote, "If our prospects fail here; our path being blocked up, and the interests of our family demand it, I will brave all the trials of the voyage and the climate and cheerfully accompany you across the Atlantic, because then I should feel 'well we tried the only path conscientiously open to us in our native land and it failed, therefore if evil befall us we shall be sustained by the belief that it was in the path of duty and in the order of providence.'"[44] One can hardly blame Catherine for her natural fear of traveling across the Atlantic in the middle of the nineteenth century. Such travel was most uncomfortable in the best of circumstances and often treacherous and dangerous in difficult ones. One can only imagine the course of Catherine's and William's lives had they taken that step of faith and sailed to America.

William was troubled by a second difficulty. It was increasingly clear to him that the Reform movement was going nowhere. It had no organization, no Methodist discipline after the order of the Wesleyan discipline, and no central government. And its members were constantly engaged in disputes and arguments. William needed a more substantive and fixed denominational identity and affiliation and he also wanted that for his people at Spalding. Catherine was in full agreement with those wishes. They would both begin to look elsewhere for a denominational home. William would begin seriously considering the Methodist New Connexion denomination.

That denomination arose in this way. After the death of John Wesley in 1791, various Methodist denominations began to spring up in spite of Wesley's continual protestations during his lifetime that Methodism was not a separatist movement. The Methodists endlessly discussed matters of organization, polity, and the extent of the use of revivalism. The Reform movement developed as a result of such discussion and no little dissension over these and other issues. One young minister who wanted reform within Methodism at the end of the eighteenth century was Alexander Kilham, born into Methodism at Epworth in Lincolnshire, the birthplace of the Wesleys. He published pamphlets pushing such reform.[45]

> The principle changes which he advocated were, that the travelling preachers should be authorized to administer the sacraments, and that the laity should have equal power with the ministry in the government of the organization. He supported his arguments by casting serious reflections on the existing management of affairs, and by alleging that abuses had already arisen, which he believed could only be effectually dealt with by introducing delegates from the laity both in the Annual Conference and into the district meetings.[46]

The issues Kilham raised were not unknown to Wesley himself, and Wesley's own resolution on these matters never pleased everyone; in fact, they often caused dissension among his Methodists. The force of Wesley's personality, his autocratic leadership, and his ability to argue his positions with an acute, Oxford-trained mind kept Methodism basically connected. Nevertheless, even during Wesley's lifetime some wished to press the reform issues that Kilham and others later espoused, while others, desiring to remain clearly under the authority of Anglicanism, knew that such measures would eventually lead to expulsion from the Anglican community. Kilham was, nevertheless, much more influenced by the democratic impulses unleashed in the broader culture at the end of the eighteenth century. The growing democracy within Methodism reflected a political and social ethos that Wesley disliked and weaned much of Methodism away from autocratic control.

Kilham's reform measures were too radical for some of Methodism's leaders, and he was expelled in 1796. He published a magazine espousing his views, which eventually evolved into the *Methodist New Connexion Magazine*. He also purchased the Ebenezer Chapel in Leeds as a place to preach, all along hoping for a reconciliation with Wesleyan Methodism. In July 1797 it became apparent that no such reconciliation was forthcoming. Kilham and three other ministers resigned and formed the Methodist New Connexion, maintaining, of course, Wesleyan theology but establishing a constitution based on the reform measures for which Kilham and others had been fighting. Chief among those measures, and appealing to William Booth, was lay representation in the governing of the denomination. When Kilham died, at age thirty-six, on December 20, 1798, he was honored by some and vilified by others. Nevertheless, by then the denomination was established. Some Reform societies, convinced that reconciliation with the Wesleyan Methodists was impossible, joined with the Methodist New Connexion, and William considered doing likewise with his independent circuit at Spalding. He took such a proposition to the quarterly meeting of the circuit, but the motion failed. However, he resolved to join the Methodist New Connexion denomination himself, regardless of the Spalding circuit's direction. New Connexion Methodism appeared to offer William what he had been looking for in a denomination: a thoroughly Wesleyan theological base, a strong emphasis on revivalism, and a governance that included representation from the laity and preachers alike.

Voluminous correspondence flowed between Catherine and William regarding this decision. Catherine naturally had her decided opinions on the matter. She completely favored the move to New Connexionism and stated so many times. William, however, wavered in his decision. Many of the parishioners of the Spalding circuit were trying to entice him to stay with them, with the promise of providing a home, a horse, and the prospect of immediate marriage rather than having to wait the four years' probationary period before being married, which was New Connexion policy. Also, some London Reformers tried to lure him to the Hinde Street circuit at an annual salary of one hundred pounds, while other friends were pressing to persuade William that his gifts were as a revivalist and that he should launch out in an independent ministry unfettered by any denominational structure or bureaucracy.

Meanwhile, William commenced correspondence with the Reverend Dr. William Cooke, "one of the leading ministers, and an ex-president of the New Connexion."[47] Finally, at the advice and counsel of Catherine, it was decided that William should enter the New Connexion ministry, and in 1854 that providential step was taken. Church historian Owen Chadwick wrote, "Catherine had links with the Methodist New Connexion, and in 1854 persuaded him to join it."[48] Precisely what those links were is difficult to say. In any case, it was Catherine who clearly, calmly, and rationally established the soundness of the move to New Connexion Methodism in William's mind. She encouraged him to put aside the advice of friends and the enticements of salary and benefits. If it was right in principle for William to go over to New Connexionism, then he should do it. In one letter to William, probably written in January 1854, she frankly wrote, "I wish you prayed more and talked less about the matter. Try it, and be determined to get a clear and settled view as to your course."[49]

It was customary in the nineteenth century for clergy outside of the established church to receive ministerial training by studying with an experienced minister, learning the trade, as it were, under the watchful eye of a senior pastor. So William moved into the house of Dr. Cooke on February 14, 1854, with a few other students and began preaching the next day at the Brunswick Street Chapel. His apprenticeship began with a view toward ordination in New Connexion Methodism. William was still trying to develop the study habits recommended by Catherine but he confessed that he found the academic side of his training difficult and, for him at least, perhaps actually uninspiring. "That William did not make a good theological student goes without saying. Into the speculations of philosophy he never entered, and for the laborious study of theology it is quite certain that he could never have had a fruitful inclination. . . . Yet he was conscious in himself of a need for knowledge, and agonized more than was good for his health over intellectual deficiencies."[50] However, he excelled in his preaching, for which he had a natural talent and an obvious love. Dr. Cooke more than once observed that many people entered into the kingdom of God through Booth's preaching—and he may have been especially moved when his own daughter became a Christian under Booth's ministry.

Catherine and William were pleased that William had begun his ministerial training, and they were overjoyed to be together again in London. They had been separated for a long time. Now they could begin to map out their common future.

Dr. Cooke eventually decided to suggest William as the superintendent of the work of the denomination in London. William, however, did not believe himself ready for such a responsibility, so he offered to become the assistant to whomever the Conference appointed. There were funds for only one position, though. The dilemma was solved by William Booth's friend in need, Edward Rabbits, "who had followed him into New Connexion, and who now offered to pay the salary of a second pastor, provided that Mr. Booth was appointed to the post. To this arrangement the Conference subsequently agreed."[51] Reverend P. T. Gilton was appointed as pastor, and Booth was to assist him. William was delighted with the prospects of beginning his ministry in the security of a small, but well established, denomination. And, as Providence would have it, some of Booth's labors included preaching in the East End of London, in Wapping. In later years the East End would become very familiar territory to Catherine and William, for this was where The Salvation Army had its start.

William was unanimously received into the Conference—no surprise to Catherine who was confident both of William's abilities and of God's leading—with the exceptionally good news that he would have to wait only twelve months before he and Catherine could be married. They would not have to postpone marriage for the usual four years of probation for a new minister. This privilege was extended to William apparently because the leaders of New Connexion Methodism recognized William's abilities for preaching and evangelism and decided that marriage at the end of the first year of probation would not unduly interfere with his training.

Meanwhile, Catherine did not sit idly by anticipating the development of William's career. In 1854 she wrote an article for the *New Connexion Magazine* "on the best means for retaining new converts."[52] This article is important not only for its content but for the fact that this is the earliest extant publication of Catherine Mumford. Hundreds of articles and many books would follow in the course of her lifetime.

Of most interest in this article is that, in developing her last point about the need for new converts to be put to work in the church, she finishes the article with pointed language about both women and men being used in the service of God's kingdom. This would become the central most critical theological issue for Catherine. Before writing the article, she had argued with her pastor over the issue of women's equality with men, and perhaps this stimulated her to begin thinking seriously about the subject. It is extremely important to note that as early as 1854, even before her marriage to William Booth, she was making public pronouncements on this subject, such as, "The capacity of every young convert, male and female, should be ascertained, and a suitable sphere provided for its development."[53] She then went on to write the following:

Methodism, beyond almost any other system, has recognized the importance of this principle, and to this fact doubtless owes much of its past success; but has it not in some measure degenerated in this respect, at least with regard to its employment of female talent? There seems in many societies a growing disinclination among the female members to engage in prayer, speak in love feasts, band meetings, or in any manner bear testimony for their Lord, or to the power of His grace. And this false God-dishonoring timidity is but too fatally pandered to by the church, as if God had given any talent to be hidden in a napkin or as if the church and the world needed not the employment of all.

Why should the swaddling-bands of blind custom, which in Wesley's days were so triumphantly broken, and with such glorious results thrown to the moles and the bats, be again wrapped round the female disciples of the Lord Jesus? Where are the Mrs. Fletchers and Mrs. Rogers of our churches now, with their numerous and healthy spiritual progeny? And yet who can doubt that equal power in prayer and the germ of equal usefulness of life exist in many a Lydia's heart, smothered and kept back though it may be?I believe it is impossible to estimate the extent of the church's loss, where prejudice and custom are allowed to render the outpouring of God's Spirit upon His handmaidens null and void. But it is a significant fact that in the most cold, formal, and worldly churches of the day we find least of female agency.

I would warn our societies against drifting into false notions on this subject. Let the female converts be not only allowed to use their newly awakened faculties, but positively encouraged to exercise and improve them. Let them be taught their obligations to work themselves in the vineyard of the Lord, and made to feel that the plea of bashfulness, or custom, will not excuse them to Him Who has put such honor on them, and Who, last at the cross and first at the sepulcher, was attended by women, who so far overcame bashfulness as to testify their love for Him before a taunting multitude, and who so far disregarded custom that when all (even fellow-disciples) forsook Him and fled, they remained faithful.

Oh that the Church would excite its female members to emulate their zeal and remove all undue restraint to its development! Then, when every member, male and female, is at work, exercising their spiritual faculties, using the talents God has given them on purpose to be used, then will our Zion become a praise in the whole earth, and men shall flock to it as doves to their windows. Yours faithfully, C.M_____.[54]

New Connexionism was struggling in London. There were only 150 New Connexion members there, and many other circuits were that size or smaller.[55] Though William was at first reluctant to go to London, once there he found an urgency in his ministry, and his journal entries show his optimism during this time. A letter to the *Methodist New Connexion Magazine* by Josiah Bates, an important New Connexion layperson in London, supports William's appraisal that things were going well. Indeed, in that letter Bates suggested that William's labors were so successful that he ought to be freed from the circuit responsibilities and appointed as an evangelist throughout the denomination.

Nothing would have pleased William more. He already enjoyed some liberty—he was free to accept invitations from other circuits to preach and conduct revival meetings, the first of many invitations being to Bristol, followed by a most successful revivalistic campaign for two weeks at Guernsey. He then went to Longton, where he recorded in his diary, "At night the chapel was comfortably filled, about 1,800 persons present;"[56] and then on to Hanley where he wrote, "I have preached twice in perhaps the largest chapel in the world. At night an imposing congregation."[57] His success came to the attention of the leaders of the movement, and the Annual Committee, which governed the denomination between the meetings of the Annual Conference, considered it wise to appoint William as a traveling evangelist and to find a substitute for him in London. He was no longer bound to the London circuit and was able to engage in a ministry for which he had obvious gifts and felt particularly well suited. He often preached to large congregations—sometimes to as many as two thousand people at a time—held long prayer meetings, and witnessed many people converted at the communion rail, following the method used so effectively by Finney.

He returned to London in May 1855. The Annual Conference of New Connexion Methodism, convening at Sheffield that year, supported the Annual Committee's decision and appointed William Booth as a traveling evangelist. William's first year of probation was completed, and the way was now open for Catherine and William to be married.

The wedding was a quiet affair held in the Congregational Stockwell New Chapel—still Catherine's place of worship until after her marriage to William—on June 16, 1855. The officiating minister was her pastor, the Reverend Dr. David Thomas. Apart from their disagreement over the issue of women's equality with men, Catherine did indeed admire the man. "Mr. Thomas called last evening to enquire how I was," she earlier wrote to William. "I do like him; he is one of the nicest men I ever conversed with. . . . I really love him and his preaching gets better and better."[58]

The only other people witnessing their wedding were Catherine's father and one of William's sisters, Emma. Why Catherine's mother was not at the wedding is unknown. A letter from William to Catherine written shortly after they met reveals Mrs. Mumford's initial displeasure with William Booth. He wrote, "The high estimation your mother has for you, led her, I conceive, to take a prejudicial view of my conduct and to make remarks which were unmerited and unjust and calculated to wrong my soul. But it is over now."[59] All evidence suggests that her initial dislike for her future son-in-law quickly passed, so some other reason, such as illness, must be the explanation for Mrs. Mumford's absence from her only daughter's wedding.

Catherine and William's honeymoon was brief, only one week at Ryde in the Isle of Wight. However, it became immediately obvious that a partnership had begun in the lives of two become one. Catherine and William sustained both their love for and friendship with each other for the thirty-five years of their marriage, strengthening each other in the face of great obstacles and difficulties in what would eventually become a remarkable shared ministry. All of this was possible, they often reflected, by God's grace alone.

3

The Gathering Storm
❧

The Booths and New Connexion Methodism

It was time for preaching to begin again. From their honeymoon on the Isle of Wight, Catherine and William sailed straight to Guernsey, where William had earlier conducted a successful evangelistic campaign. On the trip to Guernsey this time, however, he was joined by his new wife, despite Catherine's dread of sailing. There is indication in a letter to her mother that at times, after arriving in Guernsey, she was too sick to go hear her new husband preach. In any case, the newlyweds were well received. They stayed with Mr. Ozanne, who had hosted William during his previous visit. Before leaving Guernsey, Catherine wrote the following in the album of a friend on July 20, 1855, indicative of what was uppermost in her mind: "The woman who would serve her generation according to the will of God, must make moral and intellectual culture the chief business of life. Doing this she will rise to the true dignity of her nature, and find herself possessed of a wondrous capacity for turning the duties, joys,

69

and sorrows of domestic life to the highest advantage, both to herself and to all those within the sphere of her influence."[1]

A trip to Jersey for revival services followed, and then they went back to London, their home base. Catherine's continual ill health, though, made it clear that she would not always be able to travel with her husband. Catherine was ever welcomed in her parents' home, so she stayed there when William set out for York. This period of separation, coming only about six weeks after the wedding, was difficult for the couple. During their frequent separations, they kept in touch through extensive correspondence, William sharing the results of the revival and Catherine providing her husband with wisdom and counsel, which was generally well received.

William moved from York to Hull, where Catherine joined him. When Catherine was well enough to travel with William, her letters to her parents are informative. Her letters reveal that two things bothered her about this itinerant life. She was, first of all, constantly troubled by physical illnesses of one sort or another and likewise incessantly concerned and usually fussing about William's health. Some of her hand-wringing was warranted but some was unnecessary, for her obsession with matters of health was obvious her whole life. She dwelt far too frequently on the subject of physical problems and perhaps placed too much confidence in her belief that her relief from suffering would come through vegetarianism, hydropathy, and homeopathy. Second, she longed for established home of her own, with her own furniture, her own garden, and her own servant. She quickly tired, as anyone would, of setting up an apartment every few weeks and living temporarily in unfamiliar surroundings with strangers. The troubles with this kind of nomadic existence would become even more exacerbated when they would have children. But Catherine was resigned to this kind of life, at least for the present. "With the exception of the drawback of a delicate body and being without an abiding home, I have all I want," she wrote to her parents in October 1855.[2]

In spite of often difficult circumstances, Catherine and William were delighted to be together, and Catherine accompanied her husband next to Sheffield. One letter reflects her pleasure in meeting John Unwin, a leader among the Reformers and a friend of James Caughey, who came to hear William preach. She also met and heard Luke Tyerman, the biographer of John Wesley.

Catherine was pleased that the article she had written for the *Methodist New Connexion Magazine* on training young converts was published subsequently by the *Canadian Christian Witness*. She was equally pleased, it would seem, to meet her new mother-in-law, for William's mother paid them a visit in Sheffield.

Catherine's greatest pleasure, however, came in witnessing the evangelistic meetings. She wrote frequently of the crowded churches, the powerful preaching, the protracted prayer meetings, and the numbers of people who were converted during one meeting or a whole campaign. Finney's measures for conducting revival meetings were proving effective in winning people to the Lord. It was obvious to Catherine that she and William had found, by God's grace, a place of service for the kingdom. She was often elated in relating the scenes of those evangelistic meetings and felt more at home in a chapel meeting than in her parlor. She had not yet begun her own preaching ministry, but that would follow in a few brief years.

Catherine's love of the natural world and her enjoyment of it is evident in her correspondence at this time. It might be said that here she was a true daughter of Romanticism, unlike Wesley. He was decidedly pre-Romantic and more the product of the Enlightenment, with a rational approach to the natural world, thinking of that world as less to be admired than controlled. One of the joys of Catherine's life, however, was to admire God's creation and rejoice in its beauty, tranquility, and order. She often described to her parents the sights she had seen—the foliage, the beautiful sky, the lush green fields, the waterfalls, the rocks of Middleton Dale, or the ocean—"that enchanter of all my soul."[3] She enjoyed walking and absorbing the rich scenery in many of the places William's preaching took them. During a period of rest at Chatsworth, Catherine, despite her continual protestations about her ill health, managed to walk nine miles in one day, all along admiring the scenery.

The Booths moved next to Dewsbury, where inflammation of the lungs prevented Catherine from attending some of the meetings of the revival. She was able to go to the last meeting, which was held in the Wesleyan Chapel and crowded with more than two thousand people, because she had recovered during their month's stay at Dewsbury. Catherine ascribed her mending health to her practice of homeopathic medicine. In a letter to her parents, she wrote of the "superiority of homoeopathic treatment, by which I have been spared the misery of blisters, purgatives, and nauseous doses, and the tedious weeks of convalescence attendant on them."[4] Homeopathy, introduced in the late eighteenth century, had become very popular in Victorian England. This medical practice consisted of administering tiny doses of drugs or other therapies that would in healthy persons produce symptoms similar to those of the illness being treated. This was supposed to lead to a cure. Catherine was likewise convinced of the value of hydropathy, also in vogue in the nineteenth century, by which water was used to treat diseases. Patients either bathed in it or drank it.

William was highly commended for his revival services at Dewsbury, and Catherine was, in spite of her physical ailments, rejoicing in the results of the revival, her loving relationship with her new husband, and the good prospects for the future with New Connexion Methodism. This was obviously a settled time in their lives, but Catherine's sometimes too introspective Methodist nature caused her to write to her mother:

> I often think that God is trying me by prosperity and sunshine, for I am, so far as outward things go, happier than I ever was in my life. Sometimes my heart seems burdened with a sense of my unmerited mercies, and tears of gladness stream down my cheeks. I tremble lest any coldness and want of spirituality should provoke the Lord to dash the cup from my lips, even while I am exulting in its sweetness.[5]

They were on to Leeds in December 1855 and January 1856. Catherine was especially pleased to get there because they were billeted in a home where there were no children—"quite a recommendation," she wrote to her mother, "seeing how they are usually trained! I hope if I have not both sense and grace to train mine so that they shall not be a nuisance to everybody about them, that God will in mercy take them to Heaven in infancy, but I trust I shall have, and I am learning a few useful lessons from <u>observation</u>."[6] Perhaps these reflections were brought about especially at this time because she was well into her first pregnancy and apparently was overly anxious that her children be polite and respectful at all times and obedient to their parents. Catherine simply could not countenance disobedience in children!

It comes as no surprise that the Leeds campaign was successful, more than eight hundred conversions being recorded. Some of the revival meetings were held in the famous Ebenezer Chapel in Leeds, the place of the forming of New Connexion Methodism almost sixty years earlier. Again it is Catherine's correspondence to her parents that provides the clearest firsthand expression of what transpired in those meetings, confirmed by the reports in the *Methodist New Connexion Magazine*. As usual, Catherine was sometimes unnecessarily concerned about "the uncertainties of health"[7] and unduly dwelt on her own and William's health problems.

Catherine wisely insisted on a brief vacation following the Leeds campaign. "It will be thirteen weeks on Saturday since we left Chatsworth, and he has had no rest since, so I have taken the matter into my own hands, and for no power on earth will I consent to any more toil until he has recruited a bit. We leave here all well next Friday, and go to Hunslet to spend a week at one of the principal friends."[8] Perhaps there had been some disagreement over this matter, for William dropped a note to Catherine's parents informing them that "she gave me a curtain lecture on my 'blockheadism, stupidity,' etc. . . . However, she is a <u>precious</u>, increasingly precious treasure to me, despite the occasional dressing-down that I come in for."[9] Perhaps the assessment of W. T. Stead about Catherine was correct after all: "Although she never commanded, she frequently led."[10] She indeed had an increasing sense of the indisputable correctness of her own opinions about a variety of matters, including when to take vacations.

The next two months were spent in Halifax, where there were more than six hundred converts. The time in Halifax was especially remembered by the Booths, however, because it was there on Saturday, March 8, 1856, at half-past eight in the evening that their first son, William Bramwell, was born. He was named after "an exceptional English evangelist" who emphasized holiness doctrine.[11] In later years Catherine reflected, "I had from the first infinite yearnings over Bramwell. I held him up to God as soon as I had strength to do so, and I remember specially desiring that he should be an advocate of holiness. In fact we named him after the well-known holiness preacher, with the earnest prayer that he might wield the sword with equal trenchancy in the same cause."[12]

Shortly after the birth of William Bramwell, the Booths were off to their next engagement at Macclesfield, where Mrs. Mumford joined them to assist Catherine with the baby's care and with Catherine's recuperation. The women from the silk factories who attended Booth's revival meetings were especially solicitous toward Catherine and the new baby. It was at Macclesfield that William baptized his new son, along with thirty other babies, in a service separate from the revival meetings. Catherine Bramwell-Booth, a daughter of William Bramwell Booth, perhaps defensively wrote that having William Bramwell baptized along with other babies "was arranged in case a separate service should imply that the evangelist's child was in any way 'special.'"[13] However, Catherine Booth herself gives no indication of this but as usual attributes the baptism of many babies at a special ceremony as an opportunity for evangelism, "making it the occasion for a special demonstration, and an appeal to parents to consecrate their children to the service of God."[14]

At the Annual Conference of New Connexion Methodism, it was decided that William Booth be reappointed as an evangelist for the Connexion for another year, undoubtedly at the request of many laypeople and ministers who had greatly benefited from his ministry in their circuits. With this vote of confidence by the denomination, and with the certain knowledge that this was the service to the body of Christ for which William was best fitted, the Booths then moved on to Yarmouth for yet another campaign and from Yarmouth back again to Sheffield. They were delighted to go to Sheffield because it was a town known for being receptive to revivalism, as it had been when James Caughey preached there in 1844. Author Norman Murdoch refers to Sheffield, a city with a population of more than 100,000, in this way: "A predominantly working-class city with iron and steel industries. . . . The religious climate included an evangelical Church of England and a strong revivalist tradition. . . . Methodism was the strongest sect, although from 1834 to 1844, it had declined from 4,950 to 4,307 members."[15] William was in Methodist country, and the success of his ministry at Sheffield, primarily among the Methodists, was attested to by the fact that about twelve hundred people attended the farewell tea in honor of William and Catherine, and two thousand persons heard William Booth's concluding two-hour sermon. In a letter written to her mother during this campaign, Catherine expressed her longing to live nearer her parents, little realizing that one day she and William would move to London permanently.

From Sheffield the Booths moved on to Birmingham. The Birmingham ministry was significant because of the use of street meetings held for evangelistic purposes. Such meetings would become characteristic of the Booths' ministry later in The Christian Mission and The Salvation Army. Following Birmingham, they went to Nottingham, the place of William's birth. Here William was well received, in spite of his personal misgivings about a prophet not being honored in his own country and opposition from the Reverend P. J. Wright, who will be mentioned later. After a brief rest in London, where the Booths took the opportunity to hear Spurgeon preach, William proceeded to a revival campaign in Chester while Catherine and William Bramwell remained with the Mumfords in London.

William reiterated in a letter to Catherine his pleasure in speaking to the common people, much like Wesley in the preceding century. He referred to them as "the poor country folk" or "the simple-hearted country people,"[16] and preferred this ministry in the provinces to ministry in the city. The correspondence from William to Catherine during this time at Chester has been preserved, but unfortunately, Catherine's responses have been lost. So we see the Chester campaign only through William's eyes. His love for Catherine was growing, as was his love for his first son, whom he affectionately called "Sunshine." His letters also reflect his continual confidence that his beloved Catherine would be able to help him out of fits of depression, anxiety, and despair—constantly a battle for him. It is clear in one of his letters to his wife that Catherine was still trying to convince William of the value of homeopathic treatment for his physical ailments, perhaps especially for his dyspepsia. William was still skeptical but yielded to what he considered Catherine's better judgment on this matter. He wrote:

> If it does not get better I shall go to the homoeopathic doctor. Chester is either blessed or cursed with three of them. But as you deem it a blessing, I am fain in this, as in many other respects, to pin my faith to your sleeve, and with me there the controversy ends! So I throw up my cap and shout "Hurrah for homoeopathy!" with its infinite quantity of infinitesimal doses, in whatever society I may be where the question is mooted. All because I have such a blessed little wife, in whose judgment I can confide on matters physical.[17]

Following the revival meetings at Chester, Catherine and William both went to Bristol, which had been part of the "great triangle" of John Wesley's Connexion, and from Bristol to Truro and St. Agnes. The Booths had never been to Cornwall and were enthralled to be in a bastion of Methodism, established ever since the Wesleyan revivals of the eighteenth century.[18] One author raised the question of why Methodism had become so strong in this area, and offered the following reasons.

One factor which has struck several observers is what may be termed "ecclesiastical geography," that is to say, the pattern at least of Methodist success and failure which seems to correspond to the areas of weakness and strength respectively in conventional Anglican parochial ministry. The areas of Anglican weakness and Methodist strength tend to be where parishes were large, especially where settlements were scattered: in industrial areas; in towns; where single landowners did not dominate; where churches and clergy were lacking or inactive. In southern agricultural parishes with compact territory, single landowners and resident clergy Methodism was much less successful. It has been calculated that well over half the Methodists were in areas where the organized religion was weakest. Whitefield and Wesley certainly felt they went to "sheep without a shepherd" and sometimes were stared at as if a clergyman were a strange animal: "Why did you not come before?" said miners to Wesley in the North-east.

Social, economic and political factors tend to bulk large in modern accounts of religious history, though analysis of the Revival in these terms remains at a rather elementary stage. Evangelicals tended to be apolitical, tacitly or openly to endorse the scriptural injunction to "obey the powers that be" as given by God, no doubt an implicitly "conservative" stance. In moral terms there were some signs that for their own reasons evangelicals shared the impression purveyed by opposition politicians out of office that government and society were corrupt and immoral and irreligious.

. . . More obviously, Methodism appealed very selectively in terms of occupation and social status . . . and it has often been observed that Methodism did seem to attract more of the craftsmen and industrial workers than the less skilled and agricultural labourers. This also helps to account for the geography of distribution.[19]

It is important to remember, in this context, that the results at William's revival meetings were remarkable. Many people were converted—from the divine side of things, through the ministry of the Holy Spirit in their lives. From the human side, success was due largely to the new measures of revivalism Finney had introduced on the American scene. Such measures were popularized in England through Finney's book *Lectures on Revivals of Religion* as well as through his first visit to England from 1849 to 1851. William used these measures very effectively. However, it must also be said that the majority of those coming to his meetings were regular chapel attenders. Many of the converts were rededicating their lives to the Lord, others were seeking sanctification, while still others had been backsliders. In any case, the large number of people who went forward to the mercy seat in Booth's meetings must be put in proper perspective, especially in this Methodist stronghold where people had witnessed countless similar revivals.

The Booths found that they had to contend with what was common in the Methodist revivals of the preceding century—an emotional religious response to the gospel that included "outbreaks of crying and fainting"[20] as well as an unusual reliance on the part of some on such supernatural manifestations as dreams and visions. The Booths were not as accepting of such manifestations as Wesley and some of the early Methodists had been. Catherine and William found that such religious excitement could be merely superficial and rejoiced at what they perceived to be a more rational and careful response to the gospel— people seeing themselves as sinners and responding to God's grace by kneeling at the communion rail, which Catherine, following Finney and American Methodists, now referred to as the penitent form. Nevertheless, such principled response was not without emotion, and William himself, writing to the Mumfords, recounted the following:

> We had a very glorious stir last night, such a meeting for excitement and thrilling interest as I had never before witnessed. The people had been restraining their feelings all the week. Many of them had been stifling their convictions. But it burst out last night, and they shouted and danced and wept and screamed and knocked themselves about, until I was fairly alarmed lest serious consequences might ensue. However, through mercy, all went off gloriously, twenty-seven persons professing to find salvation. Praise the Lord forever![21]

There was a delicate balance in these Cornish meetings between allowing the excitement to include ecstatic singing and jumping up and down and gently guiding the meetings and even controlling them so that decency, order, and decorum might prevail and the meetings could be brought to a good and satisfying conclusion. On the one hand, the revivalists portrayed the specter of sin and hell, which raised the emotional temperatures in the listeners; while on the other hand, the preachers assured their audience of the grace of God and the conscious and ordered moral life required by him. This brought serenity to the hearers. There was certainly much to be learned here about conducting public meetings that would be helpful to both Catherine and William in their later ministry.

At the conclusion of this revival, Catherine expressed for the first time in earnest that she longed for a settled home, having now been married for almost two years. The wandering life was beginning to take its toll on her, especially because she was ill so much of the time. She was of two minds, however, because she still wanted to travel with her husband, and she was determined to keep their son, affectionately called Willie, with them rather than place him in someone else's care, even Mrs. Mumford's.

> Nor can I make up my mind to parting with Willie, first because I know the child's affections would inevitably be weaned from us, and secondly, because the next year will be the most important of his life with reference to managing his will, and in this I cannot but distrust you. I know, my darling mother, you could not wage war with his self-will so resolutely as to subdue it. And then my child would be ruined, for he must be taught implicit, uncompromising obedience.[22]

In Catherine's opinion, merely controlling a child's will was not enough. Rather, a child's will must be subdued, not so much after the manner prescribed by Locke in the eighteenth century, but after the fashion of Wesley who believed, following his mother, Susanna, "that a child's will must be broken . . . before it could be moulded according to its parents' wishes and so prepared for independent (correct) action later."[23] Catherine never wavered from this principle, and many years later wrote the following regarding the rearing of children.

The first and most important point is to secure OBEDIENCE. Obedience to properly constituted authority is the foundation of all moral excellence, not only in childhood, but all the way through life. And the secret of a great deal of the lawlessness of these times, both towards God and man, is that, when children, these people were never taught to submit to the authority of their parents; and now you may convince them ever so clearly that it is their duty, and would be their happiness to submit to God, but their unrestrained, unsubdued wills have never been accustomed to submit to anybody, and it is like beginning to break in a wild horse in old age. Well may the Prophet enquire, "Can the Ethiopian change his skin, or the leopard his spots? Then may ye also do good that are *accustomed* to do evil." God has laid it on parents to begin the work of bringing the will into subjection in childhood; and to help us in doing it, He has put in all children a tendency to obey. Watch any young child, and you will find that, as a rule, his instincts lead him to submit; insubordination is the exception, until this tendency has been trifled with by those who have the care of him. Now, how important it is, in right training, to take advantage of this tendency to obedience, and not on any account allow it to be weakened by encouraging exceptional rebellion! In order to do this, you must begin EARLY ENOUGH. This is where multitudes of mothers miss their mark; they begin too late. The great majority of children are ruined for the formation of character before they are five years old by the foolish indulgence of mothers.[24]

Note that even Catherine's reflections on child rearing were based ultimately on a redemptive purpose. Subjecting the will of small children was preparatory, Catherine believed, to the more free response of the will in later life to submit oneself to God's saving will. The freedom of the will, for Catherine, was as much humble submission to God as it was reaching out to him.

Catherine may have had some sense that their nomadic lifestyle would soon come to an end for the time being, but not as a result of their decision. There were some problems in New Connexion Methodism. All was not well. The success William enjoyed during his evangelistic campaigns, as well as his growing popularity, evidently were cause for jealousy among some fellow New Connexion ministers. This may have begun at the conclusion of William's second visit to Sheffield. Following his revival, at a special farewell meeting in the Temperance Hall in Sheffield, William was highly praised for his ministry and, as a token of appreciation from the people of Sheffield, was presented with a portrait of himself. This incident was favorably reported in the *Methodist New Connexion Magazine*.

The visit to Nottingham during the next month, in spite of the success of the meetings, was in some way spoiled by the superintending minister of Nottingham, the Reverend P. J. Wright. Wright, although consenting to the invitation extended to William, opposed both him and his work of revivalism. He would become one of William's chief antagonists. Attacks against William and his revival by the press, as had happened at Chester, could be understood and interpreted by both Catherine and William as infidel ravings of the world against the work of the church. However, attacks from within the Methodist movement, which was raised expressly for the purpose of revivalism, were not only difficult to understand but unconscionable as far as the Booths were concerned. For all their human failings, neither William nor Catherine ever demonstrated any jealousy against other people engaged in the work of the Lord and, in fact, rejoiced that such work was being done. What they understood as jealousy of William's success they simply could not comprehend. Theirs was indeed the catholic spirit prescribed by Wesley when he and his Methodists were under attack from other Christians.

There was growing opposition by a group of ministers within the Connexion, that was certain. Such antagonism against William is inexplicable except to say that there had always been resistance against some of the revivalistic measures of James Caughey, who was about to launch his second visit to England, and Charles Grandison Finney, who also would return to England for a second revivalistic tour in 1858. The emotional religious meetings certainly were disconcerting to those who wished for quieter and more orderly ones. Religious respectability was indeed at risk. Also, the success of so many of these revivals of Caughey or Finney or Booth was in a sense an indictment on the often lackluster ministry of the local preachers who had been laboring unsuccessfully for so many years, often in the shadow of the itinerant evangelists. Itinerants were also perceived as free from Conference discipline. What one author has well stated concerning Caughey might also be said of Booth at this time: "Threat to authority caused 'settled ministers' to point with envy at their itinerant brothers' freedom. Caughey had come to England without an invitation and had remained for five years without any official connection to a Methodist Conference. His popularity had kept him in demand even when circuit superintendents preferred that he stay away. More ominous, he had encouraged 'irregular ministers,' uneducated men like Booth, who might overrun the denomination.[25]

However, as easy as it is to dismiss one's enemies as either jealous or unmoved by the workings of God's Holy Spirit, not all opponents of Caughey or Finney or even of Booth were compelled by base motives. There were serious questions about revival measures used to control people's emotions, which placed doubt on the authenticity of some conversions. There were also reasonable reservations about the lasting results of thousands of conversions both for the local churches and for impact on society. What moved Booth's opponents at this time is difficult to say. Jealousy was without question a factor, perhaps even among the majority of the opposition. But certainly there were some who had honest concerns about the whole revivalistic enterprise. Catherine, however, would never see it this way. To oppose William was to oppose the will of God and the call of God. It was that simple. Also, there is no question that both Catherine and William were finding it difficult to submit to the authority of their leaders, some of whom they did not respect. In later life, this particular personal struggle would be conveniently forgotten when Booth, like Wesley before him, as the autocratic leader of a movement would demand obedience to his explicit authority. Catherine had always had an implied authority to which people submitted.

The ministers of the Connexion were reappointed at each Annual Conference, and in 1857 the Conference met at Nottingham. By a vote of forty-four to forty, William Booth was removed from his position as an evangelist and directed by the Conference to take a regular circuit. He was informed of this action by a letter from his friend, Josiah Bates; and this was followed by a letter from a minister at the Nottingham Conference, which revealed the influence of the Nottingham Superintendent, P. J. Wright, in convincing fellow ministers to vote against Booth's continuing as an evangelist in the Connexion. Wright, together with a Dr. Crofts, was one of the principal speakers during the Conference on this particular matter. He had probably been envious of Booth's influence since the revival in Nottingham during the previous year, and it is not apparent that he was moved by lofty ideas about the nature of revivalism.

Booth responded to the Conference by a letter addressed to the secretary, requesting the Conference to provide reasons for this change of appointment and defending his record as an evangelist with the denomination during the past three and a half years. The Conference responded that there were three issues at stake and notified William of such. First, there were the travel expenses needed for this ministry. Some thought the expenses of an evangelist were exorbitant. Second, some believed that Booth, for such a young man in the Connexion, was too influential due to his many contacts during his travels. Finally, it was held by some that Booth's ordination into the ministry of the denomination would depend, to a large extent, on his ability to be a regular circuit preacher and to be in charge of a circuit. Such abilities could not be rightly judged unless Booth actually had a circuit. The latter reason was certainly not an unreasonable justification for the decision of the Conference, but the first two reasons were patently absurd.

William wrote a letter to the Mumfords explaining the action of the Conference in which he resigned himself to their decision and the will of the Lord. "However, I leave the matter with the Lord. My work and my reputation are in His hands. I wait the manifestation of His will, and wherever He points there will I try to go."[26] Catherine, however, was not nearly so serene about the matter! She wrote:

> You will see from William's letter what has been the subject of our thoughts, and the cause of the anxiety we have experienced during the last few days. I have felt it far more keenly than I thought I should; in fact, it is the first real trial of my married life.
>
> Personally considered I care nothing about it. I feel that a year's rest in one place will be a boon to us both, and especially a relief from the wearying anxiety which my dear husband has experienced of late. But as a manifestation of the spirit of a handful of ministers towards him in return for his toil—as an exhibition of the cloven foot of jealousy, and as a piece of rank injustice in allowing lying reports to be reiterated in open Conference, and this without any formal charges having been brought or any inquiry as to their truthfulness instituted, I regard as little better than an old priestly persecution over again, and am ready to forswear Conferences for ever! However, we shall see. We can afford to wait. A year's rest will be an advantage to William's mind and body. Time will do great things— the people will be able to look at and contrast the year's returns. Our friends, whom this discussion has proved to be neither few nor feeble, will spread their own report of the matter, and perhaps next Conference the trumpet will sound on the <u>other side</u>. Anyhow, if God wills him to be an evangelist, He will open up his way. I find that I love the work itself far more than I thought I did, and I am willing to risk something for it, but we shall see.[27]

William journeyed to the Conference at Nottingham and probably argued his case there. Should he be made to take a circuit, he asked for Derby because there was only one minister appointed there and no superintendent above him. Booth clearly wanted to be free from the supervision of a superior. He continued to manifest an independent spirit, supported in this by Catherine, which, ironically, he would not allow in others under his command after the founding of The Salvation Army.

The Conference reiterated its decision to send him to a circuit, but it was not going to be Derby as Booth requested. He was sent to the Halifax circuit, with living quarters in Brighouse. Booth went quietly, believing that after a year in the Halifax circuit the Connexion would reappoint him to the position of an evangelist, and he would be instrumental in building up the Connexion across Britain. This in spite of the fact that he was encouraged by some friends to leave the Connexion and launch out into an independent ministry, after the fashion of James Caughey. Booth already knew, however, that evangelistic work without the support of a denomination was ephemeral. He would remain with the Connexion and obediently follow orders—for the moment at least!

For a change, William was quite optimistic about his future in the denomination once the crisis was past, while Catherine was pessimistic, doubting that the motives of William's jealous, self-seeking opponents would ever change. Those enemies were, for Catherine, beyond hope of seeing past their own selfish interests. Nevertheless, for the sake of the ministry and the family, she acquiesced to William's optimism, and the Booths moved into their first permanent home.

In spite of William's hope for the future, both his and Catherine's spirits were low on entering this new appointment. Going to Brighouse was a move contrary to their every instinct. The superintendent of the Halifax circuit "was a sombre, funereal kind of being, very well-meaning no doubt, but utterly incapable of co-operating with Mr. Booth in his ardent views and plans for the salvation of the people."[28] Brighouse was known as "one of the most obscure and least successful circuits."[29] And Catherine's health was not good. Added to that, the accommodations evidently left something to be desired. Catherine wrote to her mother shortly after arriving at Brighouse in early summer of 1857 that "it is a low, smoky town, and we are situated in the worst part of it."[30]

This period of transition was all the more difficult for Catherine because she was pregnant with her second child. Soon after arriving at Brighouse, the second Booth son, Ballington, was born on July 28, 1857. He was named after an uncle of Catherine's.

Brighouse, however, was not a total loss for one critical reason. It was here that Catherine decided to lead a class of female members who attended the chapel (men and women generally did not meet together in the Methodist class meetings), and she also began to teach a girls' Sunday school class. So the important public ministry of Catherine Booth began in this least likely of places (that beginning and its following successes will be dealt with in another chapter).

The year 1858 brought some brightness to Catherine and William through their contact with James Caughey. Both Catherine and William had great admiration for the evangelist. His preaching on the doctrine of holiness and his evangelistic emphasis influenced the Booths. Catherine was not above comparing her husband to Caughey. In a letter to her mother dated October 22, 1857, she wrote, ". . . for <u>considering</u> the difference in the <u>circumstances</u> of each, he has had <u>greater</u> success than Mr. Caughey and many have said they prefer him as a preacher. Then why should he be fettered and chained down by envy and jealousy when he might be preaching to crowds every night; but God will undertake for him and put him in his right place, help us to pray for it."[31]

Caughey had returned to England during the previous year. In February 1858 the Booths went to hear him at Sheffield. Arrangements had been made for Caughey to baptize Ballington Booth. This was a memorable event in the Booths' lives. Catherine had written to her mother earlier that "Mr. Caughey is now laboring at . . . Sheffield with great success. . . . I intend to hear him soon and take baby to be baptized by him, we are deferring it on purpose; there is no other man I would rather did it than his father except Caughey and he may not be in England when another is born."[32]

In a letter written on February 5, 1858, Catherine recounted at great length to her parents the occasion of meeting Caughey:

We took tea with Mr. Caughey at the same table and Wm had some conversation with him. Then on Wednesday we dined with him where he is staying and enjoyed a rich treat in his society. He is a sweet fellow, one of the most gentle loving humble spirits you can conceive of; he treats us with great consideration and kindness; conversed with Wm on his present and future position like a <u>brother</u> and a friend and prayed for us most fervently. On Thursday morning he called at Mr. Wilkins and baptized our boy in the presence of a few friends, it was a very solemn and interesting ceremony. He asked for him the most precious of all blessings and dedicated him to God most fervently. Afterwards he placed his hand on his head and blessed him in the name of the Lord. He wrote me an inscription for my Bible and took leave of us most affectionately expressing the deepest interest in our future and desired to know the proceedings of the next Conference in William's case.[33]

Catherine showed her genuine affection for this mentor in that same letter by concluding with these words: "I pressed one fervent kiss on his hand when he took leave of me, and felt more gratified than if it had been Victoria's."[34]

Caughey was made aware of William Booth's present dilemma with New Connexion Methodism and had experienced a similar problem himself with the Wesleyans in America. Catherine shared some advice that Caughey had given to William in a letter to her mother dated February 8, 1858.

Mr. C. advises him to wait till he is ordained before he takes any steps, his advice was very cautious but he said perhaps Wm would be compelled to "<u>cut loose</u>" if so there was plenty of room for him both here and in America, but I shall not hear of <u>America,</u> of course this is <u>strictly confidential</u>. I think Wm will take a circuit another year but we shall not stop here. They want him at Halifax. I don't know how it will be yet.[35]

The work at Brighouse was not exceptional, and the year was marked with many disappointments for the Booth family. Naturally, as the year progressed, both Catherine and William wondered about what the deliberation of the Annual Conference would be regarding their future. William was hopeful still that he would be reappointed as an evangelist with the Connexion.

Catherine was pessimistic still, and as the Conference drew near, Catherine's fears seemed more realistic than William's faith. The rumors were that William would stay in a circuit, and it was most probable that he would be reappointed to Halifax. Both, however, were resigned for a difficult circuit somewhere for another year if William was not appointed as an evangelist. The prospect of living for another year at Brighouse was indeed a depressing one.

At the Annual Conference at Hull, William Booth was ordained to the New Connexion Methodist ministry into full connexion, his four years of probation having come to an end. The next order of business that would affect the Booths had to do with the matter of appointments. There were, to William's credit, many circuits that petitioned to have him, but a lay delegate at the Conference from Gateshead, a town of fifty thousand located just across the Tyne from Newcastle, must have been particularly persuasive. The Conference appointed William Booth to Gateshead. "The resolution of Conference," Catherine wrote, "we have not yet seen. I do not feel as anxious about it because I feel confident God will open our way either in, or <u>out</u> of the Connexion and I don't care much which. I have no fears about the future if we are only ready to do his will at all risks and I think we have both come to that decision."[36]

In spite of Catherine's growing misgivings about New Connexion Methodism, she in any case was glad to get away from Brighouse. "I feel just like anyone liberated from prison getting from that hated Brighouse."[37]

Catherine and William were again on the move—this time to Gateshead.

4

Gateshead
❦

The Turning Point

Thank God, the Booths might often have said, for Gateshead!
Life for the Booth family was considerably better here, and
Catherine and William were sure they had at last found a place
of ministry worthy of their talents. The church at Gateshead was
described by Frederick Booth-Tucker, one of the Booths' sons-
in-law, as "the converting shop," claiming that it was so dubbed
by the local population on realizing the impact the Booths were
having at Gateshead. Help was indeed needed for this struggling
circuit, and the people at Gateshead were as delighted to welcome the Booths as the Booths were to meet them.

The Bethesda Chapel had a seating capacity of 1,250, so it
was large enough for William's dramatic preaching impulses,
which came alive while speaking to large congregations. He was
a restless preacher, roaming back and forth on the platform while
he preached. And Catherine may have shocked some members
of the congregation when, at the conclusion of William's sermon on the first Sunday night, she stood before the congrega-

tion and prayed. Catherine agreed to be one of the class leaders of the church. She wrote to her parents in June 1858, "I have consented to meet a class again, provided that I can have it at home, as the chapel is more than half a mile distant, and it is uphill coming back"[1]—no inordinate request for a frail woman who was now six months pregnant. Soon after settling into life at Gateshead, the eldest Booth daughter, Catherine, was born on September 18, 1858. Beginning at the birth of this first daughter, Catherine always taught her sons that the daughters were equally important.

Neither Catherine nor William approached their new ministry in conventional ways. The whole town of Gateshead was seen as their parish, and an entire day of prayer preceded the revival services at the Bethesda Chapel. Notices of special revival meetings were distributed from house to house, Catherine herself responsible for 150 houses. Lists of names for whom the congregation desired salvation were made, and times of fervent prayer were set aside in the chapel. One sees the influence of Finney in these methods. The Booths held that a slumbering church had to be brought alive and were likewise convicted that conducting special revival meetings shortly after their arrival was the best means of doing so. According to Catherine the meetings were a success, with many people professing faith.

Catherine was present at a public meeting where new converts were recognized in the chapel at the conclusion of the first great revival at Gateshead under William's direction. She wrote to her mother:

> I ventured to chapel on Tuesday night to the public recognition service. The persons brought to God since we have been here were admitted by ticket into the body of the chapel, while the old members and the public occupied the gallery. It would have done your soul good to have seen the bottom of the large chapel almost full of new converts, most of them people in middle life, and a great proportion men.
>
> William gave them an address composed of various counsels respecting their future course, which if they adopt they will do something for this poor world of ours.

On the whole it has been a glorious year for this circuit, such an one as nobody expected to see. And I believe William has become the most popular and beloved minister either in Gateshead or Newcastle. All praise unto Him, Whose doing it is![2]

These Gateshead meetings introduced a religious novelty to the town—that of street meetings. Booth-Tucker records,

The members were organized into a procession every Sunday evening and paraded the streets from five to six o'clock, singing as they went, and stopping at suitable intervals for the delivery of brief and pointed exhortations to the unconverted persons who crowded round the ring. On several occasions bands of men were sent out by the publicans to sing down the processionists, who not unfrequently started singing a hymn to the same popular tune, thus defeating the would-be disturbers with their own weapons.[3]

The only aspect of the whole enterprise that bothered both Catherine and William was the use of bazaars to raise money for the church and the revival meetings. Catherine attended the bazaar the first day, and that was enough for her! She wrote to her mother that overall this method of raising money for the gospel

has been a dissipating, godless affair, and has exerted a very evil influence on our people. There has been a deal of lotterying, which is little better than gambling, and the foolery and display in dress has made us sick at heart. William says he will write a pamphlet on the subject, but I don't know whether he will find the time. I am sure someone ought to set forth the secularising, worldly influence such occasions exert on the church. It is most baneful.[4]

A nasty accident in which Catherine and her two young sons were thrown from a carriage happened in the autumn of 1858, and it could have been much more serious but for divine assistance. Catherine held to a belief in Providential intervention much the same as Wesley did. Catherine's intense love for animals has already been noted. She wrote about the incident to her parents:

"I am sure the <u>horse</u> was not to blame. It is a sweet creature and never did such a thing before, but the rising of the shafts frightened it."[5]

As life for the Booths at Gateshead became settled, there would be important decisions made, new directions sought, and critical turning points found in the path of ministry available not only to William but to Catherine as well. One such turning in the road was something that proved to be a prelude to a public ministry for her.

She was on her way to the chapel for Sunday services and, passing along a densely populated street, noticed the way people, especially women, were loitering around the doorsteps of houses or leaning out the windows, apparently without direction or meaning in their lives. Catherine had to overcome a natural timidity and a fear of speaking with strangers but she records that she was moved by her conscience to speak with some of the people she saw and invite them to the meetings at the chapel. She felt it would be selfish of her to enjoy the services for herself alone and quite un-Christian not to witness about the love of God in Christ that compelled her to go to the chapel in the first place. Her natural inclinations set aside, she began speaking to people she met on the streets, even knocking on the doors of some homes. She was delighted with the reception she was given. People listened to her politely and were not rude or defiant. It was as though they were relieved that someone finally paid attention to them. She explained the gospel in simple language and invited the people to the meetings at the chapel. Some promised they would go.

Catherine then encountered a woman on a doorstep who said she would never be able to go to church because of her wretched appearance and because her husband was a mean drunkard (a common term for the alcoholic of that day) who would never permit it. With the woman's permission, Catherine accompanied her into the house to meet this man. Perhaps to her own surprise, and certainly to the astonishment of the wife, the husband, though drunk, received Catherine quite well. A long conversation ensued between Catherine, the husband, and the wife, and she learned of the troubles of this family living in deplorable conditions in a two-room flat. Catherine was deeply moved and not only bore witness to the gospel and prayed with the couple but elicited a promise from the husband that he would sign a total abstinence pledge, ever a cause of top priority on Catherine's agenda.

William must have been greatly concerned when Catherine did not arrive at the chapel that Sunday until the conclusion of the sermon and the commencement of the prayer meeting. However, Catherine was convinced that this new venture set her on two distinct avenues of service, both of which would later be characteristic of The Christian Mission and The Salvation Army. First, she returned to the home of the drunkard the next day with the total abstinence pledge in hand, and he signed the pledge as promised and even listened respectfully to her closely reasoned argument on the evils and dangers of drink. That prompted her to seek out others so afflicted, and she saw a ministry to alcoholics as uniquely hers. "The Lord so blessed my efforts that in a few weeks I succeeded in getting ten drunkards to abandon their soul-destroying habits, and to meet me once a week for reading the Scriptures and for prayer."[6]

Second, she had learned the value of visiting people in their homes. "From that time I commenced a systematic course of house-to-house visitation, devoting two evenings per week to the work."[7] To Catherine's credit, such visitation was done despite the circumstances, and she describes her meeting with people, and even conducting cottage prayer meetings, in hovels where there was no furniture, no place to sit, and no ventilation. Indeed, she later recalled one experience where she found

a poor woman lying on a heap of rags. She had just given birth to twins, and there was nobody of any sort to wait upon her. I can never forget the desolation of that room. By her side was a crust of bread, and a small lump of lard. . . . I was soon busy trying to make her a little more comfortable. The babies I washed in a broken pie-dish, the nearest approach to a tub that I could find. And the gratitude of those large eyes, that gazed upon me from that wan and shrunken face, can never fade from my memory.[8]

It is undoubtedly through Catherine's influence that, after the founding of The Salvation Army, one of the standards of service for its officers was: "Each officer is expected . . . to spend 18 hours (weekly) in visiting from house to house, and to spare no possible effort besides for the good of souls."[9]

The ministry prospered in Gateshead, and William had reason to be optimistic when he attended the Annual Conference of the Methodist New Connexion in Manchester in 1859. He was certainly pleased that the circuit officials wished for him to be reappointed to Gateshead, but in spite of his affection for that place and for those people, he still desired to get back into evangelistic work on a full-time basis. Catherine consented to this but insisted that if the Conference agreed, arrangements would have to be made for the family to settle in a central town in the district and William could minister in the circuits surrounding the town. This would allow Catherine and the children to have a settled life for long periods of time in one place while William was preaching. It would also allow the family to see husband and father at least once a week. So it was decided that at least for 1859–60 William would continue ministering at Gateshead, a prospect that pleased the members of the chapel, whose membership had increased from thirty-nine to three hundred during the previous year. William, however, was disappointed.

At the turn of the new year, on Sunday morning, January 8, 1860, William Booth was uncharacteristically late for the service—but he did arrive in time to preach. He had been unavoidably detained because earlier that morning, Catherine had given birth to their second daughter, Emma Moss Booth. The work at Gateshead proceeded at its usual pace, with large congregations on Sundays and revivalistic meetings in other towns in the circuit. Not long after Emma's birth, Catherine began a public ministry of preaching (this will be described in detail in the next chapter).

Catherine's natural abilities of leadership had been demonstrated in countless ways both to her husband and to her growing family. However, such skills would be required in a larger arena and were indeed needed at Gateshead during William's second year of appointment there. Such demands for public leadership constituted a second turning point for Catherine. William became quite ill in the summer of 1860, described later by Booth-Tucker as "nervous prostration and complete break-down."[10] St. John Ervine's assessment of William at this time is more pointed. He wrote, "William, so resentful about the refusal of the Manchester Conference to appoint him to evangelistic work that he did not attend the next Conference, had a complete breakdown."[11] Whatever the cause of William's incapacity, a period of rest and recuperation away from Gateshead was required as well as hydropathic treatment under the direction of a Mr. Smedley at his clinic in Matlock. William's absence forced Catherine to assume the many responsibilities for the business of the circuit.

Despite William's illness, he and Catherine sustained their usual detailed correspondence, and it provides an account of William's medical treatment as well as his progress toward recuperation. Catherine's life alone was difficult. At one point, all the children came down with whooping cough, and Catherine understandably described her own complete exasperation in a letter to her parents. As might be expected, though, homeopathy came to her rescue. She wrote to her parents, "I am giving them appropriate homoeopathic remedies, with their feet in hot water and mustard at night, and water bandages on their chests. So far this treatment answers well and they are progressing as favourably as could be expected."[12]

In that same letter Catherine revealed something of her domestic life and her child-rearing methods. She was greatly concerned that the children not take on the attitude of the world, and in this letter she demonstrated that she was particularly worried about their apparel. She reproached her mother, though not doubting her mother's good intentions. She wrote:

Accept my warmest thanks for the little frock you sent. We like it very much. There is only one difficulty, namely, it is too smart! I shall have to give you full and explicit directions in future as to the style, trimming, etc., for we really must set an example in this respect worthy of imitation. I feel no temptation now to decorate myself. But I cannot say the same about my children. And yet, oh, I see I must be decided, and come out from among the fashion-worshipping, worldly professors around me. Lord, help me! Don't think I am reflecting on you. But we must do violence to our fancies for Christ's sake. Bless you! I am sure your kindness is fully appreciated and highly prized![13]

Writing a year earlier on this same subject, Catherine assured her parents that William had similar views on the need for simple dress as an appropriate expression of being different from the world. These good Methodists were in keeping with a Methodist culture of separation from the world. One wonders if they had read John Wesley's sermon, "The Use of Money," in which he wrote the following:

And why should you throw away money upon your children, any more than upon yourself, in delicate food, in gay or costly apparel, in superfluities of any kind? Why should you purchase for them more pride or lust, more vanity, or foolish and hurtful desires? They do not want any more; they have enough already; nature has made ample provision for them. Why should you be at farther expense to increase their temptations and snares, and to pierce them through with more sorrows?[14]

In spite of the care of four sick children, the youngest being only four months old, Catherine undertook the necessary circuit responsibilities for her absent, ailing husband. The interruptions of the household did not prevent her from the business of preparing sermons, and Catherine indicates in her letters that her preaching engagements—basically substitutions in her husband's absence at this point—kept her extremely busy primarily on Sundays in many places in the circuit. She generally preached for an hour or more. She must have astounded herself at times, because only a year earlier speaking in public was out of the question. In a letter dated September 26, 1859, she wrote this to her parents: "I received a unanimous invitation from our leaders' meeting the other night, to give an address at the special prayer meetings this week but of course declined. I don't know what they can be thinking of."[15]

Preaching suited Catherine, though, and her letters both to William and her parents indicate her delight in this ministry. She was greatly humbled, no doubt, by the prayer of a "good brother who could scarcely put three words together." He earnestly prayed, Catherine wrote to her husband, "that God would crown my labours, seeing that He could bless the weakest instruments in His service."[16]

Catherine's preaching also suited the lay leaders of the Gateshead circuit, as the continual invitations to her testified. Both recognition of Catherine's considerable efforts as well as gratitude for her devoted service were given at the quarterly meeting of the circuit, and a resolution was made that, should William return by Christmas, he would be asked to preach one sermon and Catherine the other. William did return with restored health, and he and Catherine shared the responsibilities of preaching on Christmas Day at the Bethesda Chapel, a good beginning in late 1860 to what would continue to be a shared ministry for the next thirty years. In an 1861 New Year's Day letter to her parents, Catherine wrote, "At a society meeting held last week they passed a resolution that some blanks be left on the next 'plan' for Sunday nights at Bethesda, and that I be requested to supply them."[17] Catherine Booth was well on her way toward fulfilling her principal vocation—preaching the gospel. This was indeed a turning point in her life that would eventually influence thousands of women and men.

There was, however, a third turning point in Catherine's life then, brought about perhaps partly by both her preaching and other events of her life and certainly giving direction and purpose to future preaching. In 1861 Catherine, according to her own testimony, was fully sanctified.

The doctrine of sanctification was not new to Catherine and William. Both of them were reared in a Methodist tradition that consciously kept alive John Wesley's preaching and teaching on the doctrine of entire sanctification. Wesley preferred to speak of it as perfect love, manifested primarily in fulfillment of Jesus' commandment in Matthew 22:37–39: "'You shall love the Lord your God with all your heart, and with all your soul, and with all your mind.' This is the greatest and first commandment. And a second is like it: 'You shall love your neighbor as yourself.'" Wesley taught that, at the moment a person is justified and subsequently born again by God's grace through faith, sanctification begins through the ministry of the Holy Spirit in the believer. The Christian is then exhorted to fulfill the commandment of Hebrews 6:1 and "go on toward perfection," appropriating perfect love by faith. Such a perfection was not an absolute perfection, which is reserved for God alone. Nor was it a sinless perfection that rendered the believer incapable of further sin, although there were preachers during Wesley's day who taught this. Freedom of the will was inherent in the human condition both before and after salvation, and this implied that one may always choose to say no to God in disobedience. Nor was it human perfection, for this side of heaven the believer will never have perfect knowledge and will never be free from the temptations, afflictions, and infirmities that are part of this life below.

What Wesley taught was that it was possible to be perfect in love—having the perfect intention of loving God and our neighbors. In this perfection the believer is free from sin as willful transgression of God's law, but because of human imperfection he or she is never free from ignorance and mistakes. Such a perfection does not, on the other hand, mean a ceasing from growth in God's grace but continues to provide direction for such growth until a person dies. Wesley affirmed that "it is constantly both preceded and followed by a gradual work."[18] It is likewise capable of being lost should a believer choose for some reason to rebel against God. Finally, it does not eliminate the need for good works nor does it deny the importance of the moral law of God, which were accusations frequently brought against Wesley and his followers. As to the question of whether or not such full salvation was instantaneous, Wesley responded:

An instantaneous change has been wrought in some believers. None can deny this. Since that change, they enjoy perfect love; they feel this, and this alone; they "rejoice evermore, pray without ceasing, and in everything give thanks." Now this is all that I mean by perfection; therefore, these are witnesses of the perfection which I preach.

"But in some this change was not instantaneous." They did not perceive the instant when it was wrought. It is often difficult to perceive the instant when a man dies; yet there is an instant in which life ceases. And if ever sin ceases, there must be a last moment of its existence, and a first moment of our deliverance from it.[19]

Volumes have been written on this subject, but it suffices to point out four things here that are critical to any understanding of what this doctrine meant to the Booths. First, while some have denied the centrality of the question of perfect love in the thinking, preaching, and writing of both John and Charles Wesley, such denials belie the fact that this doctrine was crucial to Wesley's understanding of a complete picture of salvation. This included faith working through love in response to the mandate of Scripture and witnessed by the tradition of the church, by reason, and by experience. It is true, as is often the case, that his followers were not always as careful, precise, or clearly biblical in explaining this doctrine, which led some of them to the aberrant conclusion of belittling the doctrine of justification by faith in favor of exalting the doctrine of sanctification by faith. Naturally, Wesley would have nothing to do with such thinking.

In general, what was critical to John Wesley was shared by his brother Charles. The early Methodists learned this doctrine as they did others, not only by hearing and reading the sermons of John, but by singing the hymns of Charles. In his excellent study of Charles Wesley, John R. Tyson wrote, "The numerical predominance of sanctification terms in his hymns is overpowering. Holiness and perfection words occur in excess of six hundred times in Charles's late hymns alone, and this count does not include those many times in which the doctrine was implied or stated without the application of distinct sanctification terms."[20]

Second, to Wesley one of the many consequences of the fall was our loss of God's image in which we were originally created. Wesley understood the image of God to mean the moral image—moral rectitude; a perfect love of neighbor; and a life orientated by justice, mercy, and truth. The doctrine of sanctification was his answer to the problem and perplexity of evil. Perfect love entailed, among other things, a restoration and complete renewal of the image of God in people, or—in keeping with the Wesleyan therapeutic metaphor for salvation—it was a healing of the disease of sin.

> Ye know that the great end of religion is to renew our hearts in the image of God, to repair that total loss of righteousness and true holiness which we sustained by the sin of our first parent. Ye know that all religion which does not answer this end, all that stops short of this, the renewal of our soul in the image of God, after the likeness of Him that created it, is no other than a poor farce and a mere mockery of God, to the destruction of our own soul. . . . By nature ye are wholly corrupted; by grace ye shall be wholly renewed.[21]

Third, Wesley never nullified the doctrine of justification by faith with this doctrine of sanctification by faith. The sinner is justified by grace through faith, and the righteousness of Christ is not only imputed but also imparted to the sinner so that he or she is truly born again and begins a life of holiness. Wesley wholeheartedly affirmed the biblical and Reformation understanding of justification by faith, although some of his followers were not as careful in doing this and relegated justification as secondary to the doctrine of sanctification. However, Wesley was also influenced by the early church and by an increasing Catholic spirituality that developed from early Christianity. This spirituality viewed the Christian life as growth in the grace of God, often analogous to a pilgrim here on earth, by which the individual moves closer and closer to God. This idea was sometimes best demonstrated in the life and spirituality of the mystic.

Indeed, it may be said that one of Wesley's most important theological contributions was bringing together the Protestant notion of justification and the Catholic vision of sanctification. He held these two visions of the Christian life in tension in such a way that both emphases were critical, and one should not be preached without the other. "Wesley had worked a miracle by taking the two great principles separated at the Reformation, 'the early Protestant doctrine of justification by faith and the Catholic appreciation of the idea of holiness or Christian perfection,' and joined them 'in a well balanced synthesis.'"[22] Wesley's imagery, now well-known, was first used in 1746 to envision the working together of his central doctrines. He wrote in a letter, "Our main doctrines, which include all the rest, are three: that of repentance, of faith and of holiness. The first of these we account, as it were, the porch of religion; the next the door; the third, religion itself."[23]

Fourth, it must be emphasized that Wesley's teaching was carried into the nineteenth century by those who considered themselves to be devoted followers of him and his theology, but they weren't always as careful and precise as he was. Both Catherine and William, for example, were reared in a Wesleyan tradition, and both of them, through the preaching they heard and through participation in the class meetings, were exposed to more than merely general Evangelical theology of their time. They knew the fundamentals of Wesleyan doctrines, had command of much of the Wesleyan language by which such theology is shaped, and envisioned the Christian life largely as John Wesley did. However, concentrating only on Catherine for the moment (although the same may be noted of William), it must be said that for all her reading and native intelligence, Catherine did not have Wesley's comprehensive breadth or theological vision. There is no blame here, simply a facing of facts. Wesley was reared in an Anglican tradition during the Age of Reason. He was trained at Oxford University, was a fellow at Lincoln College, Oxford, and read widely from the Scriptures, from the classics, from theologians and philosophers, and from the historians and scientists of his time. He knew the biblical languages as well as German, and he was able to converse in Latin as well as English. Catherine was not so trained and did not deal with many of the finer details of Wesley's theology, such as Wesley's concept of *ordo salutis* (the order of salvation), his developed understanding of the relationship of prevenient grace to justifying grace and accompanying grace, his use of the analogy of faith as a central hermeneutical principle, or his constant use of the quadrilateral (a term that he himself did not use but which included an appeal to Scripture, reason, tradition, and experience). Neither in her writing nor her preaching did Catherine demonstrate a command of these and other detailed and precise theological issues and she could not have been expected to do so.

She was, though, certainly Wesleyan, especially in her emphasis of the glorious revelation of God in Christ witnessed by the written revelation of God in Scripture and confirmed by personal experience. She held to the universal provision of Christ's death on the cross available to all who believe by faith, but she did not carefully work out as Wesley did the precise relationship of faith and the law. She also believed that after a person is justified by faith, the process of sanctification begins in that believer. The way of holiness, she taught, is inaugurated at the new birth, but for many, perfect love is received some time subsequent to conversion and in a second crisis experience. Total consecration on the part of the believer was a precondition to this full and complete work of grace. Such conformity of the human will to God's will was certainly a possibility, Jesus being a perfect example. This leads to an understanding of Catherine's reception of perfect love in her heart, a critical turning point of her life at Gateshead.

Catherine believed, with Wesley, that she had been saved from the guilt of sin when she was justified by faith, and thereby restored to the favor of God, but that sin had not been conquered in her life. "To conclude," Wesley wrote in his sermon "The Spirit of Bondage and of Adoption," "the natural man neither conquers nor fights; the man under the law fights with sin, but cannot conquer; the man under grace fights and conquers, yea is more than conqueror, through him that loveth him."[24] As a believer Catherine felt she still carried with her the root of sin and thereby suffered from pride and selfishness. Earlier entries in her diary, kept periodically between 1847 and 1848, reveal such a self-awareness as well as a seeking after holiness. On November 28, 1847, she wrote:

> My desires after holiness have been much increased. This day I have sometimes seemed on the verge of the good land. Oh, for a mighty faith! I believe the Lord is willing and able to save me to the uttermost. I believe the blood of Jesus cleanses from all sin. And yet there seems something in the way to prevent me from fully entering in. But I believe today at times I have had tastes of perfect love. Oh, that these may be droppings before an overwhelming shower of grace. My chief desire is holiness of heart. This is the prevailing cry of my soul. Tonight "sanctify me through Thy truth—Thy word is truth!" Lord, answer my Redeemer's prayer. I see this salvation is highly necessary in order for me to glorify my God below and find my way to heaven. For "without holiness no man shall see the Lord!" My soul is at times very happy. I have felt many assurances of pardoning mercy. But I want a <u>clean heart</u>. I want to love the Lord with all my heart and my neighbour as myself. Oh, my Lord, take me and seal me to the day of redemption.[25]

Now, many years later at Gateshead, she perceived that she had been progressing in holiness since those yearnings were first expressed. However, she knew that the image of God had not been fully restored in her life whereby she could say that she loved God with all her heart, soul, and mind and her neighbor as herself. She wished for perfect love. She longed for the royal way of love. She prayed to be "saved from the power and root of sin and restored to the image of God."[26]

There is no question that early in 1861 Catherine gave more careful attention not only to her own spiritual condition in general but to the doctrine of sanctification in particular. She indicated in letters to her parents that the doctrine of holiness had once again come to the attention of her heart and mind and that she was determined to preach the doctrine more carefully and deliberately, thereby bringing it to the attention of the people. Subsequent letters attest to her doing so, even though she herself had not yet entered into the promise of perfect love.

There are many reasons why this Wesleyan doctrine came to her awareness, perhaps in a revitalized way, at this particular time in her life. One was that she was convinced that the Scriptures spoke of this doctrine and that the doctrine was central to the biblical message. Her continual attentive study of the Bible, greatly increased now that she had begun a preaching ministry and needed to study the Bible closely for her sermons, continued to bring the doctrine to light. Indeed, central to her debate with both Calvinism and Plymouth Brethrenism was that these theological systems appeared, to Catherine at least, to deny the full weight of the atonement. Not only does God count the sinner as righteous, but he imparts righteousness so that the believer can affirm his or her personal righteousness. The heart is renewed, and Catherine dismissed what she labeled as substitutional atonement as a weak shadow of the full story of the gospel.

She had also been recently influenced by the American holiness preacher Phoebe Palmer. She was drawn to Palmer both as a woman preacher and as an exponent of the holiness doctrine. As early as September 16, 1859, Catherine wrote to her parents: "The celebrated Mrs. Palmer of America authoress of 'The Way of Holiness,' 'Entire Consecration,' 'Economy of Salvation' is now in Newcastle speaking every night in the Wesleyan chapel and getting 30 and 40 of a night up to the communion rail. I intend to hear her when I return."[27]

Catherine reiterated in another letter on September 26, 1859, that she intended to hear Palmer as soon as was possible, although it is not clear if she ever did so. Nevertheless, she continued reading Phoebe Palmer and indicated in a letter to her parents dated January 21, 1861, that she had been reading Palmer's *Faith and Its Effects,* and she then urged her parents to read it. As one writer noted,

> Even a cursory reading of *Faith and Its Effects,* the book to which Catherine refers in her letter, makes it clear just why she found it to be so helpful. If the thrust of American holiness preaching was to write the word "now" over the experience, then Phoebe Palmer added the vital word "how." She speaks, more than anyone else of her time,

to the sincere seeker, such as Catherine Booth, who longs to claim
the desired blessing but does not know how to do it. In effect what
she does is to give a biblical explanation for her own experience.[28]

Catherine was beginning to understand that full salvation came
simply by consecrating everything to God.

Another reason for Catherine's reflections on this doctrine has
to do with what was happening at the Bethesda Chapel. The witness of several people at Gateshead regarding their experience of
entire sanctification, much like the Methodist witnesses of the
previous century who were so important to Wesley's explanation
of the doctrine, caused both joy in Catherine's heart for their
experience as well as personal anguish that she had not yet
attained such an experience. A particularly revealing letter to her
parents written on February 4, 1861, shows some of the struggle Catherine was encountering during this time of her spiritual
journey. "Pray for me," she wrote. "I only want perfect consecration and Christ as my all, and then I might be very useful, to
the glory, not of myself, the most unworthy of all who e'er His
grace received, but of His great and boundless love. May the Lord
enable me to give my wanderings o'er and to find in Christ perfect peace and full salvation!"[29]

Finally, it is important to note specifically what was going on
in Catherine's life at this time. Part of the reason for so intense
an inner struggle was the possibility of an itinerant life again, if
William was reassigned as an evangelist with the Connexion. Her
struggle over this matter will be mentioned again later, but it is
sufficient here to say that Catherine's introspection presently
caused some rather harsh self-analysis. In the letter mentioned
above, she wrote, "Oh, what a fool I have been! How slow, how
backward, how blind, how hindered by unbelief! And even now
some bolts and bars are round me, which my foolish heart will
not consent to have broken down! O unbelief, truly it binds the
hands of Omnipotence itself!"[30]

In all of her correspondence, one of the most critical letters is
that dated February 11, 1861. Written to her parents, it describes

in detail Catherine's resolution of the unbelief and inner turmoil mentioned in previous letters. She admitted she had been recently absorbed in the pursuit of holiness and then related the following, using largely the language of Phoebe Palmer: "In reading the precious book 'The Higher Life' I perceived that I had been in some degree of error with reference to the nature or rather <u>manner</u> of sanctification, regarding it rather as a great and mighty work to be wrought in me <u>through</u> Christ, than the simple reception <u>of Christ</u> as an <u>all sufficient</u> Saviour <u>dwelling in</u> my heart and thus cleansing it every moment from all sin." She then provides a detailed description of giving attention for two days on this subject, of her continual searching the Scriptures and praying, and of the final surrender of the will to God and the resolution of her struggle while kneeling in her parlor at home. In the language of consecration used by Caughey and Palmer, she laid all on the altar. Following that she wrote, "From that moment I have dared to reckon myself dead indeed unto sin and alive unto God through Jesus Christ my Lord." She continued with a recitation of her consciousness of her awful sins of the past as well as the rebellion of her heart and the awareness of her own unworthiness, "but then I said the Lord has not made my salvation to depend in any measure on my own worthiness or <u>unworthiness</u> but on the worthiness of my Saviour. He came to seek and to save that which was <u>lost</u>. Where sin hath abounded grace doth much more abound."[31]

The matter was settled. Catherine was clear not only about the truth of a biblical doctrine but about the living reality of full salvation in her own life. The righteousness of Christ was not only imputed but imparted as well in holy living. Next to the doctrine of women in ministry, the doctrine of holiness would be the most critical and central one in Catherine's writing, teaching, and preaching for the remainder of her life. She wisely included in her teaching Wesley's therapeutic image of holiness as healing, as well as his emphasis on holiness as a restoration of the image of God in the believer. She likewise continued to press home the human responsibility of consecration—leaving the world and giving of oneself, in complete abandonment in faith, to Christ for the sake of his kingdom.[32]

Catherine was now ready to face, with William and their family, the fourth turning point in her life. Catherine and William had to decide whether to press the issue of William's leaving a circuit ministry and reentering an evangelistic ministry. William's time at Gateshead had in no way dampened his evangelistic fervor and he resolved once again to become an itinerant evangelist, if possible within New Connexion Methodism. He had consented to the wishes of the denomination, so perhaps now was the time to act on conviction. Catherine had been struggling with the decision but was frank to admit she had to come to a resolution in her own heart and mind by finally submitting herself to the will of the Lord on this matter. She had become settled at Gateshead and was becoming used to a calm domestic life after many years of wandering. Understandably, she did not wish to go out on the road again—the responsibilities of mother and father for a growing family would make anyone hesitate rather than welcome another unpredictable change. Her struggle was genuine but so was her resolution. In 1861 she committed herself to following what she believed to be the Lord's leading in this and all other matters, regardless of the consequences. She was prepared to go—or stay.

The Booths had no intention of leaving New Connexion Methodism. Aside from what they considered to be some unworthy leadership in the movement, they knew and respected many people in the Connexion. They also had learned to love the people to whom they ministered and had in turn been nurtured by them. The work at Gateshead was prospering, and it is beyond dispute that the denomination reaped the benefits of the Booths' ministry whenever and wherever they preached. Nevertheless, it was time, both Catherine and William believed, to test the waters again.

William wrote a lengthy letter on March 5, 1861, to the retiring president of the Methodist New Connexion, the Reverend James Stacey, in which William carefully, deliberately, yet respectfully outlined his views regarding his future with the denomination (a copy of which Catherine sent to her parents).[33] He pressed home his conviction that, although he had not been an itinerant evangelist for the denomination for four years, he still firmly believed that this was the work to which God had called him and for which he was best suited. That belief, he averred, was supported by the witness of many people in the denomination. With the time for his reappointment at hand, William was convinced that the timing was providential for reassignment into evangelistic work.

It is of interest to note his mention of Catherine in this letter, and he refers to her own resolution of this matter. "The Lord has removed several other obstacles out of my way. Among others, my dear wife has voluntarily consented to the separation which my going forth would involve. In fact, in this matter, we have both been enabled to offer our all to God, being willing to submit to any self-denying circumstances He may appoint in order to do His will."[34]

Booth further reminded Stacey that the reasons for his being appointed to a circuit had now been fulfilled, and surely the denominational leaders were completely satisfied with his ability to provide leadership within the denomination. His evangelistic skills, moreover, had long since proved beneficial to New Connexion Methodism, and so he submitted a detailed plan to the president presenting how his itinerant work could be supported by the denomination.[35]

In a letter to her parents written only a few days before William's letter to the Reverend Stacey, Catherine revealed that William had sought some counsel on this matter. In the letter she shows some disappointment with James Caughey, the man whom she so admired. Catherine simply wrote, without explanation, that "William has written to Mr. Caughey and another friend and neither of them seem disposed to risk any advice. Mr. C. is evidently afraid but our trust is not in man and if we take the step it will be solely trusting in the Lord."[36] Perhaps she did not feel like kissing Caughey's hand as she had done three years previously! There is no indication as to why Caughey acted as he did.

The Booths could now only wait for their request to be forwarded to the Annual Conference and for the deliberations of that Conference. In the meantime, the ministry was flourishing in both the circuit and the district. Catherine had herself launched a rather heavy preaching schedule, which brought success to the work as well as considerable notice among members of the denomination that Mr. Booth's wife was preaching! Catherine must have been especially delighted during this period because it was at this time that her father, under her influence, came back to the Lord.

The Annual Conference for 1861 was held in Liverpool and commenced on Monday, May 20. Both Catherine and William attended and were uplifted by the presence of their old friend and supporter, Edward Rabbits. A wealthy Methodist layman, Joseph Love, was also present, promising to help support William financially, if need be, in his ministry as evangelist. This colliery owner had the means to do so, as did some of his friends. Therefore, any denominational concern about financial arrangements for William could be dismissed, even aside from the obvious fact that the numbers of people who would attend the revival meetings would guarantee the financial support of the ministry.

William's request finally came to the floor of the Conference. The matter was forwarded by the Reverend J. Stokoe, and he presented the arguments, already decided at a district meeting at Durham, in favor of assigning William Booth to evangelistic work for the Connexion. However, the Booths' old nemesis, P. J. Wright, was present once again with fresh arguments against this proposal and he was supported by ministers of the Connexion, some of whom most certainly were small-minded people, jealous of their own feeble power, who supposedly spoke against evangelistic work from some principled argument. It would be difficult for even the most objective interpreter of these events to support Ervine's contention in his biography of William Booth that "Wright undoubtedly was stiff in his resistance to Booth, but there is no warrant for the assumption that he had not the interests of religion and his church as fervently at heart as any person who approved the Booth proposal."[37]

The debate ensued, and William was allowed to read the letter he had written to Stacey in March. But Booth was evidently not persuasive enough, for an amendment was proposed (ironically by the Booths' friend Dr. Cooke) that Booth be assigned to a circuit again but that arrangements be made for him to conduct revival services where and when possible. The amendment carried by a majority vote, and a compromise was again imposed on William Booth that had not worked at Gateshead because his pastoral responsibilities prevented him from doing the extensive evangelistic work outside of Gateshead that he desired.

The crisis was at hand, and the turning was about to be made. Precisely what happened next is impossible to say, and the accounts vary considerably. Booth-Tucker records this very dramatic account of Catherine's reaction when the vote on the amendment carried:

This was more than Mrs. Booth could endure. She had been sitting at a point in the gallery from which she and her husband could interchange glances. It had been with difficulty that she had restrained her feelings hitherto while listening to the debate. But at this stage she was overcome with indignation. She felt that Dr. Cooke had sacrificed their cause in the interests of peace rather than righteousness. But for his suggested compromise she believed that they could have carried the day with a triumphant majority.

Rising from her seat and bending over the gallery, Mrs. Booth's clear voice rang through the Conference, as she said to her husband, "Never!"

There was a pause of bewilderment and dismay. Every eye was turned towards the speaker in the gallery. The idea of a woman daring to utter her protest or to make her voice heard in the Conference produced little short of consternation. It was a sublime scene, as, with flushed face and flashing eye, she stood before that audience. Decision, irrevocable and eternal, was written upon every feature of that powerful and animated countenance. Her "Never!" seemed to penetrate like an electric flash through every heart.

One, at least, in that assembly responded with his whole soul to the call. Mr. Booth sprang to his feet, and waived his hat in the direction of the door. Heedless of the ministerial cries of "Order, order," and not pausing for another word, they hurried forth, met and embraced each other at the foot of the gallery stairs, and turned their backs upon the Conference, resolved to trust God for the future, come what might, and to follow out their conscientious convictions regarding His work.[38]

Such a scene would indeed make great theater, and Harold Begbie in his two-volume work on William Booth, *The Life of General William Booth the Founder of the Salvation Army,* virtually retold the story as he read it in the Booth-Tucker account without any critical comment. However, St. John Ervine, the author of *God's Soldier: General William Booth,* written fifteen years after Begbie's biography, strongly disagreed, as he often did, with Booth-Tucker's dramatic account. Indeed, Ervine insisted, "The story is good, but not quite true,"[39] and based his criticism on three observations.

First, eyewitness accounts of other people at the Conference differ significantly from what Booth-Tucker recorded. One eyewitness, Mr. Gibson, who was sitting near Catherine in the gallery, did not hear her say anything at all but did recall some general excitement after the vote. "I just saw Mrs. Booth and her friends rise up and move towards the steps of the gallery."[40] Booth-Tucker failed to record that, before a motion was made, the discussion was to continue behind closed doors. "Visitors sitting in the gallery were requested to withdraw."[41] Catherine and others were already moving out of the gallery. Catherine was near the stairs leading to the back of the church, when she may have uttered something; then the doors were ordered closed by Dr. Crofts, the president of the Connexion who presided at the meeting.

Second, Ervine makes the strong point that this kind of compulsive action was not in keeping with what we know of William. The story

> is, indeed, irreconcileable [sic] with Booth's character, for he was not the impulsive and thoughtless person that he must have been had it been accurate. He was, throughout his life, a man extraordinarily conservative in his habits and most cautious in his procedure. He had, moreover, a deep love of the Methodist Church which prevailed to the day of his death. Many of his staunchest friends were in its ministry, and he never uttered a sentence which showed that he had lost his love for it. His circumstances, too, were such that only a fool, incapable of responsibility, could have flung away his office in the ill-tempered fashion in which William Booth, who was far from being a fool, is said to have flung his away. A man, married to a delicate wife, the father of four delicate and nervous children, and under financial responsibilities to other relatives, does not thoughtlessly resign his office and go "out to face the consequences of his act."[42]

Ervine later reiterated, "The accounts of this scene are not clear, nor is there any hope of making them clearer, but one thing is certain, that Booth did not spring to his feet, as his son-in-law asserted, and wave his hat to his wife, and leave the Methodist New Connexion there and then."[43]

What is true is that Catherine was prepared, more than William, to leave the Methodist New Connexion. Some act of defiance against Connexion authority is not out of character for Catherine at this time of her life. Indeed, she had written this to her parents following the Conference: "Then, I ask, does the security of our bread and cheese make that right which should otherwise be wrong when God has promised to feed and clothe us? I think not, and I am willing to trust Him, and suffer if need be in order to do His will."[44]

Finally, Ervine is convinced that Booth-Tucker was corrected about what happened at this Conference by members of New Connexion Methodism who were present, which would account for the fact that in Booth-Tucker's abridged version of Catherine Booth's life the story is not told. This is indeed strange, in that the story portrays high drama in Catherine's life and would make for good reading even in an abridged version. Also, Catherine Bramwell-Booth is sparing in her account of this incident. She wrote that after the compromise was suggested, William looked up at Catherine, who stood instantly to her feet and answered William "Never." Then, "She made her way to the exit, William met her at the foot of the stairs, where they embraced and walked out."[45] None of the drama Booth-Tucker records— indignation, bewilderment, dismay, consternation—was granted in Bramwell-Booth's account. What Booth-Tucker termed "The Resignation Scene" was probably much milder and more calculated on the part of Catherine than was possible for the romantic Booth-Tucker to admit. However, what is certainly clear is that the Booths were about to turn in a new direction.

Soon after leaving the Conference deliberations and going to the home where they were staying, Catherine and William received Dr. Cooke, who tried to persuade them to accept the generous compromise of the Conference. It had been decided that William would be appointed as Superintendent of the Newcastle circuit, "one of the most important in the Connexion, although Catherine thought little of it."[46] The Booths felt they could not give their attention to governing a circuit while trying to conduct evangelistic meetings. Neither of them was content with the compromise.

William was invited back to the last session of the Conference on a Monday morning and he accepted this invitation. He made one final appeal, but it was determined that he should conform to the wishes of the Conference and report to the Newcastle circuit where he had been assigned. Catherine was in favor of immediate resignation, allowing for grave personal difficulties as a result, but quite willing and resolved to leave the consequences with God. William, as ever, was more cautious, hoping for a healing of the wound. The Conference could not technically accept his resignation for another year, and perhaps, thought William, the attempt could be made during that year to superintend the circuit *and* conduct revival meetings. An assistant minister would substitute for William during his absence. The circuit officials were pleased with this arrangement. So the Booths, with their four children, moved to Newcastle. Catherine wrote to her parents in June 1861:

> Our position altogether is about as trying as it well could be. We have reason to fear that the Annual Committee will not allow even this arrangement with the circuit to be carried out, and if not, I don't see any honourable course open but to resign at once and risk all; if trusting in the Lord for our bread, in order to do what we believe to be His will, ought to be called a <u>risk</u>. . . . I am sick of the New Connexion from <u>top</u> to <u>bottom</u>. I have lost all faith in its ministry and I see nothing for it but a slow consumption. . . .
>
> The President has written to know the nature of the arrangements . . . with the Newcastle circuit. William will send them, and if they object I shall urge him with all my might to resign.[47]

In the meantime William began preaching outside the circuit, first inauspiciously at Alnwick and then seeking preaching engagements because many of his fellow ministers were wary of inviting him to their churches for fear of the Conference's displeasure. They did not wish to be entangled in any ongoing dispute between William Booth and New Connexion Methodism.

William also made a trip to London to speak with some gentlemen about various independent ministries of revivalism in Britain, and with one independent group he preached in the open air twice near the Garrick Theater. He was testing the possibilities of an independent revivalism apart from his denomination, but none of the ministries about which he inquired appealed to him. At this time of his life, at least, he earnestly hoped to remain with New Connexion Methodism. Catherine thought otherwise. "The <u>people</u> of <u>all denominations</u> and of no denomination at all, are exceedingly anxious to keep us. I cannot speak however for the Priests, neither do I care much whether they are anxious or not."[48] So wrote Catherine to her parents near the end of November 1861, expressing her determined feelings since the Annual Conference. Ervine is correct in his assessment of both Catherine and William at this time: "Catherine, undoubtedly, was ready, even eager, to leave the Connexion, but William undoubtedly was not."[49]

A letter from Dr. Crofts written on July 16, 1861, expressing, inexplicably, a reprimand from the Annual Committee to Booth for not yet fulfilling the pastoral duties of the Newcastle circuit, became a signal to both William and Catherine that their good intentions and promises to the Methodist New Connexion were not being taken seriously. Even the most impartial observer of the unfolding events and the struggles between the Booths and the denomination would have to conclude that the denomination was being controlled by small-minded bureaucrats, unable, even for the sake of the gospel and the kingdom, to rise to the occasion of supporting one of their own during a time of personal introspection and obvious good will. The July 16 letter from Crofts displays a deplorable lack of leadership resulting in his inability to guide the deliberations of the denomination toward a solution beneficial for all concerned. Such incompetence was apparently widespread and doubtless stifled other talented, energetic, and visionary ministers of that denomination.

It comes as no surprise that both Catherine and William were by now fully exasperated in their dealings with the narrow-minded element of their denomination. Perhaps they wondered how such uninspiring and unimaginative people rise to positions of leadership in the church. The long view has vindicated the Booths' final separation from New Connexion Methodism, made formal by William's letter of resignation written on July 18, 1861, to the Reverend H. O. Crofts, D. D., president of the Methodist New Connexion. William's resignation was formally accepted at the Annual Conference of the denomination meeting at Dudley in June 1862. Catherine kept referring to it as "our resignation" and rightly so, for surely she was influential in her husband's decision. Likewise, she was willing to suffer the consequences, along with her husband and children, of such an action and to place herself totally and without reservation in the hands of her Lord. "So, now the step is taken," Catherine wrote, "we both intend to brace ourselves for all its consequences and manfully face all difficulties. The Lord help us and show us His salvation! Continue to pray for us."[50]

The Booth family moved to the Mumford home in London. Some resting place was needed, as was a base of operations from which to fulfill the invitations coming from several churches. This move away from the security of a denomination to the uncertainties of an independent revivalist ministry was indeed one of the most dramatic—and important—turning points in the lives of all concerned. There was a new wrinkle in the story, however, which, ironically, would help to bring some security to the seemingly rootless family. Because Catherine had entered into a public ministry of preaching, invitations to preach and conduct revival meetings now came to both of the Booths. Catherine would do her share in supporting the family financially during this wilderness experience.

5

Settled Views

Women in Ministry

We now examine Catherine's very determined views of women in ministry. Many allusions have been made to this matter, which was of critical importance to Catherine. This was not a mere practical dispute for her—that women should be used for ministry because there were not enough men to fill the pulpits or supply the missionary quotas. No, this was a theological matter, at the heart of which was this question: Are women and men being faithful to the biblical vision of the kingdom of God, in which all the gifts, talents, energies, and abilities of all the people, female and male, are used in the service of the church for the sake of that kingdom? Is the church living out in faithful witness the implications of Galatians 3:28, that "there is no longer Jew or Greek, there is no longer slave or free, there is no longer male or female; for all of you are one in Christ Jesus,"—which Catherine understood as a biblical mandate for ministry, not just a salvation promise?

Catherine became convinced that to deny female ministry was to deny the full grace of God and to do irreparable harm to the cause of the kingdom. Next to the doctrine of holiness, this doctrine of ministry would become the central doctrinal and practical focus for Catherine until her death.

She did observe some limited female leadership in the Wesleyan circles in which she was nurtured. Many women were engaged as leaders in the class meetings and Sunday school classes Catherine attended. However, that was generally the extent of female participation in the ministry of the church. After the Mumfords moved to Brixton, they joined the chapel of the Reformers known as the Binfield House, situated on Binfield Road, Clapham, and here for three years Catherine taught a senior Sunday school class of fifteen girls ranging in age from twelve to nineteen, a small but favorable beginning of what would later be a long and extensive public ministry of preaching and teaching.

It was not until 1853, however, that Catherine gave public expression to heretofore private convictions about women's rights. Her initial concerns were with the traditional prejudices against women having any equality with men in England—social, intellectual, or spiritual. Her views of female ministry would evolve gradually as a result of her own thought and experience, and in due course her thinking became more concentrated on the specific issue of women's equality with men in the pulpit.

The circumstances, alluded to in chapter 2, were these: In 1853 Catherine began attending the Stockwell New Chapel, a Congregational church near her home. The Reverend David Thomas was the pastor, a man whom Catherine personally admired and who officiated at her marriage to William.[1] Little did Thomas know that this young woman was listening intently one Sunday when he referred to woman's moral and intellectual inferiority in his sermon. This was too much for Catherine to take, and she took it upon herself to correct her pastor's seriously mistaken ideas in a lengthy letter.[2] Though Catherine did not identify herself as the writer of the letter, one cannot help but surmise that Thomas found out it was she who had taken him to task, although there is no record of this. At the conclusion of the letter Catherine trusted that the recipient would not

> judge me harshly for withholding my name. I began this letter hesitating whether I should do so or not but there being nothing in it of a personal character, or which can at all be influenced by the recognition of the writer, and it being the furthest from my thoughts to obtrude myself upon your notice, I shall feel at liberty to subscribe myself an attentive hearer, and I trust a mental and spiritual debtor to your ministry.[3]

Whether or not Thomas ever discovered the writer of the letter is unimportant. The letter is revealing for demonstrating the formation of Catherine's initial arguments in favor of the equality of women with men. While the limitations of Catherine's education are evident in some of the style of the writing and in some misspellings, the force of her argument nevertheless is clear and certainly would have caught the attention of the original reader. In response to what Catherine believed to be "views so derogatory to my sex, and which I believe to be unscriptural and dishonoring to God,"[4] she went to great lengths in the letter to defend women's "perfect equality"[5] with men, which would become self-evident in the broader culture should women be allowed the same intellectual maturing as men.

> Her training from babyhood, even in this highly favoured land, has hitherto been such as to cramp and paralyse, rather than to develop and strengthen, her energies—and calculated to crush and wither her aspirations after mental greatness rather than to excite and stimulate them—and even where the more direct depressing or dissipating influence has been withdrawn, the indirect and most powerful stimulus has been wanting. What inducement has been held out to her to cultivate habits of seclusion, meditation, and thought? What sphere has been open to her? What kind of estimate would have been formed of her a few generations back, had she presumed to enter the temple of learning, or to have turned her attainments to any practical account?[6]

Catherine's initial appeal in her debate was to the natural moral equality of women with men that any objective observer would be forced to conclude. And if the doors of the academy would be opened to women as well as men, women's intellectual as well as moral equality would be brought to the fore.[7] Then, thought Catherine, her intellectual abilities would be recognized and truth would rise triumphant over customs, prejudices, institutions, and cultural norms that have insisted on the natural inferiority of women both morally and intellectually.

She was further convinced that the church has particular responsibility for uncovering and condemning the mistaken notion of women's inferiority, because such thinking of necessity circumscribes and hinders the work of the gospel intended by Jesus Christ and clearly mandated in the Bible.

> Oh that the Church generally would inquire whether narrow prejudice and lordly usurpation has not something to do with the circumscribed and limited sphere of women's religious labors, and whether much of the non-success of the Gospel is not attributable to the restrictions imposed upon the operations of the Holy Ghost in this as well as other particulars! Would to God that the truth on this subject, so important to the interests of future generations, were better understood and more practically recognized.[8]

In this spirit Catherine advised her own minister to investigate the matter carefully and rationally: "Permit me, my dear sir, to ask whether you have ever made the subject of women's equality as a <u>being</u>, the matter of calm investigation and thought? If not I would, with all deference, suggest it as a subject well worth the exercise of your brain, and calculated amply to repay any research you may bestow upon it."[9]

The central issue in Catherine's thinking at this time was that of women's natural equality with men. The specific subject of women in ministry supported by a clear biblical and historical argument had not yet surfaced. Indeed, this matter did not yet exist for Catherine because she herself had not yet entered into an active preaching ministry. It would be many years before that would be the case.

As has been mentioned, before meeting William, Catherine had already decided what kind of a man she would marry. Of supreme importance, of course, was that there must be

> oneness of views and tastes, any idea of lordship or ownership being lost in love. There can be no doubt that Jesus Christ intended, by making love the law of marriage, to restore woman to the position God intended her to occupy, as also to destroy the curse of the fall, which man by dint of his merely superior physical strength and advantageous position had magnified, if not really to a large extent manufactured.[10]

By the time of her engagement to William, Catherine was convinced that there had to be a meeting of their minds beyond the ideal of the equality of women to the practical issue of female ministry. Some of the lengthiest correspondence from Catherine to William after their engagement deals with this matter. This was still quite theoretical for her—she had no practical personal experience of preaching. William was not totally ignorant of this subject, and at the invitation of his friend Rabbits, heard the preaching of a woman in London by the name of Miss Buck. W. T. Stead records that William "left the chapel saying that he should never again oppose the practice (of women preaching), since Miss Buck had certainly preached more effectively than three-fourths of the men he had ever listened to."[11]

The most crucial and direct letter from Catherine to William on the subject of women in ministry is dated April 9, 1855, just before their marriage in June. This is a lengthy epistle of sixteen pages dealing with many matters, but the heart of it exemplifies Catherine's most precise thinking to date related to women in ministry. She wrote:

> If on that other subject you mention, my views are right, how delighted I should be for you to see as fully with me on it too; you know I feel no less deeply on this subject, and perhaps you think

I take rather a prejudiced view of it; but I have searched the Word of God through and through, I have tried to deal honestly with every passage on the subject, not forgetting to pray for light to perceive and grace to submit to the truth, however humiliating to my nature, but I solemnly assert that the more I think and read on the subject, the more satisfied I become of the true and scriptural character of my own views. . . .

Oh I believe that volumes of light will yet be shed on the world on this subject; it will bear examination and abundantly repay it. . . . I believe woman is destined to assume her true position, and exert her proper influence by the special exertions and attainments of her own sex. . . . May the Lord, even the just and impartial one, overrule all for the true emancipation of women from the swaddling bands of prejudice, ignorance, and custom, which, almost the world over, have so long debased and wronged her. . . . Oh, what endears the Christian religion to my heart is what it has done, and is destined to do, for my own sex; and that which excites my indignation beyond anything else is to hear its sacred precepts dragged forward to hear degrading arguments.

Oh for a few more Adam Clarkes to dispel the ignorance of the Church, then should we not hear very pygmies in Christianity reasoning against holy and intelligent women opening their mouths for the Lord in the presence of the Church. . . .

. . . If indeed there is in "Christ Jesus neither male nor female," but in all touching His kingdom "they are one," who shall dare thrust woman out of the Church's operations, or presume to put my candle which God has lighted under a bushel? . . . Oh, it is cruel for the Church to foster prejudice so unscriptural, and thus make the path of usefulness the path of untold suffering. Let me advise you, my Love, to get settled views on this subject and be able to render a reason to every caviller, and then fearlessly incite all whom you believe the Lord has fitted to help you in your Master's work, male or female, Christ has given them no single talent to be hid in a napkin, and yet oh what thousands are wrapped up and buried, which used and improved would yield "some thirty, some sixty, yea and some an hundred fold." . . .

If you gain anything by what I have writ, I should praise God on hearing it, otherwise I do not desire you to answer this.[12]

William's reply on April 12, 1855, was not exactly what Catherine was hoping to hear from her betrothed. He responded:

The remarks on <u>Woman's</u> position I will read again before I answer. From the first reading I cannot see anything in them to lead me for one <u>moment</u> to think of altering my opinion. You <u>combat</u> a great deal that I hold as firmly as <u>you</u> do—viz. her <u>equality</u>, her <u>perfect equality</u>, as a whole—as a <u>being</u>. But as to concede that she is man's <u>equal</u>, or <u>capable</u> of becoming man's equal, in intellectual attainments or prowess—I must say <u>that</u> is contradicted by experience in the world and my honest conviction. You know, my dear, I acknowledge the superiority of your sex in very many things—in others I believe her inferior. <u>Vice versa</u> with man.

I would not stop a woman preaching on any account. I would not encourage one to begin. You should preach if you felt moved thereto: felt equal to the task. I would not stay <u>you</u> if I had power to do so. Altho', <u>I should not like it</u>. It is easy for you to say my views are the result of prejudice; perhaps they are. I am for the world's <u>salvation</u>; I will quarrel with no means that promises help.[13]

The disagreement over this caused some strain in Catherine and William's relationship. William later referred to this as the "first little lover's quarrel, and the only serious lover's quarrel we ever had."[14] Booth-Tucker himself, not one to see any flaws in the founders of the Army, admitted such when he wrote:

their first serious difference of opinion arose soon after their engagement in regard to the mental and social equality of woman as compared with man. Mr. Booth argued that while the former carried the palm in point of affection, the latter was her superior in regard to intellect. He quoted the old aphorism that woman has a fibre more in her heart and a cell less in her brain. Miss Mumford would not admit this for a moment. She held that intellectually woman was man's equal, and that, where it was not so, the inferiority was due to disadvantages of training, a lack of opportunity, rather than to any shortcomings on the part of nature. Indeed she had avowed her determination never to take as her partner in life one who was not prepared to give woman her proper due.[15]

Stead's reaction to this in his biography of Catherine Booth is even stronger than Booth-Tucker's. Stead asserted, "It would even appear that the argument between them rose to such heights as to threaten a breaking off of their engagement. Mrs. Booth was on this question ready to resort to ultimatums, and Mr. Booth was led by his passionate love for one woman to recognize the justice of her claim for all her sex."[16] Catherine Bramwell-Booth, probably as a corrective of Booth-Tucker and Stead, noted, "At this time Catherine may have grieved a little that in theory William did not take the matter of woman's right to preach very seriously, but she was fully content with him when the time came to *act*. Then he proved himself to be one of the 'mighty and generous spirits.'"[17]

The dispute was obviously settled, and it is a tribute to William that he was both convinced and convicted by Catherine's arguments for perfect equality of male and female, including intellectual equality, and for women in ministry. Stead is correct in his summary statement of the resolution between the couple:

> Mr. Booth, in spite of his usual inflexibility of purpose, has always been singularly open to conviction. Can we wonder then that he succumbed to the logic of his fair disputant? And thus a vantage ground was gained, of which the Salvation Army has since learned to make good use. It became henceforth an essential and important doctrine in their creed that in Jesus Christ there was neither male nor female, but that the Gospel combined with nature to place both on a footing of absolute mental and spiritual equality.[18]

Catherine Booth's most notable public defense of female ministry came as a result of an incident in 1859. Phoebe Palmer, the American Methodist holiness preacher, began a four-year speaking tour in England along with her husband. She already had a large following in America. Her Tuesday holiness meetings in her home in New York City had become widely known, and she began preaching outside of her home. Two of her works, *The Way of Holiness,* published in the 1840s, and *Faith and Its Effects,* published in the 1850s, were widely read in America and England, and there is evidence that Catherine had read these and other books by Palmer.[19]

"The Palmers' Newcastle Revival of 1859 was hailed as the 'Evangelical Alliance Revival'"[20] in order to avoid identification with English sectarianism. Catherine made reference to Phoebe Palmer's preaching at this revival in letters to her parents dated September 16, 1859, and September 26, 1859, in both letters expressing her desire to hear Palmer. Unfortunately she was unable to do so. The Reverend Arthur Augustus Rees of Sunderland, an Independent minister in a neighboring town to Gateshead, publicly attacked Phoebe Palmer's right to preach, citing "Reasons for Not Co-Operating in the Alleged Sunderland Revivals." In a letter to her mother dated December 25, 1859, Catherine wrote that Rees's comments were originally "delivered in the form of an address to his congregation and repeated a second time by request to a crowded chapel, and then published!"[21]

Catherine responded in a pamphlet titled *Female Teaching: or the Rev. A. A. Rees versus Mrs. Palmer, Being a Reply to a Pamphlet by the Above Named Gentleman on the Sunderland Revival,*[22] incensed by Rees's "stuff,"[23] and moved to respond quickly by the rumor that Rees was going to publish yet another pamphlet on the same subject. Catherine, by her own admission, worked diligently on this pamphlet, fully supported, she records, by William. In fact, William did the copying for Catherine, but the argument was Catherine's alone, and she took full responsibility for the contents of *Female Teaching.*[24]

It is important to note that Catherine Booth had not yet entered into a public ministry and therefore was not defending her own personal right to preach but the principle of female ministry. She "does *not* apply the argument to herself. She is not claiming her *own* right to preach."[25] Basically there are three broad arguments to her pamphlet. First, she dealt with the fact that people wrongly confound "nature with custom."[26] It is customary, she admitted at the outset, that women have not preached, and Catherine conceded that "want of mental culture, the trammels of custom, the force of prejudice, and the assumptions of the other sex with their onesided interpretations of Scripture, have, hitherto, almost excluded her from this sphere."[27] However, she continued, it would be wrong to thereby assume that woman is not by nature fitted to preach. In fact, argued Catherine,

> Making allowance for the novelty of the thing, we cannot discover anything either unnatural or immodest in a Christian woman, becomingly attired, appearing on a platform or in a pulpit. By *nature* she seems fitted to grace either. God has given to woman a graceful form and attitude, winning manners, persuasive speech, and, above all, a finely-toned emotional nature, all of which appear to us eminent *natural* qualifications for public speaking.[28]

With this assertion, Catherine makes an important departure from Phoebe Palmer. This holiness teacher did not defend woman's natural right to preach the gospel based on biblical principle. Indeed, she understood that basically women have a different sphere of influence from men. She did allow that women could preach under the influence of the Holy Spirit and thereby tended to see women as passive receivers of a gift to preach. Catherine, on the other hand, demonstrated that woman had a natural right to preach, along with men. "Mrs. Palmer's argument emphasized passivity and receptivity; Catherine's vision gave women authority as women to preach. Catherine had issued a call to action."[29]

Second, Catherine responded to scriptural objections. She held to her views of female ministry, as far as she was concerned, *because* of the Bible and not in spite of it. She affirmed that could her convictions on this subject be demonstrated as forbidden in the Bible, she would gladly relinquish such a view. Her approach to the Bible in the pamphlet was twofold. She dealt with the objections to women in ministry generally cited by the divines. Then she underscored those passages and stories in the Bible that not only supported female ministry in principle but specifically provided legitimacy and vision for such ministry. While Catherine Booth "did not break any new hermeneutical ground,"[30] she nevertheless brought the issue of female ministry to light once again within a specific set of circumstances, and she did so primarily by dealing with the biblical texts. "Although Catherine's pamphlet was not based on original Biblical scholarship, it was, nevertheless, exceptional. The mere fact that it was written by a woman was unusual."[31]

She began by examining the two most common scriptural passages used by those who opposed female ministry. The first passage encompassed 1 Corinthians 11:4–5, and 14:3–4, and 31. Catherine affirmed what the 1 Corinthians 11 passage asserted— that both women and men were praying and preaching in the Corinthian church in fulfillment of Acts 2:17. Paul reprimanded both the men and the women in the Corinthian church for their impropriety, stipulating the proper way to pray and preach in that Greek cultural setting—men with their heads uncovered and women with their heads veiled. Catherine then raised the question of how to reconcile 1 Corinthians 14:34–36, where women were admonished to "be silent in the churches," with chapter 11. This was done, she averred, by understanding that the speaking referred to in chapter 14 was different from that referred to in chapter 11. "Taking the simple and common-sense view of the two passages, viz., that one refers to the devotional and religious services of the church, and the other to its political and disciplinary assemblies, there is no contradiction or discrepancy, no straining or twisting of either."[32] Without this understanding, one would have to draw the absurd conclusion that Paul was contradicting himself in 1 Corinthians—admonishing women to preach in chapter 11, and forbidding them to do so in chapter 14. Scripture, for Catherine, had to be understood in context.

The second objection to female ministry commonly came from 1 Timothy 2:12–13. Catherine began her exposition by giving the passage a fair and thorough examination, concluding that there is no proof "that the apostle here refers to the conduct of women in the church at all."[33] The teaching referred to in this passage, as far as Catherine was concerned, as both the context and the grammatical construction of the passage clearly implied, was to a domineering teaching done privately in the home, "which involves the usurpation of authority over the man."[34] In her mind, it is never warranted to interpret this passage as a prohibition of public preaching and teaching.

Catherine's primary scriptural concern, however, was not with the two so-called problematic passages, which could be clearly explained, but with the positive witness of the Bible for women in ministry. Although she cited some important women in the Old Testament, such as Deborah, Huldah, and Miriam, to support her argument, her primary interest was with the witness of the New Testament and the many women who prayed, preached, and ministered in various ways—Anna, Philip's daughters, Priscilla, the Samaritan woman, Phoebe, Junias, Euodia, Syntyche, and others. However, there were three New Testament passages that provided the theological legitimacy and foundation for such ministry, and Catherine built her argument on these.

The first constituted the many Gospel references to Jesus' treatment of women, specifically his commission to Mary Magdalene in Matthew 28:9–10. Here was the first public announcement of the resurrection, proclaimed to a woman, who was then to become the teacher of the rest of the apostles. Catherine understood this as not coincidental but intentional on the part of the Lord. Woman had been blamed for being the first in transgression, so to set the record straight, as it were, she is the first to know about the atonement for such transgression. She says the following about Mary Magdalene in *Female Teaching*:

> Mary was expressly commissioned to reveal the fact to the Apostles; and thus she literally became their teacher on that memorable occasion. Oh, glorious privilege, to be allowed to herald the glad tidings of a Saviour risen! How could it be that our Lord chose a *woman* to this honour? . . . One reason might be that the male disciples were all missing at the time. . . . Woman was there,

as she had ever been, ready to minister to her risen, as to her dying, Lord—

> "Not she with traitorous lips her Saviour stung;
> Not she denied Him with unholy tongue;
> She, whilst Apostles shrunk, could danger brave;
> Last at the cross, and earliest at the grave."

But surely, if the dignity of our Lord or the efficiency of His message were likely to be imperilled by committing this sacred trust to a woman, He who was guarded by legions of angels could have commanded another messenger; but, as if intent on doing her honour and rewarding her unwavering fidelity, He reveals Himself *first* to her; and, as an evidence that He had taken the curse under which she had so long groaned out of the way, nailing it to His cross, He makes her who had been first in the transgression, first also in the glorious knowledge of complete redemption.[35]

Acts 2:16–18 was a second passage critical to Catherine's argument, and as the fulfillment of Joel 2:28–29, this message by Peter at Pentecost was one of both promise and hope that "your sons and your daughters shall prophesy." Catherine often referred to this passage. The third, and most important, was Galatians 3:28, the most often quoted passage in her defense of female ministry. Matters of racial, status, and sexual distinctions were, for Catherine, the result of the fall and a sign of sin. Likewise, the abolition of these distinctions was the great sign of redemption. Obviously dismissing the contention that this passage deals only with salvation, Catherine wrote, "If this passage does not teach that in the privileges, duties, and responsibilities of Christ's Kingdom, all differences of nation, caste, and sex are abolished, we should like to know what it does teach, and wherefore it was written."[36]

In summary, Catherine maintained that the witness of Scripture, far from constraining women, justified women in ministry and indeed envisioned women as well as men proclaiming the gospel as a sure sign of the breaking in of God's kingdom, inaugurated with the life, ministry, death, and resurrection of the Christ. On the other hand, a mistaken and misled suppression of women in ministry "has resulted in . . . loss to the Church, evil to the world, and dishonour to God."[37]

The third aspect of Catherine's pamphlet, after citing many confirming witnesses of women in ministry not only from the Bible but from the history of the church, is that she supported her contention that the weight of such evidence will force the church once again to be faithful to the scriptural and historical witness. She wrote:

> Whether the Church will allow women to speak in *her* assemblies can only be a question of time; common sense, public opinion, and the blessed results of female agency will force her to give us an honest and impartial rendering of the solitary text on which she grounds her prohibitions. Then, when the true light shines and God's works take the place of man's traditions, the doctor of divinity who shall teach that Paul commands woman to be silent when God's Spirit urges her to speak, will be regarded much the same as we should regard an astronomer who should teach that the sun is the earth's satellite.[38]

Following the publication of her pamphlet, and about a year after she began preaching, Catherine was in correspondence with the Reverend J. Stacey, "perhaps the best cultured intellect in the New Connexion body, being principal of their theological college, and afterwards one of its annual presidents."[39] Stacey, now the editor of the *Wesleyan Times,* requested a copy of *Female Teaching.* Catherine responded to his request, and sent this letter, dated March 19, 1861, along with the pamphlet:

Kind and Dear Sir:

    In a letter received yesterday my dear husband informs me that you have expressed a wish to see one of my pamphlets on Female Teaching. Accordingly I avail myself of the privilege of sending you one and also a copy of Mr. Rees' in answer to which it was written.

    Altho' I think I have succeeded in answering that gentleman I am conscious that I have not done anything like justice to this very important subject but it is my intention shortly to write on it again, in which case I should esteem it a great favor if you would allow me to trouble you for a critical examination of the original with reference to a few controverted passages. For my own part I desire above all things a thorough, honest impartial investigation of the sacred Scriptures on this subject by those properly qualified for the work, and I am deeply convinced that when this is secured the present prevailing notions with reference to women's position in the Church will be driven back to the abyss of darkness and error from whence they originally issued and that the gift of prophecy to woman—one of the distinguishing characteristics of the latter day glory—will be rescued from the oblivion to which ignorance and prejudice have so long consigned it. May God hasten that day, and to this end bless even the feeble efforts of one so unworthy as yours in the love and fellowship of Jesus.

    Catherine Booth

P. S. Allow me to ask if you have seen "The Promise of the Father" by Mrs. Palmer. If not I should have great pleasure in forwarding it for your perusal. It is a large book addressed chiefly to ministers and contains much valuable matter on the subject of female agency in the Church.[40]

Stacey was unconvinced by Catherine's argument and was even sarcastic in his remarks about Adam Clarke, whom Catherine quoted in *Female Teaching*. Stacey, obviously on the defensive, wrote of Clarke,

I may observe that Dr. Clarke's authority weighs very little with me, as it has little weight anywhere. I admire him very much as a man, but as a deep thinker, or as an accurate and searching scholar, his reputation does not and cannot stand high. He knew many things rather than much. I make this remark, because I think, from a cursory glance at your pamphlet, you quote him as a chief authority. But I must read before I criticize.[41]

Catherine responded immediately on March 21, 1861:

Rev. and Dear Sir:—

    I am sorry to intrude myself on your notice again so soon, but since reading your note I feel that it is imperative on me to offer a word of explanation and that is to assure you that I had not the slightest intention of alluding to <u>yourself</u> . . . in the reference I made to the effects of ignorance and prejudice on the subject in question, but simply to the vulgar notions of the public in general. . . . But I have always entertained for you the most profound respect and esteem.

I may just observe that I did not quote Dr. Clarke so much as a first authority, as giving what appears to me a common-sense view of the passages in question, and one which does not involve the contradictions so conspicuous in some other commentators. However, I sincerely thank you for your criticisms, and shall be glad to receive more when you have leisure. If I am wrong, it is in judgment, not in heart. I am sure I only wish to know the will of God and all within me would bow in silent and loving acquiescence.

But oh, sir, <u>how can it be</u> that the promptings of the Holy Spirit and the precepts of the Word should be in such direct antagonism as Mr. Rees makes it appear? In asking this question I know that I only express the heartfelt inquiry of many of the most <u>devoted</u> and faithful amongst the female disciples of our Lord. For it is a significant fact that it is not the formal, worldly-minded professors who experience these urgings of the Spirit to open their lips for Jesus, but generally those who are most eminent for piety and unreserved consecration to the service of their Saviour. Surely there must be some mistake somewhere. I cannot but think that the mistake lies in the interpretation and application of two isolated passages in Paul's writings.

You say, my dear sir, that you do not object to female teaching in the general sense. Then you admit of a <u>qualification</u> of the passage, 'I suffer not a woman to teach'; for, taken literally, this forbids all kinds of teaching whatever. The question to be settled is, what kind of qualification do the principles and general bearing of the New Testament render necessary? To my mind, there is but one reply. Suppose commentators were to deal with some parts of the Epistle of James as they do with these two passages, what would become of the glorious doctrine of justification by faith?

I cannot but believe that a very grievous wrong has been inflicted on thousands of Spirit-baptized disciples of Jesus long since gone to their reward by the seal of silence imposed on them by good but mistaken men, who thought they were doing God service!

But I believe the Lord himself is coming out of his place to teach the Church her mistake on this subject, so important to her ultimate triumphs. I believe thousands of loving, believing hearts are pleading for the bestowment of the promise of the Father on the handmaidens as well as on the servants of the Lord. And God will in His own good time answer prayer.

Excuse me, my dear sir. I had no intention of writing at such length when I commenced. But my heart is full of feeling on this subject—not on my own account, God knows, I felt so for years before I ever admitted the possibility of speaking myself, but because it does appear to me that this subject is very intimately connected with the progress and triumph of the blessed Gospel, and because I am anxious to interest in it one whose learning and intelligence might be so helpful to the truth, and in whose nobility of soul I feel I dare rely. This is my apology for occupying so much of your valuable time.

Yours in the fellowship of Jesus,
Catherine Booth[42]

Stacey remained still unconvinced by Catherine's argument.

The timing of Catherine's entrance into public ministry is critical. As has been noted, William's appointment to the Brighouse circuit, "one of the most obscure and least successful circuits,"[43] proved nevertheless to be advantageous to his wife's ministry because it was at Brighouse that Catherine taught "a class among the female members who attended the chapel"[44] and Sunday school. "I commenced teaching a class of girls," Catherine wrote to her mother, "on Sunday afternoon in our own back parlour. I had a dozen selected out of the school for that purpose. . . . I got on well, and the children seemed well pleased."[45]

Her commitment to the temperance movement still firm, she delivered temperance addresses to the Junior Band of Hope, which was connected with the Brighouse chapel. In a revealing letter to her parents dated December 7, 1857, Catherine wrote:

If I get on well and find that I really possess any ability for public speaking, I don't intend to finish with juveniles. I very <u>much desire</u> to earn some <u>money</u> some way, and I shall by this, if I think there is any reasonable hope of success. When we were in Cornwall I went to hear a very popular female lecturer, and felt very much <u>encouraged</u> to try my hand. If I could do so, I should be able to fit in with William's efforts on his evangelistic tours nicely. I only wish I had begun years ago. Had I been fortunate enough to have been brought up among the Primitives, I believe I should have been preaching now.[46]

She reiterated this in a letter to her mother written only a couple of weeks later on December 23, 1857.

I long to repay you in some way for all your trouble and care. I hope some day to be able. If I get on and become a successful lecturer I shall be able to do so and I have strong hopes that I shall. I addressed the band of hope on Monday evening and got on far better than I expected. I felt quite at home on the <u>Platform</u>—far more so than I do in the <u>Kitchen</u>!![47]

The time finally arrived a few years later for Catherine to "try at something higher." She entered into public ministry rather inauspiciously on Whitsunday, 1860, in the Methodist New Connexion Bethesda Chapel, Gateshead.[48] This was only a few months after writing *Female Teaching,* and as one of her biographers noted, "She applied the pamphlet to herself."[49] Reflecting on the incident a few years later, Catherine stated:

I had long had a controversy on this question in my soul. In fact, from the time I was converted, the Spirit of God had constantly been urging me into paths of usefulness and labor, which seemed to me impossible. Perhaps some of you would hardly credit that I was one of the most timid and bashful disciples of the Lord Jesus ever saved. I used to make up my mind I would, and resolve, and intend, and then, when the hour came, I failed for want of courage. I need not have failed.[50]

Stead correctly observed, "Nothing is less true than that Catherine Booth took naturally to public ministry. At each successive step she was drawn forward against her own strong natural opposition."[51]

The private and anxious controversy over this issue, faced again during a period of sickness following the birth of her daughter Emma early in January 1860, was resolved on that Sunday. At the conclusion of her husband's sermon, Catherine rose from the pew where she had been sitting with her son William Bramwell and walked to the front of the chapel. Catherine recorded that "about 1000 persons were present, including a number of preachers and outside friends"[52] and stated, "My dear husband thought something had happened, and so did the people."[53] She then went on to recount the incident:

> He stepped down to ask me, "What is the matter, my dear." I said "I want to say a word." He was so taken by surprise, he could only say, "My dear wife wants to say a word," and sat down. He had been trying to persuade me to do it for ten years. I felt as if I were clinging to some human arm—and yet it was a Divine arm— to hold me. I just got up and told the people how it came about. I confessed, as I think everybody should, when they have been in the wrong and misrepresented the religion of Jesus Christ. I said, "I dare say many of you have been looking upon me as a very devoted woman, and one who has been living faithfully to God, but I have come to know that I have been living in disobedience, and to that extent I have brought darkness and leanness into my soul, but I promised the Lord three or four months ago, and I dare not disobey. I have come to tell you this, and to promise the Lord that I will be obedient to the heavenly vision."[54]

She returned to the chapel that evening and preached her first sermon, "Be Filled with the Spirit."

And so began Catherine Booth's public ministry of preaching and teaching until she was silenced by death in October 1890. Twenty years after her public confession at Gateshead, she wrote:

But oh, how little did I realize how much was then involved! I never imagined the life of publicity and trial that it would lead me to, for I was never allowed to have another quiet Sabbath when I was well enough to stand and speak. All I did was to take the first step. I could not see in advance. But the Lord, as He always does when His people are honest with Him and obedient, opened the windows of heaven and poured out such a blessing that there was not room to contain it.[55]

Her preaching ministry began almost immediately, rather to her own surprise, both at Gateshead and in neighboring towns. As early as the beginning of June we find her preaching, for example, at Newcastle, for which she received commendation from one W. H. Renwick, the Society Steward. In the meantime, the strain of the controversy that William was having with New Connexion Methodism was beginning to tell on him. In July 1860 when he was incapacitated for two weeks, Catherine filled his preaching commitments in Gateshead and other places in the circuit, preaching—as was her custom for the remainder of her life—for over an hour and sometimes for as long as an hour and a half. In September when William suffered a complete breakdown and was convinced to journey to Mr. Smedley's clinic at Matlock for hydropathic treatment, Catherine, for the following nine weeks, filled William's preaching engagements, administered the business of the circuit (she was, in effect, the superintendent of the circuit even though she did not have the title), and ran the Booth household. "You see," she wrote to William during this time, "I cannot get rid of the care and management of things at home, and this sadly interferes with the quiet necessary for preparation, but I must try to possess my soul in patience, and to do all, in the kitchen as well as in the pulpit, to the glory of God. The Lord help me!"[56]

The newspapers took notice of this woman preaching in the area. On February 24, 1861, Catherine wrote to her parents about her growing reputation and about the attention given to her in the papers, "in one of them I am represented as having my husband's clothes on! They would require to be considerably shortened before such a phenomenon could occur would they not? Well notwithstanding all I have heard about the papers, I have never had sufficient curiosity to buy one, nor have I ever seen my name in print, except on the bills on the walls and then I have had some difficulty to believe that it really meant <u>me</u>. However, I suppose it did, and now I think I should never deem anything impossible any more." In fact, earlier in the letter she wrote, "I get plenty of invitations now, far more than I can comply with."[57] Only two months later Catherine wrote, "I am just in my element in the work. I only regret that I did not commence <u>years ago</u>."[58]

Catherine provided William with great details about her ministry during his absence. She was pleased both with her own preaching and with the reception of the people. The chapel was often filled to capacity, and Catherine related stories of those who were saved under her ministry. She continued working in spite of her ever recurring bouts with illnesses until William was able to return to the circuit. Soon after his return came the events leading up to his conflict with the leaders of New Connexion Methodism and his subsequent resignation from the denomination. In the meantime, however, it was not only William who was preparing to enter into an independent preaching ministry but Catherine as well. Her abilities and skills for preaching, counseling, and administration had been well tested for more than a year since she first stood up in the chapel on Whitsunday and said, "I want to say a word." Both Catherine and William were now ready to suffer the consequences of their actions and both were likewise ready to engage in a shared ministry for the sake of the kingdom. This wife-and-husband team would cause no little stir among the churches, and it is true that many churches denied the Booths entrance not simply because they disagreed with William's evangelistic fervor but because they could never endorse a woman preaching from their pulpits.

Such discouragements notwithstanding, the Booths now believed that God had opened for them a wider ministry than simply one of awakening New Connexion Methodism through their combined evangelistic efforts. They still conceived of such ministry through the agency of existing denominations and within the doors of the churches, not having yet thought of evangelistic ministry in rented halls in the towns they visited. Such a move in that direction would give them complete independence from the churches, and eventually that is what they would do.

The first invitation following William's resignation came from Hayle in Cornwall. The minister there, Mr. Shone, was a New Connexion minister who had assisted William at Gateshead for a year and had lived with the Booth family during that time. He could not have lived with them without being influenced by Catherine, and his invitation was tellingly to both of them. Catherine and William accepted this courageous invitation happily, in spite of the fact that there was no promise of remuneration for their labors. "The earnest way in which I had been included in the invitation, and the evident appreciation and value put upon my labours, seemed to me as a cloud like a man's hand upon my horizon, and appeared to prelude the opening of a way by which we could travel together, instead of the perpetual separations to which I had been trying to make up my mind as a necessary part of the evangelistic cross."[59] So this joint ministry began in a village in Cornwall on Sunday, August 11, 1861, and would continue for many years. The Booths received other invitations in Cornwall, and a commitment originally for about seven weeks turned out to last eighteen months. Some neighboring Wesleyan chapels had also opened their doors to the Booths, and their ministry both to adults and to children was successful.

From Hayle the Booths moved to St. Ives, invited there by the congregation of the New Connexion chapel. At long last the Booth children joined their parents, after being cared for in the Mumford house. It was while the Booths were at St. Ives that a letter addressed to "My Dear Mrs. Booth" reached Catherine. It was a letter from Mrs. Phoebe Palmer and, although lengthy, is worth quoting here.

My Dear Mrs. Booth:—
    Yours of several weeks since, announcing your decision to leave the New Connexion, was received. Pardon my long delay in answering it.

I do not doubt but the step that you and your excellent husband have taken will result in your both having a much brighter crown to cast at the feet of the world's Redeemer. There is a danger of permitting earthly position and the fear of grieving friends whom we love, and who we know love us, to keep us from following on the narrowest part of the narrow way. Oh, may you ever be numbered with those who follow the Saviour closely! I need not say that if you do this your path will sometimes lead through evil as well as good report. But it is enough for the disciple that he be as his Master.

We rejoice in what the Lord is doing by you. Glory be to the Triune Deity! My faith grasps great blessings for you. I do not doubt but the Captains of the Armies of Israel will go out before you and permit you to see multitudes saved.

Through the grace of our Lord Jesus Christ, we have been permitted to see between three and four thousand added to the household of faith during the past year. We are now in the midst of an extraordinary work. We entered upon our labours here very unexpectedly.

My dear Dr. Palmer was taken so ill with a severe cold, which threatened to settle permanently on his lungs, that we had written to disengage ourselves from numerous places, and came here in view of being at the nearest point to America, or some more congenial climate. We, of course, did not intend to commence work here. But, owing to some peculiar circumstances, we have found ourselves again in the midst of our blissful toil of gathering sheaves for the heavenly garner.

My object in writing to you now is to ask whether your devoted husband and yourself will be able to come and take our place. I have sometimes thought that we might in some way be permitted to work into each other's hands, and thus increase the revenue of praise to our Lord and make our union in heaven the sweeter. I have been deeply interested to hear how you have borne the consecrated cross, as a collaborator with your excellent husband.

Doubtless the time hasteneth when truth, in relation to the gift of prophecy as entrusted to the daughters of the Lord Almighty, must triumph. Then, perhaps, those who have endured the crucifying process as pioneers in this work will not be forgotten.

But I must hasten to give some particulars in regard to the object of my writing just now. The gentleman with whom we are guests is a local preacher among the Wesleyans. He is wealthy, and is expending well-nigh all his available means in building chapels and supporting missionaries for the working classes. He has lately lost his only child, and has recently expended the 10,000 pounds which would have been her fortune in adding two or three new chapels, so that he has now six places of worship all owned by himself.

For two or three weeks after we came Dr. Palmer still continued too ill to labour, but I began in a small sort of a way to do what little good I could in one of these newly opened chapels. God began to revive His work, and several adults were saved, and a wonderful work commenced also among some of the children attached to the day school.

Dr. Palmer getting a little better, we concluded that we would be answerable for a few services the succeeding week at a more central place, Richmond Hall. Evening after evening we have continued our labours, and the work has increased in interest, till now the number of the subjects of the work is over three hundred. The ground, as you will observe, is neutral. Our host is unwilling that we should leave until he may hear of another to take our place and carry on the work, as he is all devoted to its interest, and is hoping in God that it may go on with increasing power all the winter.

If you are able to come, we are assured that the Lord of the harvest will give to your united labours many souls. Please write as soon as possible. Dr. Palmer joins me in affectionate salutations to Mr. Booth and yourself.

Ever yours in Jesus,
Phoebe Palmer.[60]

Note the value Phoebe Palmer placed on Catherine's ministry as well as William's. Catherine's preaching was gaining attention. Unfortunately, however, the work at St. Ives and other commitments prevented Catherine and William from accepting the gracious invitation extended by Mrs. Palmer to go to Liverpool, and Catherine regretfully declined.

The ministry at St. Ives, lasting from September 30, 1861, to January 18, 1862, was successful, and the register recorded that 1,028 persons were converted during that period. To Catherine's delight, it was during this Cornish campaign that her own father came again to the Lord. Also, in a letter to Mrs. Mumford dated October 18, 1861, Catherine stated, "We have also the pamphlet *(Female Teaching)* on the go. I have finished the emendations for the new edition, but William has to complete the copying for me. There will be considerably more matter than before, and I think it is much improved."[61]

From St. Ives the Booths moved to St. Just, and from this place Catherine provided vivid descriptions of the revival services, the preaching, and the religious fervor of the penitents who came forward to kneel at the communion rail to ask forgiveness of sins and receive salvation. One of the initial revival meetings lasted until 3:00 A.M., and although the Booths were opposed by some for calling sinners to come forward to the communion rail, they, like Wesley before them, defended the practice. This served the same purpose as the "anxious seat" did for Finney in his revivals, and Catherine was well aware of Finney's "new measures," having incorporated many of them into her own and her husband's revivals.

While in St. Just, Catherine began meetings for women only; this would continue to be a feature of her revival work. Catherine addressed such issues as fashion, child rearing, the responsibilities of women to preach, and the adoption of children. "It will be a happy day for England," Catherine remarked at one of those meetings, "when Christian ladies transfer their sympathies from poodles and terriers to destitute and starving children."[62]

In the middle of 1862 the Booths moved to Penzance. However, as has been mentioned, the Annual Conference of New Connexion Methodism at its meeting at Dudley in June of that year officially accepted William's resignation. Now that the break was official, so to speak, there were churches, both New Connexion and Wesleyan, that would not allow William or Catherine Booth into their pulpits. Indeed, the Wesleyans at their Annual Conference of 1862 passed an official resolution banning both William and Catherine and Dr. and Mrs. Palmer from Wesleyan pulpits. Even the Primitive Methodists showed antipathy toward revivalists. Antagonism had arisen, apparently among some influential ministers, to William's revival measures and to any woman preaching the gospel. The planned meetings at Penzance did not take place in the Wesleyan chapel there but in a smaller chapel in town.

A fifth child was born to Catherine and William while they were in Penzance. Herbert Booth was born on August 26, 1862, and only one month later, on September 28, 1862, Catherine and William began revival meetings in Redruth. They were invited there by members of the Free Methodist chapel. Completing their Cornish revivals at Camborne, many thousands professed conversion and several hundred holiness of heart.

They decided, by God's grace, that their next appointment would be at Cardiff, in Wales, and there they made a departure in their revivalism measures that would characterize their ministry as it evolved into The Christian Mission and later into The Salvation Army. Instead of using churches at Cardiff for their revival meetings, they rented a circus—a large indoor circular arena—paying fourteen pounds for two weeks. Booth-Tucker describes the reason for this departure:

> The recent action of the various Conferences, in refusing the use of their chapels to evangelists, forced upon Mr. and Mrs. Booth what became afterwards one of the most distinctive and successful features of their work, the use of public and unsectarian buildings. True, they continued for some years to labour principally in the chapels of various denominations. Nevertheless, they drifted more and more in the direction of popular resorts.
>
> By this course they secured, in the first place, the largest buildings in the town, and could thus reach a greater number of people. Again, they were unembarrassed by denominational differences, and went on common ground where all Christians could unite. Finally, they could secure the attendance of the non-church-going masses, toward whom their hearts were increasingly drawn out.[63]

Preaching in these new surroundings did not deter or intimidate Catherine. Rather, as her correspondence shows, she was inspired. She continued to see her preaching as both personally satisfying and as a living witness for the agency of women in the proclamation of the gospel. "I have every reason to think that the people receive me gladly <u>everywhere</u>, and that prejudice against female ministry melts away before me like snow in the sun."[64]

Friendships were made, nurtured, and sustained at Cardiff that would be very important to the Booths in their subsequent ministries, even well into the days of The Salvation Army. John and Richard Cory, wealthy ship owners, were among the company of those who invited the Booths to Cardiff. The Booths also became friends with Mr. and Mrs. Billups. Catherine, after leaving Cardiff, carried on a lengthy correspondence with Mrs. Billups, who became a lifelong and trusted friend until her death in 1883. Catherine would name their sixth child Marian Billups Booth.

Assured of such support, Catherine and William left Cardiff for England, pleased with the fruits of their ministry and satisfied with their endeavors—even if carried out primarily in a circus. The circumstances mattered little to them as long as the work of the kingdom prospered. A campaign was begun in Newport, but Catherine was ill with influenza and was not able to participate. She did join William for subsequent revivals. The ministry back in the provinces was well under way, and all the measures of revivalism that proved to be successful for winning souls and raising up saints were at the Booths' disposal. Catherine preached frequently, open-air meetings were held (where William preached sometimes for over an hour), children's meetings were common, workingmen and workingwomen were encouraged to tell their conversion stories in the meetings and thus minister to people of their own class.

Posters announced not only the preaching of Catherine and William Booth but the testimonies of "converted pugilists, horseracers, poachers, and others from Birmingham, Liverpool, and

Nottingham."[65] Such were joined by converted drunkards and gamblers as the Booths discovered the great effect on working-people of hearing their own speak to them in their own language about the evils of life that they were also contending with and how conversion gave them liberty. This method would be used to great effectiveness in the ministry of The Christian Mission and The Salvation Army.[66]

At Walsall Catherine had to preach in all the meetings for two weeks, William being unable to preach because of a seriously injured leg. As usual, Mr. Smedley's hydropathic treatment was tried and evidently proved beneficial. At the conclusion of the Walsall engagement both Catherine and William visited Mr. Smedley's Hydropathic at Matlock, which pleased Catherine immensely, both for the rest it ensured as well as for the treatment itself. She was a genuine convert to such treatment for all kinds of ills.

In March 1864, after a long and arduous itinerancy, the Booths secured a house in Leeds that would become a center for their continuing ministry. The sixth Booth child, Marian Billups Booth, was born on May 4, 1864, while they were at Leeds.[67] The coming of this daughter proved some sorrow for the Booths, and a certain air of mystery surrounds Marian's life. She was an invalid. St. John Ervine, following Booth-Tucker, simply states, "This child, soon after her birth, became subject to convulsive fits and is still delicate."[68] Evangeline Booth, Marian's younger sister, recorded, "At a very early age smallpox weakened her health and she could not profit by study as did the rest of us, nor in later years take part in public life."[69] Begbie's account is different. He wrote, "Marian, . . . following an accident, developed serious physical weakness, and was only reared to an invalid life with considerable difficulty."[70]

In spite of Marian's condition, and in only five weeks, Catherine was preaching again. However, Catherine and William had agreed on a new strategy. They decided they would increase their effectiveness for God's kingdom by conducting separate campaigns, so in 1864 Catherine began conducting revival meetings on her own for the first time. She shows evidence of joy at the results of such meetings, but there is no question that this was a very difficult time in the Booths' personal lives. Their separation was a strain, the care of the children was often made difficult by inept and sometimes dishonest governesses, the Booths were in debt, and Catherine's health was in jeopardy again—her spine was bothering her. William briefly considered joining the Independents in Nottingham, demonstrating that he realistically did not see a future in a ministry apart from denominational support. St. John Ervine is rather hard on William at this juncture. He wrote:

> It seems not to have occurred to him that a delicate woman, delivered of six children in nine years; constantly embarrassed by insufficiency of money; left for long spells to manage her difficult brood, one of which, a baby, suffered from convulsions; and continually agitated by his health and the emotional excitements of revival meetings, had little time in which to divert her mind with reading, that her mind, indeed, was already over-diverted, and that what she needed was rest, some security of means, and a settled life.[71]

But things were about to change. Catherine wrote to her mother, "I should like to live in London, better than any place I was ever in."[72] Catherine could not have known that only months after writing that letter her desire would be granted. At the beginning of 1865 Catherine and William Booth moved to London. The future was opening up to them in unexpected and exciting ways—by God's grace!

Catherine's parents, John Mumford and Sarah Milward Mumford.

Catherine Mumford shortly before her marriage in 1855. She and William were engaged in 1852.

William Booth in 1856, from a portrait to mark his evangelistic ministry in Sheffield

This was Bramwell Booth's favorite portrait of his mother.

William and Catherine with their family in 1862: Katie, Emma, Willie (Bramwell), Herbert (the baby) and Ballington. Three more children were born into their family.

William at the time of Catherine's last illness. Catherine's physician diagnosed her breast cancer in 1888. For William's final tribute to Catherine at the burial site (October 1890), see pages 294-97.

One of the last photographs of Catherine.

Catherine and William, on a soap box preaching, in a London street.

6

The Beginning of a Mission

1865

While William preferred ministry in the provinces, Catherine looked forward to moving to London for three reasons. She wanted to be near her aging parents, for whom she felt an increasing responsibility. She had never adjusted to the nomadic ministerial life and had often expressed a desire for a more settled existence. St. John Ervine characteristically wrote, "She had had enough of being God's gipsy."[1] Her own growing ministry could well be accommodated by moving to London, and she envisioned that if she accepted local London preaching engagements, she would be able to travel home rather than spend long periods of time away from her family.

After this move to London, Catherine and William would often be apart, either because of separate preaching engagements or because they became so involved in their work in London—he in the East End and she in the West End. However, their love for each other was a constant theme in their relationship, and neither partner begrudged the other time away from the home for the sake of the gospel. There was mutual support throughout their growing ministry for the work that the Lord had laid on them, and their times of separation were made more bearable by long correspondence as well as by their anticipation of being with each other again. Catherine and William remained friends as well as lovers throughout their thirty-five years of married life, and there is every indication that their love and respect for each other increased with the passing of the years.

The final reason, however, certainly was the most important, proving to be the motivating impulse for this providential transition. Catherine received an invitation from the superintendent of the Southwark circuit of Free Church Methodists, located in southeast London in the suburb of Rotherhithe. William had long ago recognized and supported his wife's abilities, so he encouraged Catherine to accept this, the first of her many invitations to speak in London. He was also convinced that, although this move to London was contrary to his own personal wishes, it was nevertheless possible that such was the providential leading of the Lord in their lives. William continued a series of meetings at Louth in Lincolnshire while Catherine moved to London.

On February 26, 1865, she began preaching at Rotherhithe, and her concluding meeting was held on March 19, 1865. The clever handbill that advertised the meetings read, "Come and hear a woman preach!" At the conclusion of these successful meetings, the Booths decided their permanent home would be London. They found a residence at 31 Shaftesbury Road in Hammersmith, and the children were moved there from Leeds. William promptly left for Ripon in Yorkshire to fulfill a previously promised preaching engagement, while Catherine's next invitation came from another and larger Free Church Methodist chapel in Grange Road, Bermondsey,

a squalid part of South London, densely inhabited by very poor people, many of whom lived on casual labour at the docks. She had seen degradation and misery in many provincial towns, and in Gateshead had striven with drunkards in homes of extraordinary squalor, but nowhere had she seen such appalling poverty as she now saw in Bermondsey; and her infinitely gentle heart was deeply wounded by the sorrow and suffering and vice that she saw everywhere about her.[2]

During this time she "was invited to attend a meeting of the Midnight Movement for Fallen Women, at which two or three hundred prostitutes were present, and she spoke to them so fervently, as one sinful woman to another, that some were stirred and responded to her appeal to reform their lives."[3] This was Catherine's introduction to the cruelty and viciousness directed at women in England. She had not realized this existed, and her awakened conscience would help to shape some of her future ministry. "The paltriness of the efforts put forth to minimize the evil staggered her, and the gross inequality with which society meted out its punishments to the weaker sex, allowing the participators in the vice to escape with impunity, incurred her scathing denunciations."[4]

Her last preaching engagement that spring was in Deptford in the south suburbs, "to which she made a strenuous journey from Hammersmith by the new underground from Pread Street, near Paddington Station, to Moorgate Street, took a cab to London Bridge, then rail to Deptford and a cab to the chapel."[5] For ten weeks, in any weather, Catherine made this journey to preach. At the conclusion of the meetings, usually about midnight, she reversed this route. Understandably, she decided against the invitation to extend her ministry at Deptford. This was a difficult journey for any able-bodied person—male or female—but Catherine was not well at this time and was once again pregnant. She continued to preach but took engagements much nearer to her Hammersmith home.

William, in the meantime, completed his ministry in the north and moved to London. Two gentlemen, R. C. Morgan and Samuel Chase, editors of a paper called *The Revival,* the name of which was changed to *The Christian* in 1870, invited William to preach in Whitechapel. These gentlemen were interested in revivalism among the poor and working classes and had heard of William's successes. The invitation came in spite of the fact that they were initially opposed to Catherine's preaching because they believed that the Bible prohibited women from doing so. In fact, they advised William to admonish his wife against such activity in the future! Obviously, they did not know either William or Catherine very well at the time, and in spite of suffering the remonstrance of Catherine herself for their views, they persuaded William to lead a mission in the East End of London for six weeks. The name East End was commonly used by the 1880s, designating a place of extreme poverty, desolation, and despair. Characterized by high unemployment, the East End and its good citizens were preyed upon by the criminal classes. The climate bred prostitution, drunkenness, and crimes of all measure and description. Diseases were rampant, and fatalities from a wide variety of causes were common. In spite of it all, William accepted their invitation, and on Sunday, July 2, 1865, he began preaching in a tent in an unused Quaker burial ground. It was an unspectacular, inauspicious beginning of his ministry in London, but he persevered, often in inclement weather, having finally to hire halls for the Sunday services "because the dribblings from the leaky tent washed the unsaved away."[6] The many holes in the old tent also made the meetings difficult when the wind blew through it, and it appears that using the tent was discontinued after August 27.

Now they needed to rent an indoor facility. For the first Sunday services in September, Professor Orson's Dancing Academy, also known as the Assembly Rooms, located on 23 New Road, Whitechapel, was secured. Booth and his fellow workers set up enough seats to accommodate 350 people for the three Sunday services. After the street meetings preceding each service, the somewhat ragged company of undaunted Christians would march through the streets to the Dancing Academy singing all the way.

In order to support this fledgling work an organization called The East London Christian Revival Union was formed.[7] It was hoped that members of this association would financially support the ministry, and William and Catherine likewise prayed that a permanent structure could be found in which to hold religious services. An editorial in *The Revival* magazine warmly endorsed William's work in the East End of London and furthermore welcomed the ministry of Mrs. Booth. Morgan and Chase had evidently changed their minds about Catherine preaching!

Through her own preaching in London, Catherine was already in touch with the better classes of people who would have virtually no association with the inhabitants of East London. Catherine informed these people of the beginning ministry in the East End to the poor and working classes. And that struggling Mission in the East End could not have survived without the support of those in the West End to whom Catherine preached and from whom she received money.

Such financial support may have surprised even Catherine herself, given the nature of her preaching and her lectures to West End audiences. She found herself defending not only the work of the Mission but the so-called criminal classes to whom the Mission ministered. Her acrimonious attacks on the behavior of the upper classes were relentless, and Catherine turned the tables on those rather comfortable Christians, insisting that they were the real criminals for supporting the sweated trades, for employing women and children in filthy working conditions at the lowest wages possible, for laboring in the drink traffic, or for participating in the business of war. Indeed, much of the blame for the poverty and thievery of the East Enders she laid at the feet of her audiences in the West End.

She seemed to take special delight in condemning the sins of the rich because they were so quick to point out the sins of the poor. But the worst brutality and the most flagrant crimes of cruelty and injustice were committed, she was convinced, by those who were quite comfortable and complacent in parlor and chapel. Even the treatment of animals by the wealthy did not escape Catherine's condemnation, as evidenced by her remarks about foxhunting:

Here is His Grace the Duke of Rackrent, and the Right Honourable Woman Seducer Fitz-Shameless, and the gallant Colonel

155

Swearer, with half the aristocracy of a county, male and female, mounted on horses worth hundreds of pounds each, and which have been bred and trained at a cost of hundreds more, and what for? This "splendid field" are waiting whilst a poor little timid animal is let loose from confinement and permitted to fly in terror from its strange surroundings. Observe the delight of all the gentlemen and noble ladies when a whole pack of strong dogs is let loose in pursuit, and then behold the noble chase. The regiment of well-mounted cavalry and the pack of hounds all charge at full gallop after the poor frightened little creature. It will be a great disappointment if by any means it should escape or be killed within such a short time as an hour. The sport will be excellent in proportion to the time during which the poor thing's agony is prolonged, and the number of miles it is able to run in terror of its life. Brutality! I tell you that, in my judgment at any rate, you can find nothing in the vilest back slums more utterly, more deliberately, more savagely cruel than that.[8]

Catherine preached in diverse places such as the Polytechnic or the Assembly Rooms at Kensington, while William decided to cease his longings for an itinerant evangelistic ministry and devote himself fully to the ministry in the East End. In fact, in order to be closer to the East End, the family moved from Hammersmith to 1 Cambridge Heath, Hackney. In his biography of William Booth, George Scott Railton records a decisive conversation between William and Catherine regarding the future of their work together.

When I saw those masses of poor people, so many of them evidently without God or hope in the world, and found that they so readily and eagerly listened to me, following from Open-Air Meeting to tent, and accepting, in many instances, my invitation to kneel at the Saviour's feet there and then, my whole heart went out to them. I walked back to our West End home and said to my wife:—

"O Kate, I have found my destiny! These are the people for whose salvation I have been longing all these years. As I passed by the doors of the flaming gin-palaces tonight I seemed to hear a voice sounding in my ears, 'Where can you go and find such heathen as these, and where is there so great a need for your labours?' And there and then in my soul I offered myself and you and the children up to this great work. Those people shall be our people, and they shall have our God for their God."

Mrs. Booth herself wrote:—

I remember the emotion that this produced in my soul. I sat gazing into the fire, and the Devil whispered to me, "This means another departure, another start in life!" The question of our support constituted a serious difficulty. Hitherto we had been able to meet our expenses out of the collections which we had made from our more respectable audiences. But it was impossible to suppose that we could do so among the poverty-stricken East Enders—we were afraid even to ask for a collection in such a locality.

Nevertheless, I did not answer discouragingly. After a momentary pause for thought and prayer, I replied, "Well, if you feel you ought to stay, stay. We have trusted the Lord *once* for our support, and we can trust Him *again!*"[9]

Catherine's trust was well-founded, for the Booths saw their immediate financial needs providentially supplied by Samuel Morley, Liberal M.P. for Nottingham and later for Bristol and a man who had acquired an immense fortune from the textile business founded by his father. He had heard from William of the work in the East End and wrote inviting him to visit and provide an account of what the East London Christian Revival Union was all about. Mr. Morley proved to be a friend of the Booths and, in that October meeting with William, gave him a check to help support the Booth family. This money well supplemented what Catherine was making from her preaching, and the Booths were hoping for further support from some of their friends in Wales such as the Cory brothers or the Billups family. Morley would prove to be a sympathetic friend and benefactor to the Booths right through to the founding of The Salvation Army and until his death in 1886.

Christmas 1865 was not an ordinary day for the Booth family, for on that day their fourth daughter was born. She was named

Evelyne Cory Booth, the namesake of the Welch supporters of the Booths. She was popularly known as Eva and later in life she changed her name to Evangeline.[10] She, like her siblings, would become a Salvation Army officer and would be the first woman general of The Salvation Army, holding that office from 1934 to 1939.

Catherine, in the meantime, continued preaching after the birth of Eva, as was her custom, and from the middle of February until the end of April 1866, she preached for ten weeks at the Rosemary Branch Assembly Rooms in Peckham. The work was strenuous but rewarding. Once again, though, her health failed, and William took Catherine for a time of rest and recuperation to Tunbridge Wells. No doubt William needed this respite as much as his wife. While there the Booths met Henry Reed, a man of substance who had made his fortune as a sheep farmer in Tasmania. He would become a supporter of the Booths. Although he would prove to be somewhat difficult to manage—as much of an autocrat as Catherine and William—St. John Ervine's assessment is probably accurate: "Reed, in brief, was Rabbits over again, but richer."[11]

In Catherine's interest, after the return to London they decided to move to another house, one in a quieter neighborhood where Catherine, while recuperating, would not be so distracted by the sounds of the city. Finally in December 1868 the family moved to Belgrave House, 3 Gore Road, Hackney. Lodgers were taken into this larger home to offset the added expense of maintaining it, and, as would continue to be the case throughout Catherine's life, the Booth home served as kind of a second headquarters for the business of The Christian Mission and later The Salvation Army. Catherine's busy life never allowed for the privacy she so cherished.

The year 1867 opened with Catherine conducting a preaching campaign for three months in St. John's Wood and, as usual, success attended her way. Following these services a generous offer was afforded to Catherine, and one can only imagine that it was indeed tempting. Had she accepted, however, it is doubtful that she would have enjoyed the national and even international ministry and successes that she did. Booth-Tucker mentions the offer very simply with these words:

> Some little time after the services had been brought to a conclusion a deputation of gentlemen waited on Mrs. Booth, offering to build her a church larger than Mr. Spurgeon's Tabernacle. This proposal was declined, Mrs. Booth believing that she could best expend her time and strength in visiting the various important centers, from which the calls were becoming more and more numerous.[12]

The Christian Mission was progressing, but William took no salary for leading it. Two things are important here, and the invitation to build a church for Catherine underscores both. First, at this time the name of Catherine Booth was far better known in London circles than was that of William Booth. Countless people had heard Catherine preach and would not have known of William's work with a struggling mission in the East End of London save for Catherine's speaking of it. Second, it was basically Catherine's earnings through her preaching, along with the generosity of some friends, that supported the family. William had no income then, so Catherine's income put bread on the table at the Booth home.

It was suggested to Catherine that she might consider preaching at seaside resorts during the summer months, since many of the more affluent Londoners went to such places to escape the heat of the crowded city. So in the summer of 1867 Catherine first began preaching at Margate. So well was she received that she decided to spend the summer there. The children joined her, much to their delight, and the ministry proved to be beneficial in many respects. Catherine was able to support the family financially, the children were able to enjoy Margate for the summer months, and many friends were made for The Christian Mission, some of whom became its supporters.

The grandest benefit in Catherine's mind, though, was that many people were converted and some fully sanctified at her

159

meetings that summer. She believed the Lord was working powerfully. One convert, of special importance to the Booths, was one of the daughters of the Billups, the Booths' friends from Cardiff. She had attended some of Catherine's meetings in London and met Mrs. Booth again at Margate where she came to faith.

Back home the work of what was now called The East London Christian Mission was continuing. It was now obvious that many of William's converts were either not going to churches, as he advised, or were being rejected by churches because of the life from which they had come or the class of society with which they were identified. Not surprisingly, then, there was an increasing allegiance to William, to his ministry, and to his vision, and such strong support caused the Mission to grow. In its earliest days various sites had been rented for the indoor religious services, for example, the Dancing Academy. Other places included such strange venues as a stable, a shed adjoining a pigsty, a skittle alley, and a pigeon shop, a kind of nineteenth-century pet shop where people could purchase pigeons and white mice. A particularly filthy establishment, the stench was often unbearable. Nevertheless, the meetings had to go on, and at the Sunday meetings in the room behind the pigeon shop, many people encountered the grace of God for the first time in their lives.

Many of the evening meetings were held on East London's streets, and on Sundays the missioners would march from those street meetings to places like the pigeon shop for worship. These were mean streets and often unforgiving toward the converted missioners who were now living and witnessing for Jesus. The street meetings and processions were interrupted by fights, jeers, and taunts from the listening crowds, and a barrage of objects was thrown at the missioners, including dead cats and rats. However, such persecution only convinced the indomitable William and his followers that God was mightily at work convicting people of their sins, and they rejoiced to share in the sufferings of Christ.

Through the help of a man named Mr. Bewley of Dublin, the Mission was able to rent a much larger facility for its Sunday services, the Effingham Theater, and William was also able to raise funds to purchase a beer house, the Eastern Star, 188 Whitechapel Road, which became the first permanent headquarters of The East London Christian Mission. William was clearly consolidating the work, followers were joining the Mission, and by 1868 there were thirteen Christian Mission stations called preaching stations with a total seating capacity of eight thousand. And to top everything off, on April 28, 1868, the youngest Booth child and fifth daughter, Lucy Milward, was born.[13] "With the exception of Marian she was the most delicate of the family."[14] She would, nevertheless, take part in the work of the Mission, also eventually becoming a Salvation Army officer. The Booth family was now complete save for the adoption of a boy named Georgie.[15]

The East London Christian Mission was financially supported by a Council of ten men, all of whom were philanthropists and involved in religious work. Members of the Council included people like Samuel Morley, R. C. Morgan, and Samuel Chase. The Mission's first audited financial report was published under the guidance of these men, plus an oversight committee consisting of nine additional men—one of them, Nathaniel James Powell, acting as treasurer of the Mission and another, Charles Owen, acting as secretary. The audited balance-sheet covered the period of Mission work from January 1, 1867, to September 30, 1868.

The preaching stations carried on many activities, although the evangelistic meetings were the center of the work. Apart from the religious services, and depending on the particular needs of the local station, there were classes in writing, reading, and arithmetic, a Drunkards' Rescue Society, and a savings bank. In addition, there was the visitation of the sick and the poor and the establishment of a soup kitchen.[16] By October 1868 the Mission began its own magazine, *The East London Evangelist*,[17] published by Morgan and Chase, the first editors of this publication being Catherine and William Booth. Catherine was delighted to undertake another responsibility in spite of her busy preaching schedule and management of a large family and active household. She and William would no longer have to confine the reports of The East London Christian Mission to the likes and dislikes or the whims and idiosyncracies of the editors of religious periodicals in which they reported their progress. They were now free to write about their Mission as they saw fit and "to edit a paper which should advocate more advanced views in regard to the privilege of Christians and their duty in working for God."[18]

Catherine, of course, was more than an editor. She wrote many of the articles in *The East London Evangelist,* some of which were later reproduced for wider circulation in her books. Her first article for that publication was on "Prevailing Prayer," reprinted posthumously in *Papers on Practical Religion.* The "Dedication" of the paper's first issue, probably written by both Catherine and William, articulated both the work and vision of the Mission. Although rather halting in its literary form, it nevertheless set the tone for the work of the Mission and immediately recognized the ministry of many others who were likewise laboring for the gospel. It reads:

> To all earnest laborers in the Lord's vineyard; to all those who, obedient to the Master's command, are simply, lovingly, and strenuously seeking to rescue souls from everlasting burnings, through His own precious blood, who, believing in the promise of the Father, are seeking with strong cries and tears for a mighty outpouring of the Holy Spirit to stem the rising tide of error and superstition, break up the slumbers of the professing church, arrest the attention of a dying world, and clothe the religion of Jesus with its primitive simplicity, fervour and energy—to such belonging to whatever division of the Church of the living God, or engaged in whatever department of Christian effort, with yearnings of deep sympathy we dedicate the "East London Evangelist," wishing abundance of peace and prosperity in the Master's name.[19]

By late 1868 the work of the Mission was extending beyond the borders of East London, first into Norwood in the west of London in September 1868 and then into Edinburgh, Scotland, in August 1869. Catherine was invited to preach in an independent mission hall in Norwood. The workers there had been struggling to reach the working classes. She accepted the invitation, and later The East London Christian Mission was asked to take over the operation of that mission station. The Booths complied, but the benefactor insisted on regaining control of the station after the initial success of the Mission's work, so the Booths wisely withdrew.

Something similar happened in Edinburgh. An independent mission was founded there by Mr. P. Stuart, who had actually visited The East London Christian Mission and who subscribed to *The East London Evangelist* for his own mission. The Booths were invited to attend his meetings and they did so in July 1869. The work of the East London Christian Mission commenced in Scotland officially in August of that year but was closed thirteen months later for financial reasons.

Nevertheless, despite the setbacks and disappointments, some work outside the East End was successful, and Catherine's preaching at the Public Hall in Croyden was so prosperous that the call came to establish a branch of the Mission there. This was done in the summer of 1869. With the extension of the Mission's work outside of East London, the name was appropriately changed to The Christian Mission and announced in *The East London Evangelist* in September 1869 in the article titled "Our New Name." With the first issue of 1870, the publication of the Mission was changed to *The Christian Mission Magazine*.

On December 16, 1869, Catherine's mother died of cancer, an immeasurable loss to Catherine, who had been so close to her mother. Indeed, because of her mother's illness, Catherine had convinced her to give up the house in Brixton and move next door to her so that Catherine would be able to take care of her mother in her final months. Catherine allowed injections of morphine to ease her mother's pain. A boarder in the Booth household and a friend of the Booths, Miss Jane Short, recounted the death scene of Mrs. Mumford in this way:

> In those days the Booths had not given up the Communion service, and towards the last, poor Mrs. Mumford, who had suffered untold agonies from cancer, asked that the General should give her the Sacrament. I was present then, as I was also present at her death, and I cannot tell you how deeply I was affected by the beautiful tenderness of the General on that occasion. He made one feel that the whole service was deeply personal to the poor dying woman; he put his arm about her, bent his face close to hers, and said—I shall never forget it—"Take and eat this, Mother, in remembrance that Christ's blood was shed for thee," and his voice, though it trembled with tenderness, was strong with faith. I remember, too, how we were all sent for late one night, and how Bramwell and Ballington were brought to her bedside. This was the first experience either the General or his wife had had of death in their own immediate circle. They were both deeply affected. Mrs. Mumford desired to testify, and she testified in a weak and faltering voice to her unshaken faith in Christ. Afterwards, sinking back on her pillow and closing her eyes, she said, "Sing." The General sang a hymn and told the boys to sing with him, saying "Softly, softly." While we sang that hymn very quietly, Mrs. Mumford relapsed into unconsciousness, and remained unconscious until 1 o'clock the next day. Her death was remarkable. Mrs. Booth was kneeling at her side, holding her hand, and quite suddenly Mrs. Mumford regained consciousness, opened her eyes wide, and with a light on her face that was unearthly, exclaimed, "Kate!—Jesus!" and was gone in that moment.[20]

After an interlude of grieving, Catherine went back to her preaching. The growing Mission had been able to purchase the People's Market in Whitechapel Road, and following renovation, this served as a preaching station that could seat up to two thousand people, could feed up to one thousand people,[21] and during the weekdays offered a range of religious meetings as well as other services to the poor. Also, in spite of some failures, a plan of attack had been devised for the opening of more Mission stations. Speaking of the opening of the work at Croyden, Glenn K. Horridge, in his excellent work *The Salvation Army: Origins and Early Days: 1865–1900,* summarizes the plan:

> This was to be, with very few exceptions, the pattern of station (after 1878 corps) advancement adopted. If Catherine Booth or any other missioners/officers preached in an area in halls and in the open-air and received enough local support, a branch mission (station/corps) would be established. (As the Movement grew, new areas to "attack" were chosen with greater care.) Frequently this branch would be used as a "springboard" for opening corps in smaller or other towns nearby. The earliest example of this is Bromley, six miles from Croyden, which opened in October 1870.[22]

Although a good year for the advancement of the Mission work, 1870 did not begin well for the Booths personally. Near the beginning of the year, William again fell ill and was not able to carry out most of his responsibilities. The minutes for The Christian Mission indicate that he was able to chair the committee meetings; however, once again the tasks of preaching, some administration, and running the home fell to Catherine. Thanks to her capable intervention, influence, and leadership, the work of the Mission continued. After William had recuperated, he was able to again assume the responsibilities of a ministry that was still thriving.

Unfortunately William's illness was only the beginning of much sickness in the Booth family that year. Both Miss Billups, who lived with the Booths, and Bramwell contracted rheumatic fever, and Emma Booth suffered from an injury to her hand. Catherine reflected on the sufferings of her family by writing an article on "The Uses of Trial," which was published in *The Christian Mission Magazine.* Many years later, it was reprinted under that title in her book *Practical Religion* and under the title "The Christian Facing Trial" in *The Highway of Our God.* She wrote:

> Affliction occupies a large place in the economy of salvation, for though suffering is the result of sin, God takes hold of it and trans-

mutes it into one of the richest blessings to His own people. For whatever secondary causes the afflictions of the righteous may arise, whether from the sins of their forefathers, the cruelty of their enemies, their own mistakes, or the mistakes of their friends, or the malice of Satan, it is their blessed privilege to realize that the Lord permits and overrules all, and that He has a gracious END in every sorrow which He allows to overtake them. Happy the Christian who, though he cannot see this "end" at present, is able to trust in the goodness which chastens, and cleaves to the hand that smites.[23]

In spite of such family setbacks and afflictions, the Mission preaching stations expanded, largely, of course, through Catherine's preaching ministry and efforts. Mission stations were opened in Stoke Newington and Hastings as a result of her preaching campaigns, and opposition did not deter her from her work and from the accomplishment of her purposes. She found it quite unfortunate that the branch at Brighton, opened as a result of her preaching, broke off from The Christian Mission—its leaders and supporters desired an independent ministry apart from any control from a London headquarters or the autocratic Booths. Catherine journeyed to Brighton to attempt to stay the breach but she was unsuccessful.

Neither Catherine nor William looked on this move of independence on the part of the Brighton missioners favorably and they possibly misjudged their motivations. The people at Brighton apparently had superior reasons for leaving The Christian Mission as compared to those in Norwood, but the Booths failed to make such a distinction. Catherine and William also had a selective memory and probably should have remembered that they themselves had launched into an independent ministry not too many years earlier. They had also likewise led The Christian Mission down a path quite independent of any existing denomination. What these conflicts boiled down to was this: What they valued in themselves they often questioned in others. While they were certain of the righteousness of their own motives, they sometimes impugned the motives of those who disagreed with them.

And while they saw their break from New Connexion Methodism as an act of great courage motivated by God himself, similar actions by Christian Missioners or later by Salvation Army officers would be viewed with suspicion. This attitude would be reflected in Catherine and William's tightening control, such control proving in later years to be both a great strength to the Mission's ongoing work and later of The Salvation Army but also a weakness, especially as it sometimes revealed the all too human sides of the founders of the Mission and the Army.

Booth-Tucker reflected Catherine and William's attitude over the Brighton affair. He wrote of Mrs. Booth going to Brighton "to repair the mischief"[24] and he further contended that the leaders of the Brighton Mission

> did not realize that, under the specious pretext of being their own masters, so far as they at least were concerned, it was but a transfer of the governing power from those who had exercized it with single-eyed devotion and ability to those who might be actuated by selfish motives, and who could not be expected to possess the singular qualifications of the leaders of the movement.[25]

How Booth-Tucker could have known this is, of course, impossible to understand, and precisely why the leaders at Brighton could not be expected to possess the same qualifications of leadership as Catherine and William is unsupported speculation. Certainly, there were many religious leaders of the day equal to Catherine and William.

St. John Ervine is quite critical of both Booths on this very issue. "It was characteristic of the Booths," he wrote, "that they rejected authority over themselves, and at the same time sincerely and vehemently resented any question of their own authority over others, and they were remarkably successful in persuading other people to share their resentment."[26]

Such unquestioned authority and power, however, would come to the service of the Booths as they consolidated the work of The Christian Mission from their headquarters in London. William especially had been wary of committees, and it is certain that

167

Catherine, ever as autocratic as her husband and not one to appreciate people who disagreed with her views or opinions, shared this view. Until 1870 the Committee of The East London Christian Mission had governed the work of the Mission, with William as chair. However, William was moving more and more toward control of the operation of The Christian Mission.

The first Conference of The Christian Mission was held in 1870.[27] In that conference a constitution was established for The Christian Mission that was Methodistic but with three distinctions: Much power was placed in the hands of the person holding the office of general superintendent, then William Booth himself; the equality of women in ministry was insisted upon; and officeholders in The Christian Mission had to be total abstainers.[28] Catherine's hand is evident in these provisions. Regarding the first, it has been obvious by both word and deed that she had increasing regard for her own as well as her husband's authority. She certainly supported William's being the general superintendent, with all the authority of that office, as Horridge points out.

> In 1872 William Booth was too ill to attend the Conference and it was cancelled. This raises the very important question as to why Booth did not appoint another person to preside in his place as he was eligible to do according to Section III, Article 3, of *The Constitution*. It is likely that he alone knew the daily routine of the Mission and as Mrs. Booth, probably his closest adviser, was also ill, there was no one who could ensure that the Conference would be guided along William Booth's lines. Clearly even the Committee were not going to be allowed to act as substitute for the General Superintendent. This suggests that his control of the Mission was so great that he alone ruled and that his organisation continued to be autocratically controlled. His influence must certainly have been powerful for his wife wrote at the time "It would be too much to say that the work has not suffered in consequence of Mr. Booth's absence."[29]

On the issue of total abstinence, we have already seen Catherine's strong convictions held since her childhood. Insisting on total abstinence as a condition for officeholding was a departure even from the rules of New Connexion Methodism, which was used as a model for the rules of The Christian Mission. What is surprising is that Catherine evidently did not entirely win the day on this issue, because total abstinence was not required for membership in The Christian Mission but only for leadership. "The conditions of membership in the Mission were exceedingly complicated and detailed in their requirements, but while it was insisted that members should not in any way traffic in intoxicating drink, personal abstinence therefore was not more than strongly urged."[30]

Catherine's most obvious and powerful influence in the formulation of *The Constitution*, however, had to do with women in ministry. At the 1870 conference, the following stipulation was enunciated in section XII, Female Preachers:

> As it is manifest from the Scripture of the Old and especially the New Testament that God has sanctioned the labours of godly women in His Church; godly women possessing the necessary gifts and qualifications, shall be employed as preachers itinerant or otherwise and class leaders and as such shall have appointments given to them on the preacher's plan; they shall be eligible for any office, and to speak and vote at all official meetings.[31]

A Mrs. Collingridge was the first woman to hold office in The Christian Mission. She was at one time the superintendent of the Shoreditch circuit and presided at the meetings. The minutes of the Shoreditch Circuit Elders' Meeting for February 6, 1870, list Sister Collingridge as the superintendent,[32] which predates the official sanction of The Christian Mission at its conference that year.

The number of women actively involved in The Christian Mission increased, as did their influence and responsibility. In 1870, of the thirty-four delegates, six were women, including Catherine. "The idea of a mixed Conference was very unusual for the 1860s and 1870s or before, but one where women were held to be on an equal footing with men was unheard of and, in religious circles, generally considered heretical."[33] Also, Catherine's 1870 edition of *Female Ministry* proved useful as an apologetic for the somewhat radical position taken by The Christian Mission. This third edition of Catherine's pamphlet

> reflected the changes in her own position and the need to establish women's preaching within the limits of the organization she and William were building. It also provided an intellectual rationale for women's new position. It provided guidance to the membership, who might well have been wary of such an innovation, and it provided an explanation to the larger Christian community. All references to Rees and his objections to Phoebe Palmer were removed. By this time, Catherine's own career was flourishing and the Christian Mission was well-established. The particulars of Rees' argument were no longer worthy of rebuttal.[34]

The 1876 conference was very important. Booth-Tucker's recollection is not quite accurate, since he seems to have forgotten about Mrs. Collingridge, who died in 1872. However, he wrote:

> The most revolutionary measure adopted by the Conference was the appointment of women evangelists to the sole charge of stations. Hitherto they had been attached to various places to assist the regular evangelist, as a sort of irresponsible co-pastor. But now for the first time their names were published in the annual list of preachers as fulfilling the ordinary duties assigned to the male evangelists. Annie Davis, afterwards Mrs. Colonel Ridsdel, was placed in charge of Bethnal Green. Mrs. Reynolds, subsequently a major in the Rescue work, was attached to the Whitechapel and Shoreditch circuit. Miss Booth was reserved for "general evangelistic tours."[35]

The biblical and theological stand taken for women in ministry by The Christian Mission was not without its dissenters, and Begbie wrote that "many of the workers in the Mission, between 1875 and 1878, left William Booth, and some of them none too fairly. He was criticized for setting women over men."[36]

All objections and dissent aside, this was a matter of theological commitment for the leaders of the Mission, and Catherine continued to serve as the model for female ministry. Also, William had definitely come around on this matter. There is every indication that he was convinced on the theological and biblical level of the viability of women in ministry, and he acted in a way that was consistent with his own developed convictions on the subject. After all, he encouraged Catherine in the writing of *Female Teaching*, the teaching of class meetings and Sunday school classes, and the preaching of the gospel.

Another important ally, not only in the matter of female ministry but in the work of the Mission generally, was George Scott Railton.[37] He would rank next to Catherine and William in importance in the formation of the theology and ministry of The Christian Mission and later of The Salvation Army. The Booths had written a pamphlet titled *How to Reach the Masses with the Gospel*,[38] and Railton sent for it and was captivated by its vision for ministry. He gave up his prospects for training for the Wesleyan ministry and, in 1872, moved to London, joined The Christian Mission, and lived with the Booths for the next eleven years. He soon became one of the most zealous workers for The Christian Mission, serving as secretary and later becoming the first commissioner after the founding of The Salvation Army. There was great mutual admiration between him and Catherine and William. With them he had found his calling.

Like William, Railton's initial commitment to women in ministry was on the practical level—any legitimate means possible for the conversion of the world must be employed. "As soon as he saw that women were successful Missioners he was advocating that they should have equal place with men."[39] Bernard Watson wrote, "Railton was a leading protagonist, perhaps the decisive influence, in causing William Booth to give women equal place with men in Salvation Army commands."[40] The case, of course, is overstated, for no one was more influential on William regarding this matter than Catherine herself. However, Watson's general observation was seconded by Bramwell Booth: "Commissioner Railton, who was always ready for new departures, favored entrusting women with the responsibilities and authorities which we had given to the men."[41]

Railton apparently continued to operate on the practical level of what was good for the Mission and the Army with a view to the salvation of the world. However, as influential as Railton was in setting forth the doctrines of those organizations, his commitment was eventually grounded on the premise that equality in ministry was ordained by God and witnessed to in the Bible. This he surely learned from Catherine.

The direction of The Christian Mission was set with the 1870 conference. William's place of leadership was secure for the future, the requirement of total abstinence for the leaders of the Mission was firm and would eventually be more broadly applied to the membership, and the place of women in the ministry of the Mission was settled. Catherine must have been pleased with the outcome of this conference and with the formation of *The Constitution*. She had been influential in the direction of the Mission and in the writing of *The Constitution*.

As The Christian Mission prospered, others who would become leaders in the Mission and later in the Army joined the Booths in their enterprise. They were convinced of the vitality and viability of the Mission's work, were committed to the biblical and Wesleyan doctrines of the Mission, and supported the position taken on women in leadership. Bramwell Booth, though only fourteen in 1870, was beginning to assume positions of leadership, and all the other Booth children would follow his lead as health and ability permitted.

In 1871 Bramwell Booth was appointed treasurer of the Preachers' Beneficent Fund, James F. Rapson being secretary, and two years later he became *ex officio* a member of Conference. He forthwith took active part in the proceedings and served (1874) on a committee that had in hand the preparation of a concise set of Rules of the Mission. In 1875 he was appointed a member of the Conference Committee, the body dealing with the business of the Mission between Conferences.[42]

Other early leaders included Mrs. Pollett, William J. Pearson, William Corbridge, William Ridsdel, Abraham Lamb, James Dowdle, Annie Davis, and John Allen.

A man by the name of James Jermy was the first Missioner to expand the work of the Mission internationally, and for the first time Catherine and William considered the possibility of a Christian Mission beyond the borders of Great Britain. Jermy had emigrated first to Canada and then to Cleveland, Ohio. Finding the great need for the Mission's ministry in that American city, Jermy commenced such work with the help of a few newfound friends of like mind and evangelistic zeal—then he wrote to William Booth to inform him of his actions! By March 1873 there were two Christian Mission stations in Cleveland. Shortly thereafter, however, Jermy had to return to England, and the work of the Mission in America ceased. It would be resumed a few years later in the form of The Salvation Army in Philadelphia.

In spite of encouraging advances, the early seventies were difficult for the Booths. William had long bouts with serious illness, brought on frequently, no doubt, by exhaustion and worry; and Catherine often had to bear the burden of managing the Mission. There were no new stations opened in the years 1871 and 1872 due to William's illness, sometimes also due to Catherine's illness, and to the fact that more people who had leadership gifts and abilities were needed to open these stations.

William regained his health and was able once again to take full administrative control of the Mission in October 1872. This was a great relief to Catherine, because she could resume her preaching outside the confines of the Mission stations. She was most creative when she was preaching the gospel to new audiences and opening new work. Her first campaign after William's return began on March 2, 1873, in Portsmouth. The meetings began in Portland Hall, Southsea, which had a seating capacity of one thousand, but this soon proved to be too small to accommodate all who wished to hear Catherine preach. She then decided to engage a music hall for her Sunday services—it could seat three thousand! For seventeen weeks she held the attention of the crowds in Portsmouth; when the journey to and from London proved to be too difficult, she rented an apartment in Portsmouth and moved six of her eight children to be with her there.

Catherine's next major engagement was in Chatham, but this campaign was interrupted by a heart attack. That slowed Catherine down for a few weeks, but after recuperating in her home in London, she commenced the meetings again. William substituted for her in her absence, and at the conclusion of the meetings on November 23, 1873, an appeal was made for the opening of a Mission station at Chatham. This was done, again, largely because of Catherine's ministry there. While at Chatham, the Chatham *News* provided one of the few descriptions we have of Catherine.

> Mrs. Booth possesses remarkable powers as a preacher. With a pleasing voice, distinct in all its tones, now colloquial, now persuasive, she can rise to the height of a great argument with an impassioned force and fervour that thrills her hearers. Quiet in her demeanour, her looks, her words, her actions are peculiarly emphatic. She can indeed "suit the action to the word, the word to the action." And yet there is no ranting—nothing to offend the most fastidious taste—but much to enchain the attention. "The matter is full, the manner excellent."[43]

While Catherine was in Hastings at the end of 1873 for a period of recuperation for her children, most of whom had been suffering from whooping cough, she decided to take advantage of being there and held meetings at the Royal Circus, seating capacity twenty-five hundred. It is no mystery, therefore, why, in a speech at the 1874 Conference of The Christian Mission, that Mr. Samuel Morley, still a supporter of the Booths and of the work of the Mission, referred to "Mr. and Mrs. Booth, the originators of this Mission."[44] Such natural affirmation of Catherine and William's joint ministry by one who was so close to the Mission's work belies later accounts of the founding of The Christian Mission or The Salvation Army as being done by William alone. Indeed, he is often affectionately referred to as the founder, when in reality he could no more have founded or sustained The Christian Mission or The Salvation Army without Catherine than a child could be conceived by only one natural parent. In the work of The Christian Mission, as in the work of The Salvation Army, both Catherine and William were seen as the founders. That was clear.

At Catherine's instigation, a Drunkards' Rescue Brigade was organized by the Mission in 1874 to give prominence to some of the Drunkards' Rescue Societies that had been organized by local stations. This, of course, was a cause that interested Catherine since she first began to work with alcoholics and their families in Gateshead. The Booths found that the great majority of those converted in the preaching stations of the Mission were alcoholics, so Catherine's campaign for total abstinence was vigorously renewed. She preached that total abstinence was "indispensable in order to preserve those rescued out of the power of this great destroyer, but it is equally valuable to prevent others from falling into it."[45]

Catherine also found herself with added responsibilities by 1874. She had been personally responsible for the opening of many of The Christian Mission stations; and now she discovered that personal visitation and a heavy correspondence were necessary to sustain their work. In 1874 there were thirty-one Christian Mission stations; therefore she commenced a round of visitations—to Hackney, Poplar, Croyden, Bethnal Green, Kettering, Wellingborough, Barking, Chatham, and Stoke Newington. This was in addition to her preaching in places where the Mission was not yet in operation. On August 23, 1874, she began a two-month preaching campaign at Ryde, taking the younger children with her for the duration of the campaign. The older children were engaged in the Mission's work in London, Bramwell bearing administrative responsibilities, and Catherine and Ballington— only sixteen and seventeen years old respectively—already preaching in street meetings and speaking briefly or leading hymns in the indoor meetings.

By 1875 it was determined that The Christian Mission should seek legal standing. A deed poll was prepared, approved by the conference, and enrolled in Chancery "dated 5th June 1875, signed by William Booth as 'President or Chairman of Conference' and by George Scott Railton as 'Secretary.'"[46] The agenda of the 1875 conference was successfully completed in terms of the business transacted and of placing the work of the Mission on a secure legal footing. However, Catherine suffered another heart attack during the conference and this caused all who attended great concern. Catherine resorted again to hydropathic treatment, this time at the home of a practitioner by the name of Richard Metcalfe, in Paddington Green. This was much closer to the Booth home than Matlock, where Mr. Smedley's establishment was located. Her treatment was followed by a period of recuperation in the home of a friend near Canterbury.

Catherine's illness, as well as a period of recuperation needed by William because of a sprained leg, caused both of them to be away from the work of the Mission. However, they were able to supervise the work from afar. Also, the Mission in London was under the capable supervision of George Scott Railton and Bramwell Booth. And some of the other Booth children, like their mother, had already started speaking at both indoor and outdoor meetings and therefore were able to fulfill speaking engagements at various Mission stations. By 1875 the Booth children were beginning to take an active and prominent role in the work of the thirty-nine Christian Mission stations.

Catherine was surprising at times. In spite of frequent illness, she was able to balance the management of the Mission with her many family responsibilities. She was stronger than she thought. She could continue to care for her growing family while at the same time assisting with the work of the Mission. It is true that she had help at home—a servant and often a governess to care for the children. Nevertheless, Catherine's methodical discipline came to her aid when there were so many tasks to be undertaken. In later life her children bear remarkable witness that they constantly felt the care and affection of both their mother and their father even in the busiest of times.

When she was well enough to return to work in 1876, one of Catherine's first engagements was in Portsmouth, a Mission station having been opened there as a result of her first evangelistic campaign. There was trouble in Portsmouth, however, and Catherine was determined to help the cause of the Mission by her visit. After the appointments of the Annual Conference of 1875 had been announced, the evangelist at Portsmouth refused to move and had the support of some of the people in the Mission. The Booths had learned from their experience of losing the Brighton Mission and knew that constant secessions by popular evangelists would follow if this matter were not settled. By legal means the Booths held on to the Portsmouth Christian Mission, and the evangelist and some Missioners were forced out, probably to begin some other independent mission. Catherine's visit to Portsmouth, then, was political as well as spiritual. She was there to consolidate the loyal forces and show the necessity of allegiance to the governance of The Christian Mission in London. No secession from The Christian Mission would be tolerated. If evangelists or their supporters wished to begin their own work, that was up to them. But they would not be taking the property or the name of The Christian Mission with them. That was settled!

Catherine otherwise continued to occupy herself with her evangelistic meetings, correspondence, and visiting Mission stations. This was no small task; *The Christian Mission Magazine* for January 1876, in its summary of the work for the quarter ending November 7, 1875, lists thirty Christian Mission stations, the largest having a seating capacity of thirty-four hundred. The Leicester Christian Mission station was opened as a result of Catherine's two-month evangelistic campaign there. She preached in the theater on Sunday evenings and in a Congregational chapel and other chapels during the week. In a letter from Leicester to her son Ballington, Catherine wrote that the theater "was packed, and hundreds, they tell me, were unable to get in."[47] From Leicester she also wrote to Bramwell regarding the training of a Mission worker. The letter reveals Catherine's usual settled views and firm convictions and also demonstrates her continued authority in the operation of the Mission. She wrote:

> I am glad to hear that H——— did not get <u>lost</u>, at least so far as his wife and children are concerned! I do hope you will not throw a lot of money away in <u>trying</u> him, just for want of courage to tell him at once that he will not do, because I am sure that it will be thrown away. It is the <u>nature</u> of the man that is at fault, and not his <u>circumstances</u>. He is a <u>drone</u>, and nothing, no change of place or position, can ever make him into a bee. He never ought to have left his trade; he never <u>would</u> have done so if he had thought missioning was harder work![48]

Catherine attended the Annual Conference of 1876 held at the People's Hall, Whitechapel, on June 5–7, 1876. Undoubtedly at her instigation, supported by William, Bramwell, and George Scott Railton, the matter of making total abstinence a condition of membership and not only of holding office in the Mission was discussed. There was not unanimous opinion about this among the membership. "An amendment resolution was carried which went no further than to require that members should be 'strongly urged' to abstain."[49] Catherine was not yet able to carry the day in this matter, which points to the pervasiveness of the use of alcohol in the general culture, even among Christians.

However, she would win one battle at this conference. She had always had an aversion to church bazaars, as noted earlier when she expressed her dislike of them after William's appointment to Gateshead. Her continuing indignation over this practice is revealed in this piece of advice:

> I said to a lady a little while ago, who was working an elaborate piece of embroidery for a bazaar, "Why don't you give the money, and use your time for something better?" She answered, "This will sell for more than it costs." "Then reckon what it will sell for, and give the money; don't sit at home making other people's

finery, instead of visiting the sick and seeking to save the lost!" It makes me burn with shame to think how money is raised for so-called religious purposes by semi-worldly concerts, entertainments, penny readings, and bazaars at which there is frequently positive *gambling* to raise money for Jesus Christ, whom they say they love more than fathers, mothers, husbands, wives, houses or lands, or anything else on earth![50]

The Conference of 1876, then, declared "bazaars, fancy sales, spelling-bees and entertainments to be opposed to the spirit of the Mission, and therefore unadvisable and inadmissable."[51]

The remainder of 1876 was a bit rocky for the Booths, not in terms of the actual work of the Mission, but in other ways. The by now customary bouts with ill health were a problem not only for Catherine and William, but for the children as well, and especially for Bramwell. Catherine's abnormal fear of ill health had been passed on to the children, and they often thought of themselves as more fragile than they actually were. Also at this time Bramwell, while recuperating from a near breakdown in Scotland, entered into controversy over Calvinism with other Christians with whom he had contact. Catherine naturally suggested reading Finney, especially his *Theological Lectures,* published first in 1840 as *Skeletons of a Course of Theological Lectures by the Rev. Charles G. Finney.* In response to a letter from Bramwell during this controversy came Catherine's strongest sentiments about Calvinism. She wrote:

I am very glad of your letter, so very glad that you are better. Do not worry about anything at present. Remember you are there to benefit your health; to get strength of nerve and brain to fight in the future some of the giant evils of which you are only just getting a fair view now.

I expected all you say. They cannot help it; it seems a peculiarity of the awful doctrine of Calvinism that it makes those who hold it far more interested in and anxious about its propagation than about the diminution of sin and the salvation of souls. "By their fruits ye shall know them"—*doctrines* as well as men. I know just how you feel. I have felt so myself in the past. But go to the Lord for arguments, and hit right straight home at the heart and conscience. *Never mind consequences*. It may be God will bless your sling and stone to deliver His servant out of the paw of this bear of hell—Calvinism.

I only wish you understood the controversy better and could meet them theologically, but perhaps you will do best by pounding at their hearts. If you could get a meeting arranged, and talk and pray and get some anxious souls, that would help to smash up their cold and dismal creed better than anything else. Let your heart out on them, and break up their stagnant souls. Oh, how Satan laughs at their God-dishonouring theories while thousands go down to the chambers of death!

You can talk to Mr. _____ on *heart* religion. He loves God, and desires to know more of Him. Talk on experimental subjects. Read those parts of the Bible which he overlooks, and show him how much is made of human responsibility and choice and will. I long to be with you and help you.

Do not fear to speak out your convictions, but try to be gentle and courteous in manner. Mrs. Newenham has often said that if my visit to St. John's Wood had done nothing but deliver her from the thraldom of Calvinism it would not have been in vain. I spent hours meeting her difficulties and overturning her arguments. Mind you go to the Lord for yourself, and do not allow the deadly poison to infect *you*.[52]

Catherine was undoubtedly happy to see 1876 come to an end. This was so not only because her family as well as her friend and theological ally, George Scott Railton, had recovered from various sicknesses, but because she could look back on the year with gratitude to God for all that he had done for the work of the Mission in that year. The work was progressing well by God's grace, the family was working hard together for the sake of the gospel, and there were good prospects for the future of The Christian Mission.

The reason for the success of many Nonconformists, and especially of some independent missions such as The Christian Mission, was that these groups adapted to the urbanization of the nineteenth century by going to the people where they were. This the Anglican Church was slow in doing. "Its one hope lay in convincing the working-class that the Church could benefit them. However where the urban denizens congregated most, the Church rarely penetrated. It particularly did not see the need to go to the people on the streets but took the view that the people must go to it."[53] This, of course, was part of the argument that Wesley and Whitefield had with Anglicanism in the previous century. Catherine and William followed Wesley's lead and went to the people in the streets as well as in the theaters and circuses.

Furthermore, the gap between the educated clergy and the working classes or unemployed was often painfully obvious. This was true even of many of the Nonconformists, such as the Methodists, whose methodical approach to life as well as religion had raised generations of Methodists up the social ladder. The Christian Mission put working-class lay leaders to work, preaching in the outdoor and indoor meetings in the dress and language of the people they were trying to reach. Converted pugilists and gamblers, along with honest laborers and many women converts, were engaged in the business of converting those from similar backgrounds. The Christian Mission

> was an innovative organization. As soon as a man or woman was saved, the Mission asked that person to stand before a crowd and relate their experience of conversion. Other denominations insisted that evangelists required education and special training. But The Christian Mission was nothing more than its converts; it had no denominational body that could provide evangelists or training programs.[54]

This does point, however, to a dilemma that must have been raging in Catherine's mind at this time. She had a mixed view about the value of education. On the one hand, she naturally valued the life of the mind, especially in the study of the Bible and of theologians such as Wesley and Finney. Many of the early Mission preachers had neither the background nor the training to bring to bear a thorough knowledge of Scripture or theology to their messages. Some, indeed, were illiterate, and it would be interesting to know Catherine's thoughts on hearing some of their sermons. Catherine, nevertheless, kept pressing, especially on her children, the need for study and learning.

On the other hand, she knew the dangers of education and was not always able to retain Wesley's balanced view of the use of reason. She often thought that education detracted from the simple and straightforward work of the ministry and took one down useless paths of idle speculation; she was forgetting, perhaps, that such had not been the case with the Wesley brothers or George Whitefield. In spite of her fears, her difficulty in listening to some of the preaching of The Christian Mission perhaps caused her to admonish Missioners to study more of the Bible and theology! At this time, however, no formal training or education was required of the Mission evangelists.

In any case, the use of working-class preachers—even with their educational limitations—and the fervent evangelism of the Mission's leaders reinforced the momentum of many Nonconformist missions, of which the Booths' East End Mission was the greatest example and the most prosperous. "The growth of the number of stations between 1865 and 1878 had mainly been founded on the hard work and increasing reputation of the Booths, with their strong working-class appeal in language and actions, plus their use of female preachers, many of whom were placed in sole charge of stations from 1875."[55]

The work of the Mission was progressing well by the late 1870s, but Catherine could not have known at that time that her life and that of her loved ones was about to change drastically. The hard work would increase tenfold, and the ministry begun in a tent in the East End of London would reach out internationally. A fledgling Mission would indeed become a denomination whose ministry would be acknowledged and praised by both East Enders and the Queen herself. The Christian Mission was about to evolve, through a set of interesting and providential circumstances, into an Army of the Lord—The Salvation Army. Catherine Booth was on the threshold of becoming the mother of an Army.

7

Mother of an Army

The Evolution of a Mission

By 1877 William was disillusioned with the organizational structure of The Christian Mission. He was frustrated with making decisions by committees and he did not wish to answer to them—except that he wisely and instinctively knew that the financial operations of the Mission must always be open to audit from outside the organization. He had no desire to control the Mission's operations in secret; he was no charlatan on the lookout for personal gain. The opposite was true. His leanings toward a more autocratic form of government reflected his own disposition as well as the desires of those around him, including Catherine. He became convinced that a more single-minded and centralized control of the Mission would allow it to better carry out its goal and realize its controlling vision: the conquest of the world for Jesus.

William's indebtedness to John Wesley is especially important at this turning point in the governing of the Mission. William, like Catherine, was an evangelical. His loyalties were, nevertheless, not only to that broad evangelical tradition of Victorian England that had crossed denominational lines but more specifically to the Wesleyan distinctives of that tradition, which has already been evident in his relationship with New Connexion Methodism. Beginning with his early associations with the Wesleyans in Nottingham, under whose ministry he was converted in 1844, and continuing throughout his life, he would have a great appreciation for John Wesley. In a letter to Bramwell on August 27, 1876, written during the time he was considering taking more personal control of the Mission, he said:

> I have been reading Tyerman's *Wesley* in my illness and have, by comparing his (Wesley's) experience with my own, I think, derived some *important lessons*. One is that, under God, Wesley made Methodists not [only] by converting sinners, but by making well instructed *saints*. We must follow in his track, or we are a rope of sand. He laid as much stress on visiting the members privately, and in classes, as on preaching. Let us profit by the experience of those who have trod similar paths before us.[1]

William claimed that by the age of twenty he had become a great admirer of John Wesley. He said this of himself:

> I worshipped everything that bore the name of Methodist. To me there was one God, and John Wesley was his prophet. I had devoured the story of his life. No human compositions seemed to me to be comparable to his writings, and to the hymns of his brother Charles, and all that was wanted, in my estimation, for the salvation of the world was the faithful carrying into practice of the letter and the spirit of his instructions.[2]

William now understood his inheritance from John Wesley to be twofold: First, he considered himself Wesley's theological heir, especially in his understanding of sanctification by grace. He was correct in this self-assessment—he articulated the broad constructs of the doctrine very much as Wesley had a century before. Second, in the late 1870s he was beginning to see himself as a disciple of John Wesley in principles of organization. W. T. Stead noted this when comparing Booth and Wesley and claimed that William's admonition to "remember Wesley's success" was a reference to Wesley's organizational and leadership abilities.[3] Indeed, the reason why the Wesleyan movement outlasted that of Whitefield and eventually evolved denominationally was due to the exceptional organizational skills of John Wesley. Stead wrote, "The Salvation Army represented, in the General's theory, what Wesleyanism would have come to if it had not ceased to develop when its founder died."[4]

Both Catherine and William, throughout their own experiences within Methodism and now through the lessons learned in leading an independent Mission, believed that Methodism would have continued much more successfully if it had retained Wesley's autocratic control over the organization and not yielded to government by committee. The decline in Methodism was largely due, in their estimation, to its democratization, and the movement would certainly have manifested much more of its original zeal in the nineteenth century had it maintained an autocratic form of government.

However, they failed to consider two important matters. Much of what they came up against in New Connexion Methodism was autocratic, inflexible leadership. This was what caused them to leave that movement, not necessarily their frustration with the committee system. Autocracy can be a virtue or a vice—depending on who is in control. The Booths had no doubt that their autocracy would be blessed. Also, they did not consider the social context, quite different from their own, of Wesley's authoritarianism. Wesley's call for absolute obedience to his leadership and to his rules is understandable when it is recognized that "as a clerical gentleman he was, for most of the time, dealing with social inferiors as accustomed to obey as he was to command."[5] As Methodism naturally evolved, the discipline of the movement caused Methodists to move up the social ladder, and many Methodists in the nineteenth century found themselves better educated and in better financial situations than their preachers.

185

The call to absolute obedience to the minister could not possibly have worked on them as it did on their socially inferior forebears in Wesley's day. Also William and Catherine were from the same working class as many of the evangelists of the Mission and did not have the social or educational advantages of some who joined the Mission or later joined The Salvation Army. Their call to absolute obedience would have to be based on some foundation other than social standing.

At the inception of The Christian Mission, Catherine and William did not simply drift into setting up a democratic form of government. They patterned such government after what they knew—Methodism—and this entailed class meetings in the local stations, elders' meetings, quarterly meetings in the circuits, conference committees, and, finally, the Annual Conference. This leadership by committee frustrated them greatly, and they finally saw this democratization as detrimental to the Mission's goal.

> The experiment proved to be a disappointing one. Much valuable time was wasted in unprofitable debate. True, many excellent resolutions were passed. But they were left for others to carry into effect, or remained a dead letter in the minutes of the proceedings. On the other hand, the opportunity to obstruct often created the desire to do so, and useful measures were thus needlessly blocked. Sometimes the members disagreed among themselves; sometimes the committees were at loggerheads with the Conference. Mr. Booth had hoped to weld the Mission into a cohesive and self-governing organization, but after a careful experiment he became thoroughly convinced that the system was too cumbrous to be consistent with the rapid advances on which his heart was set.[6]

Both Catherine and William tended to see this inept organizational situation as the cause of a declining membership by late 1876. Added to this, there was the frustration of yet another Mission station, the Leicester Station, wishing to break off and establish an independent mission. Clearly, it was time for a change.

In January 1877 thirty-six evangelists were employed full-time by The Christian Mission. The Booths asked them to come apart on January 23–24, 1877, so they could explain the new departure they were about to take. The primary reason given for taking the Mission in a new direction was that they wished to conform its organization to its primary objective of the conquest of the world. It was decided to abolish the Conference Committee, which dealt with the business of the Mission between Annual Conferences. The Annual Conference would henceforth be viewed and run as a Council of War. Catherine and William found it advantageous to incorporate military imagery and strategy into the life of the Mission. They believed that patterning the Mission after the military, with the general superintendent in charge, would enhance efficiency. "Just as the commander-in-chief of an army gathered around him his principal officers, and received from them counsel and information upon which to base his operation, such would be their future practice."[7]

The changes announced in January 1877 were confirmed by the Annual Conference in June of that year. William was now clearly in charge. He would make the decisions and he would settle the appointments of the evangelists. It should come as no surprise that one of Catherine's wishes for the Mission, which had previously been blocked by committee, was enacted at that June Conference—total abstinence would now be required not only for the leaders of the Mission but for the membership as well. "The evangelists left the 1877 Conference with the knowledge that they were under an autocratic leadership."[8]

None of the Missioners dissented. Just as John Wesley, William's mentor in this move, was accused of "surrounding himself with flatterers: the standing temptation, indeed, of autocrats,"[9] it is possible that some of the thirty-six evangelists or some of the conference delegates could be called flatterers. Indeed, neither William nor Catherine were free from attracting those kinds of people. Nevertheless, most of the Missioners genuinely shared Catherine and William's vision for the Mission and were excited about their ministry in this Army of God. Some of the

Missioners had even been pushing the Booths in this autocratic direction. George Scott Railton had long been referring to William as General and thought of himself as Mr. Booth's lieutenant before there ever was a Salvation Army. In fact, while laid aside with a serious illness in 1876, Railton wrote *Heathen England* as a kind of apologetic for the work of The Christian Mission. "Before the name of the movement existed the idea of The Salvation Army leaps at one from every page. . . . All through *Heathen England* we see that General Superintendent, William Booth, and General Secretary, George Scott Railton, had an army on their hands."[10] Subsequent editions of *Heathen England* were well suited for explaining the work of the Army.

Another prominent and colorful Missioner, Elijah Cadman, a chimney sweep by trade and a pugilist for fun, had joined The Christian Mission after his conversion. In his October 1876 report, Cadman clearly demonstrated that "in his mind the 'army' idea was already at work—at least so far as phraseology was concerned. He wrote 'We are making a powerful attack upon the devil's kingdom . . . King Jesus is our great Commander. . . . We have an army here that will face the world, the flesh, and the devil. All are volunteers.'"[11] When Cadman was sent to Whitby to commence the work of the Mission there, he circulated a poster advertising the Mission as a "Hallelujah Army." Because Mission evangelists were prohibited from using the term *Reverend,* some substitution had to be found. Cadman decided to refer to himself as *Captain,* a title that was "not only Scriptural but popular, being commonly applied to the skippers of the coasting craft and to the leaders in mines and other inland occupations."[12] Cadman took advantage of the militarism that was in the air in Great Britain, when people were half expecting the possibility of war with Russia.

Formal expression was finally given to this increasing militaristic identification of The Christian Mission. George Scott Railton, himself present at the event, recounted how the name of The Christian Mission was changed to The Salvation Army:

The adoption of the new name for this organization was almost accidental. We were drawing up a brief description of the Mission, and, wishing to express what it was in one phrase, I wrote, "The Christian Mission is a volunteer army of converted working people." "No," said Mr. Booth, "we are not volunteers, for we feel we must do what we do, and we are always on duty." He crossed out the word and wrote "Salvation." The phrase immediately struck us all, and we very soon found that it would be far more widely effective than the old name.[13]

Initially references were made to "The Salvation Army, commonly called The Christian Mission," but eventually all references to The Christian Mission were dropped, and military terminology came into the service of this new Army. Evangelists were captains and lieutenants; elders and class leaders were sergeants and sergeant majors; and the general superintendent was simply the general.

The Annual Conference held on August 5–7, 1878, was advertised as a War Congress. Legal changes were necessary with the change of name and leadership style of the organization, so *The Deed of Annulment* was registered in Chancery as well as *The Deed of Constitution*, primarily outlining the duties, responsibilities, and powers of the general. There was, of course, some irony to this move.

He who was so much against the restraints imposed by religious elders within societies to which he had once belonged, now imposed restraints on people under him. It could be argued however that Booth had to adopt a radical autocratic system of government in order to avoid the Movement making the same mistakes of time-wasting and indecision seen in the histories of all other denominations and churches.[14]

The Booths had their dissenters, and some resigned from The Christian Mission. However, the idea of an Army was well established, as was William's authority. An Army was born, and it took advantage of the British penchant for pageantry. With uniforms, flags, bands, and marching in the streets, it attracted crowds to its meetings and soon forced itself on the attention of the British public. Military terminology continued to be developed as the Army took shape. Officers now held various ranks, the lay members of the Mission were now soldiers, and the Mission stations were called corps. The Army flag was created, the red, yellow, and blue colors of which represented salvation through the blood of Christ, the baptism of the Holy Spirit, and holiness. Likewise the motto inscribed on the flag—Blood and Fire—signified the blood of Christ and the fire of the Holy Spirit. The imagery of battling for the Lord from the pages of the New Testament justified, in the thinking of Catherine and William and their followers, this daring step they had taken. After all, had not Paul spoken of the warfare of the Church, admonishing believers to equip themselves for the spiritual battle in which they were engaged? The Army was bringing to life in the nineteenth century the New Testament imagery of warfare. "Clearly . . . by August 1878, William Booth was the undoubted head of potentially the strongest and nationally the fastest growing revivalistic force in nineteenth century England."[15]

Catherine's role during all of this change was significant, although the idea of change from the Mission to the Army should be credited primarily to William, Bramwell, and George Scott Railton, with the encouragement of some of the more enthusiastic evangelists such as Elijah Cadman. Catherine's vision of aggressive Christianity certainly provided a foundation for this new direction. The Army would understand itself as a rigorously active evangelistic movement within the church.

Once the Army was formed, moreover, Catherine became both an apologist for its doctrines and methods and a shaper of the Army image in ways both great and small. She did this in spite of the fact that, while eventually assuming the honorific title of the Army mother, she never held a rank as an officer in The Salvation Army. Neither, of course, had she ever been ordained by any denomination. Her ministry was that of a layperson both before and after the founding of the Army. She needed no authority to preach save that of God himself through the baptism of the Holy Spirit in her life and she never doubted that she was endowed with such authority. Her influence over the Army came not through any office she held but through her personal views that she considered to have the authority of the Bible behind them.

The formation of the Army did cause some opposition among both friend and foe. Catherine early on found herself defending the newly formed Army, including many of its innovative measures to attract the attention of the people and to get them saved and sanctified. Writing on October 23, 1878, only a couple of months after the first War Congress, Catherine stated:

> We have changed the name of the Mission into "The Salvation Army," and truly it is fast assuming the force and spirit of an army of the living God. I see no bounds to our extension; if God will own and use such simple men and women (we have over thirty women in the field) as we are sending out now, we can encompass the whole country in a very short time. And it is truly wonderful what is being done by the instrumentality of quite young girls. I could not have believed it if I had not seen it. Truly, out of the mouth of babes and sucklings He has ordained strength, because of the enemy, and the enemy *feels* it.
>
> In one small town where we have two girls labouring, a man, quite an outsider, told another that if they went on much longer all the publics would have to shut up, for he went to every one in the town the other night and he only found four men in them all! The whole population, he said, had gone to the "Hallelujah Lasses"! Oh, for more of the fire! Pray for our officers.
>
> Now, my dearest friend, you have access; go up boldly and in mighty faith for torrents of power to break in on the enemy's territory on every side. Our moorings are fairly cut and we are "out on the ocean sailing." The rich and respectable are giving us up on every hand, as they did our Master when He got nearer the vulgar cross, but we hear Him saying, "I will show thee greater things than these." And, money or no money, we must go on.[16]

Catherine was delighted to announce in November 1878 that a uniform would be adopted by this Army, which would give more visibility to the idea that had sprung forth in recent months. She had always been Methodistic in her approach to dress, believing in modesty and refusing to conform to the fashions of the world. She likewise believed that circumspection was necessary in ministering to the poorer classes who did not have the luxury of fine clothes. For these same reasons, Wesley, in his later years, had wished that he had copied the Quakers and adopted the use of a uniform for his Methodists.[17] He might have been pleased to see a Methodistic society take a serious and deliberate attitude toward dress, one that enhanced the mission of this Army of God.

Catherine was influential in the design of The Salvation Army uniform, especially in what the women would wear. "Mrs. Booth set herself to work to devise for the women something which would be at once plain, distinctive, and attractive."[18] She took special care in creating a suitable bonnet for the female soldiers and officers of the Army. The uniforms finally adopted met Catherine's requirements for both simplicity and modesty, serving as a sign of separation from a sinful fashion-conscious world.

Catherine was equally as important in the shaping of Army doctrine. The Deed Poll of 1878, which defined the legal standing of the Army, listed eleven essential doctrines, a refinement of the original seven doctrines of The Christian Revival Society. The tenth doctrine read, "We believe that it is the privilege of all believers to be 'wholly sanctified,' and that 'their whole spirit and soul and body' may 'be preserved blameless unto the coming of our Lord Jesus Christ' (I Thess. V.23)."[19] Catherine's commitment to the biblical and Wesleyan doctrine of holiness has already been noted, and her influence in shaping a Wesleyan vision of holiness and positioning it as central within the Army's doctrines is undoubted. Along with Wesley, she envisioned justification as salvation from the guilt of sin and restoration to the favor of God, while sanctification was salvation from the power of sin and restoration to the image of God.[20] For this she had the support of William, Bramwell, George Scott Railton, and others. When the transition was being made from The Christian Mission to The Salvation Army, William himself gave a clear and definitive statement on this doctrine in a speech titled, "Holiness: An Address at the Conference," which was later published in *The Christian Mission Magazine* for all Missioners and other subscribers to read. William was encouraged, no doubt, by the recent visit of the American revivalist Robert Pearsall Smith, his emphasis on the holiness doctrine, and the success of the Brighton Holiness Conference of 1875. In this address William said:

> Holiness to the Lord is to us a fundamental truth; it stands to the forefront of our doctrines. We write it on our banners. It is in no shape or form an open debatable question as to whether God can sanctify wholly, whether Jesus does save His people *from* their sins. In the estimation of the Christian Mission that is settled forever, and any Evangelist who did not hold and proclaim the ability of Jesus Christ to save His people to the uttermost from sin and from sinning I should consider out of place amongst us.[21]

Catherine's greatest doctrinal and practical influence was in the matter of women in ministry. Women's roles and influence in The Christian Mission would prove to be minimal contrasted with such ministry after the founding of The Salvation Army. The visibility and novelty of these women Salvation Army officers and soldiers, marching in the streets of cities and towns throughout Great Britain in their Hallelujah bonnets, accounted for much of the public attention—both good and bad—that the Army received in its early days. These Hallelujah Lasses, as they were called, caused no small stir. They attracted great attention, and the Army would not have grown as it did were it not for the ministry of these women. Time after time the crowds of people at Army meetings, often numbering in the thousands, could be attributed to the novelty of seeing these Hallelujah Lasses and hearing them preach. And Catherine Booth was their mentor.

The women in the Mission and in the Army saw Catherine as one who fearlessly and consistently took up the cause of women in ministry, not in spite of the gospel but because of it. She was the product, in many ways, of the leveling influence of the great revivalism of the nineteenth century in which salvation was available to women as well as to men, and preaching this good news was the responsibility of women and men alike. She was also open to the leading of the Holy Spirit and knew by experience the ministry of God the Holy Spirit in her own life, empowering her for ministry and sustaining her in that ministry. In her departure from the organized church, along with William, she no longer had to ask permission of any denomination to preach the gospel but was free to follow the leading of the Lord in her life. She was becoming the voice for an increasingly egalitarian movement. The women who followed her would be the product of the same forces that operated on Catherine and they would therefore enjoy the freedom of ministry that she so faithfully modeled. Her concern for the women officers and soldiers of The Salvation Army continued unabated until her death.

The women who joined the infant Army and donned that simple black uniform and bonnet were varied in personality and style. They were sometimes as young as fourteen years of age and very often only in their late teens. Nevertheless, the fact that women were preaching was what astonished the crowds. Two of the more interesting were Kate Shepherd, only seventeen years of age when she began her ministry, and Eliza Haynes. Shepherd was a Salvation Army revivalist sent in early 1879 to open the Army's work in the Rhondda Valley in Wales. She could pray and preach and establish and lead corps. And when Catherine visited the Rhondda Valley later in 1879 to present the colors—give The Salvation Army flag to the corps that had been established there— she was greeted by an estimated fifteen thousand people.

Eliza Haynes was another kind of personality altogether. Captain Carrie Reynolds was sent to Nottingham to open the work there, and her assistant was Lieutenant Eliza Haynes. The crowds were not going to the meetings in the great numbers the Captain and her assistant had expected, so Eliza took matters into her own hands.

With "Happy Eliza" on streamers fluttering from her unbraided hair and placarded across her back she dashed up and down the back streets of Nottingham shouting invitations to the meetings. Before long Happy Eliza was marching down the same streets waving her fiddle-stick to beat time for a long procession of converted ruffians who sang lustily: "I'm a wonder unto many, God alone the change has wrought."[22]

She was also successful with similar startling methods at Marylebone. There "a four-wheeler was hired. With brass instruments inside and a drum on the box, Happy Eliza took up her position on the luggage-railed roof, and drove through the streets, alternately playing her fiddle and distributing thousands of handbills which announced the coming meetings."[23] She became a household name in England, and many of her sister Salvation Army lasses heard the crowds call out to them—there goes Happy Eliza!

The Booths' daughters, to Catherine's delight, also took part in this glorious war and joined the forces of women engaged in the work. By 1877 Emma, at age seventeen, was beginning to take part in both outdoor and indoor meetings, and young Catherine, only nineteen, already having proved her speaking ability, conducted along with Bramwell a campaign in Leicester. Later at Stockton-on-Tees young Catherine held meetings with her father; between the two of them they conducted between three and four meetings every day. In spite of this success, Catherine, in a letter written from Stockton-on-Tees, fretted over her daughter's health: "Katie is still, however, but poorly, and frail, which seems to be the only hindrance to her doing an immense work."[24] In spite of her mother's fears regarding her health, Katie did conduct a service in the chapel at Gateshead, where years earlier she had been baptized.

These women preachers confounded the British public; some thought their activities were scandalous. Many simply could not condone women parading in public behind brass bands, preaching in the streets, or preaching from the pulpits in churches or behind tables in theaters. Church of England officials could not imagine women baptizing converts or giving communion—The Salvation Army would not take a nonsacramental position until

1883. "The Salvation Army was the first instance of English women giving communion as part of the official, regular work of a sect. It was a singularly shocking act."[25]

Yet, in spite of such public disapproval and even ridicule, many women were attracted to the ministry. Women from the middle class, daughters of doctors or clergymen, and women largely from Nonconformist backgrounds joined the Army, and in the Army they found opportunities for ministry and leadership not available to them in the broader culture. *The War Cry* in August 1880 reported that of the 138 corps, women supervised 46 of them. They enjoyed a religious authority in their communities that they could never have had outside the Army in British culture at that time. Pamela Walker has written:

> Despite the hardships Salvationist women endured, the work compared favorably to other employments open to women of their class. The pay was higher and more regular than most female employments. A Salvation Army Captain's salary of fifteen shillings a week compared favorably to the two shillings six pence a charwoman earned each day or the four to eighteen shillings a week a laundress could earn. Although a Salvation Army officer's wages were not as high as a school teacher's, that career was available only to women who could afford to stay in school and train. This excluded most working-class women. The Salvation Army, in contrast, paid less but required no previous training. . . .
>
> Most working-class women's occupations also demanded that workers follow orders and perform repetitive, arduous tasks for long hours under difficult and often dangerous conditions. Salvation Army work, in contrast, allowed for self-expression, originality and the opportunity to spread the truths they so fervently endorsed. Moreover it offered an extraordinary degree of independence, particularly for young single women. They could leave their parents' home and live with one or more other women in lodgings without any implied impropriety. They travelled about Great Britain. Many women chose to go to the United States, France, India or anywhere else the Army was at work. Such travel was usually reserved for elite men. Harriet Lawrance, for example, began work as a London domestic servant. On her first

evening off, she went to the Army hall and found salvation. In 1886 she commanded the open-fire in Stratford and later reached the rank of Colonel. Had she remained a domestic servant or joined practically any other denomination, she would never have enjoyed such opportunities.[26]

As the Army developed, other avenues of service would open up for women that would make use of their gifts and abilities, would provide training for their leadership skills, and would ensure the legitimization of their spiritual authority. The developed rescue work of the Army proved to be especially important in this regard.

From late 1878 Catherine was particularly busy in speaking at war councils in various towns and cities, encouraging the new officers and soldiers of the Lord, presenting the colors to new corps, defending the means and methods of this newly founded Army, and explaining the work to critics, skeptics, and well-wishers alike. During 1879 she visited fifty-nine towns. It was estimated that during her visit to Newcastle and Gateshead alone, nine thousand people were in attendance at the Sunday meetings of the various corps. The following Sunday Catherine preached to four thousand in the circus, and twelve hundred people attended the Wednesday night meeting in the Hall of Varieties.

New work was opening at a very fast pace. "On Saturday afternoon, 17th of May, Mrs. Booth presented flags in the Newcastle Circus to nine of the newly formed corps in the presence of about 4000 people, who had gathered to witness the novel ceremony."[27] And the next day, Sunday, it was estimated that 20,000 persons attended the great open-air meeting. The council of war concluded on Monday, with meetings conducted morning, afternoon, and evening.

At these public meetings, as well as in her personal correspondence, Catherine found herself defending the Army as well as carefully explaining the means and methods being used for the purpose of winning the world for Jesus. Catherine was by now convinced that the Army was the restoration in the nineteenth century of the glorious acts of the apostles in the first century, and she compared the coming of the Holy Spirit on the Army with the coming of the Holy Spirit at Pentecost. The Salvationists now were charged with the same responsibility as were the Salvationists in the upper room—to bring the entire world into subjection to its Savior. Of course, many of her hearers and readers had never thought of themselves in such lofty terms, as being equal in their tasks to the apostles of Jesus Christ. Such a theological vision empowered Catherine and William's followers, imposed a spiritual authority on their ministry, and provided theological legitimacy for the glorious work to which they were called. Catherine, like William, was a postmillennialist: she believed, even during the formation of the Army, that the Army was going to conquer the world for Christ. Her task was now to bring that vision to reality; and as the Army developed and grew, her optimism about accomplishing the conquest of the world increased. Let the sinner mock, let the churchman scoff, let the devil rage—Catherine knew that her work was no less than that of the New Testament saints. In their company she helped to lead an Army of God.

By the late 1870s the Army was growing at a remarkable rate and doing so by using methods that certainly shocked the sensibilities of many. According to Sandall, in June of 1878 there were 50 corps and 88 officers. Six months later, by December of 1878 there were 81 corps and 127 officers.[28] And by 1879 there were 130 corps and 195 officers. The increasing use of the Hallelujah Lasses, bands, mass open-air meetings, marching in the streets, and the use of the "Converted Sweep" or the "Hallelujah Giant" to speak or preach in the meetings in the language of the people caused great sensation in many circles. Particularly offensive to some people was the use of popular pub tunes with religious words. Because many of the early converts knew these tunes so well from their lives with a drinking crowd, they were able to express their newfound salvation with their singing. If the respectable people of England found this revolting or vulgar when they passed by the Army meetings, they likely found absolutely uncivilized the singing of such lines as, "The devil and me, we can't agree; I hate him, and he hates me!"

Such sensationalism brought the Army to the attention of the press, for better and for worse. Of course, the more press given to this strange new religious phenomenon, the more popular the Army became—and the more criticized. A problem arose, however, that affected the finances of this new operation. Many people who had supported The Christian Mission when it was confined to the East End and could be viewed as a worthwhile charity from a distance were now offended when the Army came to public attention. Many of these supporters were now embarrassed by the Army's means and methods—they thought of them as antics. They had been happy, and perhaps not a little satisfied, to support a small mission in a part of London where neither they nor their friends visited. But they could not support these religious zealots dressed in military uniform who were now marching in significant numbers in the main streets of the cities and towns of England disrupting the traffic and making a mockery of religion.

Many of the wealthy were beginning to withdraw their support. Catherine, nevertheless, was adamant about the work of the Army and the righteousness of its cause and most especially so when addressing wealthy friends. "I would rather die in the workhouse than sacrifice one iota of my liberty in Christ to adopt such measures as I deem best suited for reaching the masses," she wrote.[29] Mr. Morley, still a friend of the Booths and a contributor to the Army, said to William one day, "Tell your wife that I love and esteem her, but that she has got me into a deal of trouble!"[30]

Morley's fears notwithstanding, he did arrange two meetings in his London office between the Booths and some wealthy Christians who admired them personally but had serious doubts about the means and measures of the Army. In both meetings Catherine and William felt that they ably defended their work. Catherine wrote to her friend Mrs. Billups about the meetings, recounting how the Lord helped her when it was her time to speak after listening to objections about some aspects of the Army's work. She continued:

Mr. Morley assured me, with the tears in his eyes, that I had "carried them every one," and that they agreed with every word I had said. I finished by telling them that we had fought thirteen years for this principle of adaptation to the needs of the people—and this with everybody against us—and that, whether they helped us or no, we should not abandon it! We *dared* not! And we should not, if we ended in the workhouse.

Everyone seemed deeply moved. Mr. Morley assured us that they only wanted to prevent our agents from running to any great extremes, and the meeting ended beautifully.[31]

William, relating the events of these meetings to his son, Herbert, praised Catherine. He wrote, "We had quite a fight. Your mother did magnificently, and we came off with flying colours."[32]

The Army was not left without other influential friends, however. Two examples of those early supporters of the Army are indicative of that. The first was T. A. Denny, whom St. John Ervine describes simply as "a wealthy merchant."[33] Both Denny and his brother, Edward, were convinced that they should support the work of the Army. T. A. Denny had visited some Army centers in the provinces, wanting to be somewhat familiar with the Army before contributing financially. He was present at Mr. Morley's luncheon meetings and even spoke about the favorable impression the Army had made on him. He was further convinced as to the merits of this work when he heard Catherine and William speak at Mr. Morley's and he cheerfully parted with some of his money.

He would continue to support the Army but he was an exacting contributor who had decided opinions about its work, always delivering those opinions with his donations. Nevertheless, there was mutual respect between the Booths and T. A. Denny regardless of how many times they had to explain some aspect of Army theology or some new measure of evangelism to him. He certainly admired Catherine. He was influential in arranging for many of her West End visits during this time. "Your blessed wife will affect the West of London," he wrote to William, "and do more good to the cause than any other machinery that I know of. God is with her, of a truth!"[34] It was this same man who had the privilege of reading the Scriptures at City Temple in 1888 when Catherine preached her last sermon in public. William was deeply moved at the passing of this loyal friend on Christmas Day 1909.

A second friend and supporter was the journalist W. T. Stead. He met the Booths when he was editor of *The Northern Echo*. He had reported on the war council held at Newcastle and Gateshead, but it would be at Darlington where he would first actually meet Catherine. The Hallelujah Lasses, under the command of Captain Rose Clapham and assisted by Lieutenant de Vinny, had made quite an impact on this community, and a great religious revival led by these women well established the Army in that place. In fact, it was this ministry of women that first attracted his attention to the Army. Many of the converts included the worst element of Darlington's population. One of Catherine's last engagements in 1879 was preaching at the Darlington war congress. Stead's remarks about his impressions of the Army meetings in Darlington are insightful not only for giving some objective journalistic opinion about those early Army operations but also for recording Stead's initial impressions about a movement with which he would become deeply involved.

> At last I went to see the girls who had turned Darlington upside-down. I was amazed. I found two delicate girls—one hardly able to write a letter; the other not yet nineteen—ministering to a crowded congregation which they had themselves collected out of the street, and building up an aggressive church militant out of the human refuse which other churches regarded with blank despair. They had come to the town without a friend, without an introduction, with hardly a penny in their purses. They had to provide for maintaining services every week-night and nearly all day Sunday in the largest hall in the town; they had to raise the funds to pay the rent, meet the gas bill, repair broken windows and broken forms, and provide themselves with food and lodging. And they did it. The town was suffering severely from the depression in the iron trade and the regular churches could with

difficulty meet their liabilities. But these girls raised a new cause out of the ground in the poorest part of the town and made it self-supporting by the coppers of their collections.

In the first six months a thousand persons had been down to the penitent-form; many of them had joined various religious organizations in the town, and a corps or a church was formed of nearly two hundred members, each of whom was pledged to speak, pray, sing, visit, march in procession and take a collection or do anything that wanted doing.[35]

W. T. Stead was a religious adventurer; he considered himself a Christian, but he was for any means, religious or otherwise, for saving the world from itself. He was captivated both by the extremes of the Army—he was a bit of a journalistic sensationalist himself—and by the preaching of this woman named Catherine Booth. He and Catherine became fast friends in spite of the fact that she criticized some of his broad religious toleration and undoubtedly chastised him for his belief in spiritualism and his use of mediums to call people back from the dead during séances.[36] Likewise, Stead found Catherine a bit too dogmatic and narrow-minded on religious matters and thought she needed a good dose of toleration.

Stead would prove to be an invaluable friend and ally of the Army. He was of inestimable assistance to Catherine in the Maiden Tribute Campaign, a national crusade waged between 1883 and 1885 to have the legal age of girls raised from twelve to sixteen. He assisted William with the writing of his 1890 book, *In Darkest England and the Way Out,* and he wrote biographies of both William and Catherine.[37] Stead's last hours were spent on the *Titanic*. He was on his way to America to address a peace conference in Carnegie Hall.

The last positive identification was claimed by Miss Hilda Slater, on one of the lifeboats, who claims she saw Stead and the millionaire Colonel Astor clinging to a raft, endeavouring to help others until the cold forced them to release their hold and sink. Since Stead was a strong swimmer it seems certain that he could have reached a lifeboat and the possibility is that he decided not to attempt to board one of the crowded boats for fear of jeopardizing the safety of those already on board. He must have given away his lifebelt for no one saw him with one at the end.[38]

Catherine was pleased as she surveyed the Army at the close of 1879, for she was in large measure responsible for what she saw. Just as she had been in every sense of the word a cofounder of The Christian Mission, she now viewed herself in that same capacity with this new Army. Just as she was accustomed to referring to *our* Mission, she now spoke of *our* Army, *our* responsibilities, and *our* orders and regulations. It had been through her personal ministry that so many of the preaching stations had been opened, and now many of those stations were flourishing as Salvation Army Corps.

It was this mother of an Army who inspired both men and women in the ministry, primarily in the preaching side. Her personal example, however, was especially influential on the countless women from all classes, many of them in their early to middle teens, who joined the Army and ministered. They often faced fierce opposition in towns and cities alike. But had it not been for those women and for Catherine's leadership, the Army would not possibly have reached the masses as it did and would not have grown at such a remarkable rate in those early years. The great attraction in many places was the Hallelujah Lasses, and literally tens of thousands of people throughout England would leave home and pub, shop and factory to witness this new phenomenon in the history of the church, for the church had never sent forth such a concentration of women preachers who commanded such attention and who claimed such success.

Catherine continued to shape the theology of the Army, especially in that central doctrine of holiness. She likewise helped fashion all the organization of an Army—a flag, uniforms, ranks, and corps. She did this in London and also through her endless round of war councils and congresses, especially in 1878 and 1879. This new Army had to be explained to the Missioners and

203

defended before the public tribunal. Catherine remained in relatively good health as she undertook all these responsibilities; indeed, she was energized by the events and times in which she was playing such an important part. Through her preaching, teaching, writing, and being constantly alert to the necessity of defending God's Army before a disbelieving public, she helped shape and form what would in a few brief years grow into a large international missionary enterprise. This cofounder, this mother of an Army, was only at the beginning of a venture, which, by the end of 1879, with 130 corps and 195 officers primarily in England and Wales, she could not have imagined would blossom as it did.

Catherine, though, was always ready for new departures and challenges. She believed that this movement was of the Lord, and inspired and moved by the Holy Spirit, she was prepared to follow wherever the Lord led her. She would have ten more years to do so, and with an Army on the march she now saw the importance of defending the cause. She admirably and courageously set her hand to that task.

8

An Army Advances

❧

Defending the Cause

The Army commenced its international ministry in 1880 and thus began to understand itself as a missionary movement, encouraged no doubt by the great Protestant missionary enterprise of the nineteenth century. Three examples of this suffice to give a picture of the expanding religious cause Catherine increasingly defended until her death.

Brother Jermy had established two Christian Mission Stations in Cleveland, Ohio, in the early 1870s, but on his return to England in 1876, that work apparently ceased to exist. The next excursion to America was by a family of Salvationists from Coventry, England. Amos and Annie Shirley and their daughter Eliza began the work of the Army in Philadelphia, Amos having sailed first to America and secured a position in a silk manufacturing firm. He then sent for his wife and daughter, who were both, like him, Salvationists. In fact, Eliza Shirley had already become a Salvation Army officer in England. It took some effort on her part to persuade a reluctant William Booth that she should be sent to Philadelphia where, along with her family, she would begin the work of The Salvation Army in America.

When the Shirleys were reunited in America, they rented a dilapidated chair factory building on Oxford Street in which to hold services. The attendance at the early meetings was disappointing, but the Shirleys persisted, and within four months two corps were opened in Philadelphia. General Booth was apprised of their success and he sent George Scott Railton, the first to hold the rank of commissioner in this newfound Army, and seven Hallelujah Lasses to consolidate the fledgling work and increase the Army's work in America. They landed in New York on March 10, 1880. By the fall of that year "there were twelve corps in the United States, and fifteen hundred souls had been saved."[1]

At the farewell meeting in England for Railton and the seven women (who were the first to appear publicly in the newly designed Salvation Army uniform), Catherine presented the colors for the first Philadelphia corps and the first corps to be opened in New York. Catherine turned to the women, one of whom had served in the Booth household for several years, and said:

> You look young. To some people you may appear insignificant—but so do we all. So did those women who stood grouped round the cross of Christ to the proud Pharisees who walked, mocking, past. But their names have been handed down to us, while those of the Pharisees have been forgotten.
>
> I present you with these flags in the name of our great King, who bought all sinners with His blood, and who bids us go forth and sprinkle them with it. First in His name, and then in that of the General of this Army, I hand them to you, praying that God may give you, young as you are, strength to fight heroically under His banner, and to lead tens of thousands to the Cross.[2]

The next opening of Army work outside of Great Britain was, to both Catherine and William's amazement, in Australia. Edward Saunders and John Gore, both converted during Christian Mission days in England, ended up in Adelaide, Australia. Saunders was a stonemason and builder by trade, and John Gore eventually became a worker for the South Australia government railways. They did not know each other previous to the meetings of Matthew Burnett, a revivalist and temperance lecturer. They decided, after writing to General Booth, that The Salvation Army should commence work in Australia. "A hall was taken (Labour League Hall, Hindley Street, Adelaide), and on Sunday evening, 5th of September [1880] they began to hold meetings. In the afternoon an open-air meeting was held in the Botanic Park."[3] On Wednesday, January 5, 1881, Captain and Mrs. Thomas Sutherland were sent to Australia to consolidate the Australian work. At their farewell service, Catherine presented the colors for the first Australian corps. "During the first year thirty-two officers had been raised and twelve corps formed. The circulation of *The War Cry* had reached sixty-six thousand weekly. . . . At the second anniversary 3,600 soldiers mustered for 'the grandest march ever seen in Australia.'"[4]

The opening of the work in Canada was a similar story. James Jermy had occasionally conducted meetings in both Hamilton and St. Catherines while working there at his trade as a cabinetmaker. Railton had conducted meetings in Halifax in 1881 while traveling from St. Louis, Missouri, back to London. Neither The Christian Mission nor The Salvation Army were established, however, as a result of these efforts. Jack Addie and Joe Ludgate had both been converted through the ministry of the Army in England. Addie was a draper's assistant by trade and had moved to London, Ontario, with his parents. He met Joe Ludgate at a cottage prayer meeting, and like Saunders and Gore before them in Australia, they decided that they would begin the work of the Army in Canada. They must have been a sight as they conducted their first street meeting in Victoria Park on Sunday, May 21, 1882. They wore makeshift uniforms. Their helmets were adorned with a Salvation Army shield and a banner that proclaimed, "Prepare to Meet Thy God"!

As had been the case in both America and Australia, officers were soon sent to Canada to give leadership to the work. The first officer to command the territory of Canada was Thomas B.

Coombs, who at the age of twenty-four was already a commissioner. Just over a year and a half after Addie and Ludgate's first street meeting, there were more than two hundred corps and outposts and four hundred Salvation Army officers in Canada.

The early 1880s witnessed other openings of the work around the world, for example in India, Sweden, and France. And corps continued to be opened throughout Great Britain.

The work of the Army, including its theology and the aggressive means for pursuing its mission, was not without its critics and detractors. Catherine's gifts and skills were brought into most useful service in the Army's defense. She continued to be invited to speak in the parlors of fashionable West End homes or in the West End halls or theaters. "The buildings used were the well-known and fashionable St. James's, St. Andrew's, Prince's, St. George's and Steinway Halls. They were crowded to the doors."[5] During the days of The Christian Mission, Catherine's name was known throughout London by people who had scarcely, if at all, heard of William Booth. That was beginning to change. With the inauguration of The Salvation Army and the public attention it drew, largely due to its unorthodox means of evangelism, William was also becoming a household name in England. Nevertheless, people generally turned to Catherine for someone to explain, if possible, this new phenomenon in their midst. Catherine's contacts in the West End proved invaluable to that cause.

To reach the widest audience possible, many of her addresses in the West End were published in *The War Cry* and later in book form. These addresses served not only as apologetics for the aggressive evangelism of this newly formed Army of God but also as instruction to Salvationists regarding what was expected of them. Salvationist beliefs and conduct were shaped largely through Catherine's writing, and her books—such as *Practical Religion, Aggressive Christianity,* or *The Salvation Army in Relation to Church and State*—were widely read both by those within the Army and by audiences outside it. As one author has noted,

These meetings and publications helped to make The Salvation Army known to a far wider circle than could have been reached in any other way, and removed many misconceptions as to its aims and practices. But perhaps the greatest, because permanent, usefulness of the publications is that they embody the principles on which The Salvation Army is founded.[6]

Make no mistake—Catherine never passed up a prospect for evangelism and she envisioned these West End meetings as opportunities not only for defending the Army's cause but for proclaiming the good news of salvation and holiness. Her correspondence during this time is replete with accounts of people being saved during these meetings and of others entering into the experience of holiness. As far as she was concerned, defending the Army was the same as defending the time-honored doctrines and teachings of the Christian church. Defending the Army was defending Christianity. And the Army's methods, which some saw as scandalous (such as using female preachers), she presented as a fulfillment of scriptural promises.

Catherine was also intent on remaining faithful in answering the many letters that came to her, largely from people who had heard her preach and were asking for advice on matters as divergent as how to rear their children or how to be saved. She often referred to these letters in her writing and preaching, and her correspondence took an increasing amount of her time. Of course, Catherine's work was not limited to her West End campaigns nor to keeping up her correspondence. She also maintained a preaching schedule in the provinces as well as in London, and she was present at the opening of the many new corps buildings springing up throughout Great Britain.

One would be mistaken, however, with the assumption that Catherine neglected her home life during this time. Rather, she was constantly grooming her children to take part in the great salvation war, and increasingly her family life centered around both the home and the work of the Army. Indeed, some critics of the Booths may have thought that they were too single-minded about the direction of the children's lives, but the children never doubted the affection of both mother and father for them. The parents were not afraid of the battle. They long ago learned to live for something greater than themselves even if this meant falling in the fight. In every way they instilled this attitude of the life of the soldier of Christ into their children, and all the children followed them into the ministry of The Salvation Army.

With the rapid growth of The Salvation Army, immediate attention needed to be given to the training of its ministers, now called officers. And with the geographical expansion of the Army, such training was especially important. When there were only a few Christian Mission stations, the Booths and others such as Railton could oversee the on-site training of the Mission workers and somewhat measure their increase in knowledge, spiritual maturity, preaching ability, and leadership potential. This was no longer possible. The Army was sending out officers throughout Great Britain and to other parts of the world and entrusting them with critical ministerial and financial responsibilities. Catherine especially knew the value and importance of an educated mind to give clear biblical expression to a warm heart and a genuine Christian experience; and she modeled the importance of continual reading, studying, and writing regardless of the pressures of the day.

In 1880 two training homes were opened for the purpose of preparing future Army officers. A training home for women was opened under the supervision of the Booths' second daughter, Emma, and a training home for men was opened under Ballington's supervision. This initial residential training lasted from four to six months. Catherine noted that the question she was asked most by people wanting to understand the Army had to do with the training of officers. This was certainly a reasonable inquiry—Salvation Army cadets were often being commissioned as officers in their mid- to late-teens, and questions were raised about the preparation of these young people to assume the duties and responsibilities of the ministerial office.

Catherine's answer to such inquiry is important not only for her defense of the cause but for her setting forth of the vision and principles that governed the training of women and men in the early Salvation Army. She envisioned the training of officers as vocational training in one basic field: the winning of souls. Just as builders are taught to build houses and shoemakers are taught to make shoes, so Salvation Army officers are taught to win souls. To that end they were instructed in the necessity of their own heart being right with God, which comes from understanding and personally claiming full salvation (or holiness) for themselves. Catherine wrote, "We take it to be a fundamental principle that if the soul is not right the service cannot be right, and therefore we make the soul the first and chief care."[7]

Educational instruction was also required, including, if need be, reading, writing, arithmetic, history, and geography. This was not necessary for all cadets, and references from many written sources as well as the family background of several officers make it clear that many people became Salvation Army officers from the working classes or above. William Booth referred to this in an article titled "What is The Salvation Army?" written for *The Contemporary Review*. He wrote,

> The training given, however, does not purport to be so much scholastic as spiritual, the great necessity continually pressed upon everyone's attention being that of holiness of heart and life. Those who prove to be unfit for an officer's post are unhesitatingly sent back to their place in the ranks. The care exercised in selecting cadets, however, is such that this necessity does not often arise. Very few persons are received as officers who do not give up homes or positions more comfortable from a worldly point of view than the one they come to, so that the Army is pretty well secured against the ravages of self-seeking persons.[8]

Glenn Horridge reminds his readers that, like many of the Nonconformist denominations, the Army drew several of its officer candidates from the working classes.

> In fact The Salvation Army gained 93 percent of its officers from this class. As the dates of the Army's officer sample were 1878 to

211

1883, which coincided with the most rapid period of the Movement's expansion, it could be argued that the Army was reaching larger numbers of the working-class than any other denomination.[9]

Therefore, it is obvious that the training of the mind varied from person to person as there was need.

However, it is equally clear that all cadets—whether coming from a family living on Whitechapel Road in the East End or from the family of a physician or an Anglican rector—needed the third area of training: instruction "in the principles, discipline, and methods of the Army through which they are to act upon the people."[10] None could escape this training, according to Catherine, for the principles of warfare had to be learned by all who applied for Salvation Army officership. The classroom teaching was supplemented by vigorous field training. "Not only is this done in theory in the lecture room," Catherine explained, "but they are led out into actual contact with the ignorance, sins, and woes of the people. This is done by means of open-air marches, meetings, house-to-house visitation, *War Cry* selling, slum, attic and garret work, the hunting up of drunkards, the Little Soldiers' work, and, in short, by any and every kind of active warfare."[11]

Such bearing of the cross, as Catherine often described it, included above all preaching aggressively to attack the sins of people and rouse their consciences to the need of a Savior. What she despised most was insipid preaching that lulled people to sleep and made them happily at ease with their sinful, slothful, and rebellious lives. The preaching of the Army officer was geared to capture the attention of the listener and make him or her thoroughly troubled by the present state of the soul, to help the listener understand the way of salvation and holiness, and to lead the listener into such experience as God by his grace has prepared. Following this was the insistence that the gospel be lived out among the people in everyday life. "We have never had a question in our own minds," Catherine further wrote, "but that the Gospel would prove the same mighty power of God, when truly lived out by those who preach it, and energized by the Holy Spirit, as in its earlier dispensation; and the results have confirmed us tenfold in this conviction."[12]

In spite of Catherine's careful and deliberate explanations of the doctrines and measures of the Army, she was still bothered by the Army's detractors—be they police and magistrates who refused to let the Army march to its street meetings; Anglican clergy who berated the Army publicly as having nothing to do with historic orthodox Christianity and who intimated that immoral conduct took place in the Army's meetings, especially in the "All-Night of Prayer" sessions; or Lord Shaftesbury who, although a leader among evangelicals and a great philanthropist, was antagonistic toward the Booths and the Army. Catherine simply could not understand the obtuseness and ignorance of professing Christians! In late 1880 the Army opened its work in Carlisle, and the bishop of Carlisle condemned it in a sermon in the cathedral. Catherine was in Carlisle at the time and rented an old theater in order to have a platform from which to reply to the bishop. Her address, characteristic of her apologetic posture at this time of her ministry, was published under the title "The Salvation Army and the Bishop of Carlisle" in three successive issues of *The War Cry,* October 9, 16, and 23, 1880.

Catherine began with an assertion that she had made many times in similar circumstances. She said, "All I shall say in respect to the Bishop is that I feel quite certain that if his lordship is a spiritually enlightened man—if he had himself attended those meetings on which he founded his remarks, he would have come to very different conclusions."[13] She was constantly convinced that if the Army were objectively examined, and if the results of its work were carefully scrutinized, then people—even the Bishop of Carlisle—would rejoice in what they saw. This would be especially true if it could be emphasized, as Catherine did in her speaking and writing, that the working classes were disenfranchised from the established churches of nineteenth-century England and that the Army had the means and methods, as Wesley did a century earlier, of bringing religion back to the working classes and the working classes back to religion. Of that she had no doubt, and she was astonished that the Church of England could not see this as an ultimate benefit to the life of the church and the health of the social fabric of England. She had visited sixty-two towns in Great Britain in the past eleven months and knew from personal experiences what the mood was among the working classes of Great Britain. She was beginning to understand the people's feeling of alienation from a church that simply failed to reach out and minister to them.

Catherine often had to defend the methods the Army used to get to those masses, for here was an area of great criticism from many quarters. Preaching the gospel in theaters and circuses, using working-class people speaking in the language that class understood in order to win them to the gospel, adapting secular tunes to the service of the gospel as the Wesleys had done a century earlier, marching in the streets, and displaying the huge "salvation giant" or the "converted gypsy" in its public meetings—these were tactics abhorrent to many of the upper classes in England and to many members of the established church. Catherine constantly asserted, however, that the exigencies of warfare demanded the adaptation of methods to suit the occasion and the audience. "That is the great fundamental principle of this Salvation Army. The great fundamental principle is the law of adaptation—that is, making the means suitable to the end."[14]

When speaking of such adaptation, Catherine was always careful to underscore two things. First, she wanted to make clear that she spoke of adaptation

> with respect to modes and measures of bringing the Gospel to bear on the people. I do not believe in, and God forbid I should ever teach, any adaptation of the Gospel. We will retain that, and preserve it intact to the very letter. The devil has got the adaptation of that in these days. He has a gospel without any repentance, without any obedience, without any cross-carrying, without any restitution-making, without holy living, and with a sort of heaven at the end. . . . I teach no adaptation of the Gospel. I

will keep the blessed Gospel whole, as it is; but I contend we may serve it up on any sort of dish that will induce the people to partake of it.[15]

Second, she was convinced that she found support for this principle of adaptation in the New Testament. What the Army was doing was thoroughly biblical, she believed. This identification of the Army with the New Testament church provided legitimacy for the Army's work as well as for the way the Army went about that work. The institutional church may scoff; church leaders may condemn; the upper classes may show disgust. These things did not matter to Catherine. The Bible, and indeed the Lord himself, gave credence to the Army's means and methods to win the lost. That was all that mattered. In one of her lectures delivered at this time and later published in *Aggressive Christianity,* Catherine said:

We have seen that it is clearly laid down in the texts I have read that the law of adaptation is the only law laid down in the New Testament with respect to modes and measures. I challenge anybody to find me any other. While the Gospel message is laid down with unerring accuracy, we are left at perfect freedom to adapt our measures and modes of bringing it to bear upon men to the circumstances, times, and conditions in which we live—free as air. "I became all things to all men." The great Apostle of the Gentiles who had thrown off the paraphernalia of Judaism years before, yet became as a Jew that he might win the Jews. The great, strong intellect became as a weak man that he might win the weak. He conformed himself to the conditions and circumstances of his hearers, in all lawful things, that he might win them; he let no mere conventionalities, or ideas of propriety, stand in his way when it was necessary to abandon them. He suffered his limbs to be thrust into a basket, and himself let down over the wall, when necessary, for the success of his work. He who was brave as a lion, and hailed a crown of martyrdom like a conquering hero, as he was, yet was willing to submit to anything when the requirements of his mission rendered it necessary. He adapted himself to the circumstances. He was instant in season and out of season. Oh!

215

what a hue-and-cry there is about out of season Christianity; "of some making a difference"—pulling them out of the fire by the hair of the head, if needful,—never mind—*save them,* SAVE THEM. That is the great desideratum. Save them—pulling them out of the fire. Adapt your measures to your circumstances and to the necessities of the times in which you live. Now here it seems to me that the church—I speak universally—has made a grand mistake, the same old mistake which we are so prone to fall into of exalting the traditions of the elders into the same importance and authority as the Word of God, as the clearly laid down principles of the New Testament.[16]

Catherine did not have the same appreciation for tradition as John Wesley had, and there were undoubtedly times when she would have done well to consider, as Wesley had before her, the critical relationship of tradition and reason and experience in interpreting the biblical text. However, she did have the same exalted view of the Bible, and it was from several texts that she derived her principle of adaptation. In the Bible Catherine found no single and fixed order of service. She found no particular form of church government. What she discovered as she read the New Testament was the freedom of adaptation of both form and government suited to particular local needs. The conclusion of such an argument would be that therefore all forms of worship and government are thereby acceptable, as long as they do not directly contradict biblical teaching. Catherine, perhaps too eager to defend the Army's free-and-easy style of meetings, argued, however, that New Testament religious services were of the Pentecostal type—rather unconventional, controlled not by form or ritual but solely by the moving of the Holy Spirit.

Here she was a restorationist; she read the experience of The Salvation Army back into the pages of the New Testament, and likewise, what she interpreted from the New Testament provided legitimacy for the means and measures of the Army. The fallacy of her argument was that she ignored passages in the same text that admonish all things to be done decently and in order (1 Cor.

14:40). Also, she established a false dichotomy in her argument—as though worship in the cathedral is lifeless while worship in the Army comes from the heart, making it intrinsically more acceptable to God because it is clearly more biblical. Catherine's understandable enthusiasm for the Army and its ways sometimes caused her argument to be greatly exaggerated.

These faults aside, it is clear that Catherine's ecclesiology was being driven by her sense of mission. The lost had to be saved and rescued from the perils of their sinful life in rebellion against God. The urgency of the task in winning the lost demanded that all legitimate biblical means possible be used in attracting those people to the gospel and thereby to the Christ of their salvation. The institutional church is to be faulted for losing sight of such a demanding New Testament mission. In Catherine's mind, this was what the Army was all about. And for this Catherine had the authority of both John Wesley and Charles Grandison Finney. Just as John Wesley preached in the open air, allowed sinners to the communion rail, or employed women, and just as Finney introduced "new measures" to evangelism, so the Army had its "new measures." David Rightmire has well explored this pragmatic aspect of ministry in both Catherine and William in his work *Sacraments and The Salvation Army: Pneumatological Foundations.*

Innovation seems to be a mark of the Army's early history, as it responded to human need in dramatic and bold ways. Booth creatively adapted the gospel to the needs of the poor, breaking down the secular/sacred distinction prevalent in his day, involving religious means in relieving temporal problems. The success of the Army's "new measures" not only served to confirm the principle of accommodation in missiology, but also became the justification for a developing pragmatic hermeneutic. . . . As the novel methods of the early Army met with success, the Army mother began to support the adoption of every lawful means to reach the desired goals of salvation warfare. Her theology of accommodation was defended biblically, employing 1 Corinthians 9:22 as her proof-text: "I want you to note that the only law laid down in the New Testament for the prosecution of this aggressive warfare is the law of adaptation." Taking Jesus as her model, Mrs. Booth reiterates the need to accommodate the message to the understanding of the audience. The traditional forms of church and Christianity were no longer relevant to the needs of the people. Therefore, the Salvation Army pragmatically employed "new measures" in reaching their people.[17]

A wealthy gentleman who had refused to assist The Salvation Army said he disapproved of the Army's measures. Here is Catherine's response to him:

I quite agree with you that your benevolence must be directed according to your own convictions as to the best methods, and yet, I ask you, does it signify *how* men are saved if they *are* saved? If with some we have to "make a difference, pulling them out of the fire," by means as "out of season" and unconventional as those prescribed by God through Ezekiel and Hosea and Paul— if they are washed, and sanctified, and lead holy, useful lives— will the Master chide us because in the first instance we attracted their attention by a drum or a tambourine? Oh, my dear sir, if you only knew the indifferent, besotted, semi-heathenish condition of the classes on whom we operate, you would, I am sure, deem any *lawful means* expedient if only they succeeded in bringing such people under the sound of the Gospel. It is a standing mystery to me that thoughtful Christian men can contemplate the existing state of the world without perceiving the desperate need of some more effective and aggressive agency on the side of God and righteousness. It is so evident that the revolutionary, murderous spirit of multitudes of the people is only kept down by physical force, and infidelity and socialism are everywhere prevailing. I often wonder that the mere instinct of self-preservation does not lead those whose every human and personal interest is at stake to support the Salvation Army; and I often think what bitter regrets will seize the minds of those who have rejected this new departure on account of its modes when they find that it was as truly the putting forth of the Lord's own life and power as in the days of the apostles, or of Luther, Wesley, or Whitefield—all of whom were regarded by many of the religious people of their times as evil innovators and irreverent fanatics. "Is not the life more than meat, and the body more than raiment," *spiritually,* as well as physically?

I must say I feel it very keenly that, because of measures perfectly innocent in themselves, and which God has so marvelously owned, wealthy Christians should withhold their support from us in this gigantic struggle.[18]

Catherine wisely did not limit her appeal to the intrinsic value of preaching the gospel. She often reminded the wealthy that The Salvation Army was, by its ministry, protecting society from the evil forces and social chaos let loose across the invisible line in the east of London. The preservation of the social order was at stake in supporting the work of the Army to bring the heathen under the controlling influence of the gospel.

One of the greatest challenges to Catherine at this time of her ministry, however, came not from having to defend the cause at home but having to defend it abroad—in France. The Army had received invitations from sympathizers in France to begin the work there. The person chosen to "open fire" was Catherine, the Booth's eldest daughter and her mother's namesake. She had been active in The Christian Mission and was now, in her early twenties, a captain in the Army. She, along with Florence Soper, the daughter of a physician in Wales and later the wife of Bramwell Booth, and Adelaide Cox, the daughter of an Anglican vicar, were presented the colors for France by Mrs. Booth on February 4, 1881, at a farewell meeting in St. James's Hall in London. T. A. Denny and his brother were present. They had contributed the first two hundred pounds toward the amount William Booth had requested to underwrite the opening of the work in France. Present as well was Sir Arthur Blackwood, a retired captain of the Guards and a supporter of the Army since Christian Mission days.

The elder Catherine Booth could not have helped but feel both pride and concern for her daughter and the other women who were leaving for Paris. Localized persecution in England, chiefly from what was commonly called the "Skeleton Army," was still common. These were mobs, often incited by those with interests in the drinking establishment, who were especially violent against Nonconformist groups that challenged long-held religious beliefs and social customs. They used the weapons of force and intimidation as means of social control. The Society of Friends, the Methodists, the Baptists, the Congregationalists—all had at one time or another been subject to brutal attacks and reckless vandalism by such mobs. Mob violence, often overlooked by local police or magistrates, was still on the rise against the Army in 1881. Catherine might well fear that her daughter would be in physical danger if she encountered similar—or worse—violence in Paris. Indeed, Catherine confessed in a letter to a friend that she "felt unutterable things." She went on to write, "The papers I read on the state of society in Paris make me shudder, and I see all the dangers to which our darling will be exposed!"[19]

Nevertheless, Catherine gave her child over to the Lord and to his will—and over to the service of the Army. God would be able to accomplish what her daughter, relying on her own strengths and gifts alone, could not accomplish. In presenting the colors, the mother of this young captain said:

> My dear child and my dear young friends:—I consider it an honour, in the name of our Divine Commander-in-Chief, and in the name of the General of this Army, to present you with this flag, as an emblem of the office and position you sustain, and I pray that He may give you grace to uphold the truths which this banner represents, and establish on a permanent and solid basis the Salvation Army in France. Oh, that He may give you grace to carry it into the slums and alleys, wherever there are lost and perishing souls, and to preach under its shadow the everlasting Gospel of the Lord Jesus Christ, so that through your instrumentality thousands may be won, from darkness, infidelity, and vice, to Him, their Lord and their God. And in all hours of darkness and trial, oh, may He encompass you in His arms of grace and strength, and fill your soul with His love and peace; and may you begin such a work as shall roll on to generations to come, and ultimately sweep hundreds of thousands into the Kingdom of God! Amen.[20]

The reception in Paris of these young female Salvationists was less than enthusiastic. The Army rented a small meeting hall, and some of the worst people in Paris came to the meetings, attracted at first by the fact that girls were preaching the gospel in passable French. This first Army contingent did not have the privilege that some of their English sisters had of seeing thousands of people attend the Army meetings. The converts were hard won at first—by twos and threes—and the early Salvationists had to endure persecution by the anticlerical and antireligious mobs as well as contempt by the upper classes.

For a brief time shortly after their arrival, the Salvationists' meetings were stopped due to the disturbances caused by the mobs. Herbert had gone to Paris to help his sister Katie, and Catherine wrote this letter to her son, rather typical of the advice she gave to others while not always acting on such advice for herself:

> Keep your mind quiet! Lean back on God and don't worry. It is His affair, and if you have done what you could that is enough! There are plenty of other countries to save besides France, and if God's time has not yet come you cannot help it! Leave it with Him, both of you. Alas! how little we have of the faith that can "stand still and see the salvation of God." What would you do if you were put into custody for two years like Paul was? And yet that imprisonment in Rome sent the Gospel far and wide! God's ways are not our ways. He takes in the whole field at once and does the best He can for the entire world. Human wisdom never has been able at the time to comprehend His plans. But years after it has often seen their wisdom. Let us learn to trust in the dark— to stand still. I question whether it would not be best to wait till you get your large hall. However, act on Katie's judgment in this. Never mind the bit of time lost, or what the gossips say! Do what strikes you as best for the work. Poor dear Katie! Your illness will worry her. Do keep quiet, and mind these instructions.[21]

Through the intervention of Sir William McArthur, Lord Mayor of London; Lord Cairns, the City Chamberlain; and Colonel Henderson, the Commissioner of Police, the police in Paris allowed the Army to resume its work. Catherine mentioned as an aside that she and William had lunch with the Lord Mayor when they were getting his signature to support the reopening of the work in Paris.

The Army was finally able to open up corps in Paris, cadets were trained, and a counterpart to *The War Cry* called *En Avant* was published beginning in March 1882 and sold on the streets and in the cafés. Young Catherine Booth became known as the *La Maréchale* (field marshal). Other French-speaking officers from Great Britain were sent to France to assist her in the growing work. One of those officers was Arthur Clibborn, a Quaker, who married Catherine a few years later.

The elder Catherine decided to visit Paris in April 1882, her only journey to a country outside of Great Britain. She coincided her visit with the opening of a new corps. Her ministry in France served the same purpose as it had in England. First, in meeting with Christians sympathetic to the work of the Army, she found herself once again defending such work as well as the means and methods used to accomplish it. Such a ministry, necessary as it was, must sometimes have been annoying to Catherine, for she wrote to a friend while in Paris that she had "tried to scrape together patience to answer old, time worn objections to our measures."[22] However, as difficult as this was to her, it was greatly appreciated by the Salvationists in Paris, for it helped their cause in the estimation of other Christians.

Catherine was obviously more energized and challenged by her second ministry—preaching in the Army meetings. But under the worst circumstances in England, Catherine had never had to preach in such a setting. She describes the utterly desperate people in the meetings, as well as the uproar, vile shouting, and blasphemous screaming that ensued between the singing and the attempts to preach. At the conclusion of Catherine's first meeting, both Colonel Clibborn and some of the soldiers were beaten and kicked as the people departed. But Catherine was nevertheless looking forward to the next meeting with these people and exhibited great pride in her daughter as well as in the other Salvation Army officers and soldiers who were persevering in the face of such opposition. The mother of the Army returned to England satisfied that she had witnessed the progress of the Army in a completely different culture and the accomplishment of the same purposes by similar means in spite of severe opposition.

Back home she returned to her rather hectic schedule, and she and William led the advance of the Army on British soil, both in London and in the provinces. Even Catherine might have been amazed at such progress. An international headquarters was established at 101 Queen Victoria Street, within view of St. Paul's Cathedral. The Army continued to purchase properties in London and renovate them, thereby rendering them suitable as corps where the gospel would be preached. One such venture in 1882 was the Army's attempt to purchase the Eagle Tavern and the Grecian Theater and Dancing Grounds, which were attached to the Eagle Tavern. This occasion prompted the first letter Catherine wrote to Queen Victoria, informing her of the importance of this project and asking Her Majesty to contribute to this cause. Catherine wrote:

To Her Most Gracious Majesty the Queen:

Knowing your Majesty's benevolent concern for the well-being of the masses of your people, and having worked largely amongst them for twenty-three years, I venture to call your Majesty's attention to an effort now being made to transform one of the most terrible centers of demoralization for the young in the East of London into a centre of operations and influences for their reformation and salvation.

The Eagle Tavern, the Grecian Theater and Dancing Grounds, in the City Road, have become so notorious that probably your Majesty may have gathered something of the disastrous consequences of the scenes which have been enacted there for so many years past.

On behalf of the Salvation Army we are negotiating for the purchase of the lease of the whole property, and for 16,750 pounds hope to be put in possession in three weeks' time, when, by the blessing of God, we shall be able to gather 10,000 people at one time to hear the Gospel.

His Grace, the Archbishop of Canterbury, having kindly consented to head our subscription list, we have ventured to hope that it might not be impossible that your Majesty might graciously signify your approval of and sympathy with an effort which must surely commend itself to all whose hearts bleed for the ruined and friendless of this City, irrespective of their views as to our *modus operandi*. It will, I feel sure, interest your Majesty to know that many thousands of the lower and dangerous classes have already been won to temperance, virtue, and religion by the methods and spirit of this Army, to which fact many of your Majesty's officers of justice in different parts of the kingdom would gladly bear witness.

The misfortune of our only having three weeks to raise (for us) so large a sum as 16,750 pounds, for the purchase of the lease, must be my excuse for intruding this matter upon your Majesty's notice.

I herewith send a more particular description of this effort, and of our teaching and methods, in the hope that your Majesty may not find it altogether uninteresting, or irrelevant to your Majesty's highest desires for the welfare of your people.

Praying fervently that the God of grace may supply all your Majesty's spiritual need, I have the happiness to be, Your Majesty's devoted servant in Jesus,

Catherine Booth.[23]

Through Sir Henry F. Ponsonby from Windsor Castle on June 30, 1882, the Queen responded:

Madam:—

I am commanded by the Queen to acknowledge the receipt of your letter of the 27th inst., and to assure you that Her Majesty learns with much satisfaction that you have, with the other members of your society, been successful in your efforts to win many thousands to the ways of temperance, virtue, and religion. I regret, however, to have to inform you that Her Majesty cannot contribute to the fund you are now endeavoring to raise for the purchase of the Grecian Theater.

I have the honor to be, madam, your obedient servant,
Henry F. Ponsonby.[24]

While Catherine did not get the funds she requested from the queen, something far more significant was accomplished with this correspondence. Her Majesty was now informed about the working of this new society in her realm and about its central purpose. Catherine carefully placed herself and the Army not only on the side of righteousness and care for the poor but on the side of law and order, an appeal to which the queen might gladly respond. Catherine's rather conservative political nature is shown, matching her conservatism in religious matters. She would be in correspondence with the queen a few years later on a much more important matter.

In the meantime, the purchase of the Grecian Theater was only one of many projects in which the Army was engaged. Corps were being opened and expanded throughout Great Britain at a remarkable rate, the city of Manchester being only one example.

In January 1884, the eight corps (Manchester I to VIII) buildings then established held 2,000, 600, 800, 1,200, 500, 1,500, and 600 respectively. Salford I held 600 and II, 1,000. Denton held 400 and Droylsden, 300. The seating capacity was therefore 10,100, approximately 1.36% of Manchester Parish's population. . . . Between 1878 and 1883 inclusive, the Army opened twelve corps within Manchester Parish, five of these in 1883 itself. This growth corresponds with the fastest period of Army growth nationally.[25]

Both Catherine and William enjoyed great popularity among their followers, although they, like Wesley before them, certainly had their dissenters, generally disgruntled because of the autocracy of the Army's founders. When an all-day holiness convention was held for the first time in Exeter Hall in London in 1881, no fewer than four thousand people attended, the principal draw for the occasion being the preaching of the founders. Such meetings continued to be annual events in the Army, and Exeter Hall being found too small for the occasion, the Crystal Palace, completed for the Great Exhibition of 1851, was eventually used. Catherine also spoke to smaller assemblies, and one of the added responsibilities she assumed after 1881 was to lecture at both the women's and men's training homes—the training colleges for cadets who were preparing to become Salvation Army officers.

Mrs. Booth also continued her speaking around Great Britain, often at established corps and frequently at the opening of new corps. She gives glowing accounts of her times, for example, at Hull and Bristol, and had by now become quite used to speaking to audiences of three and four thousand. One of her most difficult experiences, however, took place in Sheffield in January 1882. She and William traveled there for a war council with the Sheffield Salvationists. The venue for the meetings was the Albert Hall, accommodating thirty-five hundred persons. The Army was still suffering from local persecution from the mobs in various parts of England, such opposition operating under the general name of the Skeleton Army. The most brutal assault on the Army took place on this occasion. The Sheffield "Blades," whose animosity against religion was intense, had not taken notice of the Army in Sheffield until now.

So many Salvationists gathered together drew the attention of this local gang of thugs. The Army advertised a march through the streets of Sheffield on Monday, and Lieutenant Emmerson Davison, a recent convert of the Army's and the primary object of the mob's assault, rode his horse in the march. Davison had been a champion Northumberland wrestler, and the men who attacked the Army, for whom the wrestler was a local hero, could not endure the sight of their hero marching with this Salvation Army. During the march, many of the Salvationists were beaten, and Davison had to be taken to the hospital. Fortunately both Catherine and William, who were riding in a carriage, were not harmed—the indomitable General William stood in the carriage and directed his troops during the riot! When the Booths greeted their wounded and bleeding comrades following the march,

William commented that this would be a good time to have their photographs taken!

Such persecution did bring to more focused attention the Army's difficulties in suffering unjustly at the hands of lawless and sometimes dangerous citizens of the realm. In both the House of Commons and the House of Lords, the right of the Army to march in the streets was defended, Archbishop Tait himself speaking on their behalf. Public sympathy was turning to their side, and Catherine played no small part in this being the case. It was Catherine who, through those West End meetings as well as her continual correspondence, had the attention of John Bright, M.P., or Lord and Lady Cairns.

These influential friends of Catherine did not always understand her rigorous approach to the Christian life, and may at times have been put off by Catherine's forthright denunciations of the sins of the wealthy. However, they undoubtedly respected Catherine for her convictions and, despite her occasional condemnation of the wealthy, they went to hear her often when she spoke in the West End. Some of them contributed liberally to the work of the growing Army. Many people admired Catherine, and she used this for the advancement of the Army.

In spite of localized persecution, Catherine was delighted to see the expansion and development of the Army into other countries, such as France, America, Australia, and Canada. At the end of 1882 she also presented the colors for work in India, South Africa, and New Zealand. At the same meeting Bramwell Booth presented the colors to six officers going to work in Sweden— that work having already begun under the direction of Miss Hanna Ouchterlony. She was singularly convicted about the need for the work of the Army in Sweden when she heard Bramwell Booth speak there. She visited England twice to persuade William to send officers to Sweden, but it was Catherine, convinced and moved by her Christian sister's arguments, who decided that the Army must be opened in Sweden. Bramwell supported her in this conviction. Catherine realized that the Army was fast becoming a missionary movement and she was especially aware of the importance of women in that endeavor. So Hanna Ouchterlony returned from her second visit to England with five officers to officially start the work there.[26]

Domestic responsibilities did not escape Catherine's attention even during the hectic times in her life. She was very concerned that her children find suitable marriage partners. The first Booth child to be married was Bramwell, and it would be to no one's surprise that his mother was influential in the coming together of Bramwell and Florence Soper. Indeed, Catherine encouraged her son, "You want a wife, *one* with you in soul, with whom you could commune and in whom you could find companionship and solace. . . . God will find you one, and I shall help Him."[27] Miss Soper was the daughter of a wealthy Welsh family, her father being a physician. She went to London to complete her education and there heard Catherine Booth speak in the West End. She came to complete faith in Christ under Catherine's ministry and in 1880 offered herself for service to God and the Army—to the horror of her family. She was one of the few who accompanied the younger Catherine to Paris, and—much to the dismay of her father, who had reared his daughter in cultured and refined circles—she preached in the cafés and on the streets, sold *En Avant,* and suffered the ridicule and slander of the crowds.

Dr. Soper drew the line on one issue—he would never consent to his daughter marrying a Salvationist! That was out of the question. Catherine took matters into her own hands and wrote a long letter to Dr. Soper, concluding the letter in this way:

> I believe real holy love to be one of God's choicest gifts, and I would rather one of my daughters should marry a man with only a brain and five fingers with *this,* than a man with ten thousand pounds per year without. . . . Believing that both our dear ones have conceived this love for each other, ought we not, as desiring their highest happiness, to embrace it and try to make them as happy as God intends them to be? Will not even the happiest life have enough of trial and sorrow without our embittering the morning with clouds and tears?[28]

The physician and his wife gave in to the logic of this woman and mother.

In 1882 Bramwell and Florence were married. The wedding set the tone for Army weddings to follow. It was held at an acquired and renovated orphanage that the Army had renamed Congress Hall. This building had a seating capacity of five thousand, and it was filled for the wedding. An admission fee was charged that was used to advance the work of the Army, and commitment was made by bride and groom to the Army as well as to each other. As a sign of that, they were married beneath the Army flag. The bride's father was present at the wedding, perhaps as a witness to his graciousness, but undoubtedly also as a witness to Catherine's perseverance. Both Catherine and William preached at the wedding, Catherine paying tribute to her own marriage by saying that "the highest happiness I can wish to my beloved children is that they may realize as thorough a union of heart and mind, and as much blessing in their married life, as the Lord has vouchsafed to us in ours."[29]

Catherine continued working tirelessly to answer the Army's detractors and skeptics. This new movement, however, was not without its friends and supporters, such as Mrs. Billups, W. T. Stead, and T. A. Denny. One group that particularly admired Catherine and the Army was the Quakers. There were common bonds between these groups, beginning with a simplicity of dress and moving even to a nonsacramental position, which in 1882 the Army was on the verge of taking. In that year Catherine was invited to address the annual meeting of the Quakers at the Devonshire House in London. She found it refreshing to be able to define the cause, not defend it, and to speak to its measures of adaptation before an audience of like-minded Christians, linking its history to that of the historic church. "We have been led by the Spirit as truly as were Fox and Wesley and Whitefield," Catherine said.[30]

Catherine was appreciative of the support of others and always worked to win friends for the work of the Army. She might, however, have been surprised to receive the following letter from Mrs. Josephine Butler:

> I ought not perhaps, to give you the trouble here of reading a letter from me in the midst of your arduous and blessed work; but I cannot any longer refrain from writing you a line to express—first, my joy in the advances being made by the Salvation Army; and secondly, my sympathy with you in the numberless criticisms and strictures passed upon you, your teaching and your practice. I am sure your burden is already heavy enough without anyone's adding to it by fault-finding. The attacks of enemies are comparatively easy to bear, but the fault-findings and misunderstandings of Christian people, these are what grieve and hurt. I do so feel for, and with, you that I cannot refrain from expressing myself to you. I can truly say there is not a day, scarcely an hour, in which I do not think of you and your fellow-workers, and rejoice in the tide of blessing which our eyes are privileged to see. My own duties, domestic and public, keep me from being among you as often as I would, but I doubt if there is anyone living who is more with you in spirit.
>
> About twenty-five years ago I had a kind of vision. I was in weak health, and lying on my bed. For some years I had been praying, thirsting, longing, for a great revival to come to the world, for showers of blessing, for a fresh Pentecost, in which I and mine would have a part, and which would prove such an awakening as the world has not seen since the first Apostles' times. I was like one dying of thirst, in drought, and in a wilderness.
>
> One evening I fell into a half sleep. I seemed to be transported to some dark and gloomy mountains, with my face to the east, and behind me the great wilderness of the world lying in deep darkness. Then a streak of light appeared in the east, a sweet heavenly light, and voices sounded, and music, and there was a noise as of gathering forces, and it seemed God said to me, "Behold! the answer to all your prayers. A glorious day of grace is coming; fix your eyes on it; gaze in that direction. For though it tarry it will come; it will not tarry." There was nothing remarkable in my dream except that it made such an impression on me as I have never lost. It was twenty-five years ago. I see now the fulfillment (or the beginning of the fulfillment) of that vision. I think there are many oth-

ers who have thirsted as I have, and who now rejoice as I rejoice.
I am sure you are sustained under the fire of criticisms.

   I remain, dear Mr. and Mrs. Booth,
   Yours, in the love of Jesus,
   Josephine E. Butler.[31]

Catherine was greatly encouraged by such support, and this would sustain her and her husband in the years ahead—some of them difficult and trying years for them personally and for the Army. Indeed, Josephine Butler would become one of the great allies of Catherine and William in the Purity Crusade of 1885.

A singularly important event in 1882 caused both Catherine and William to carefully consider every aspect of the Army—its mission, methods, and doctrines. The outcome of this was the consolidation of the Army's work, and the placing of the Army on an irrevocable future course. Catherine played a major part in this turning point.

By all accounts the growth of The Salvation Army was somewhat of a religious phenomenon in nineteenth-century England, and in 1882 the Army was still growing, demonstrating strength, and proving successful where others had failed in ministering to urban working classes. The reasons for such growth were many, including, as has been mentioned, the use of female ministers, the use of working-class officers and soldiers to speak to their own about Jesus and salvation, the Army's tight organization that fostered great loyalty and devotion to Catherine and William, and the Army's tactics to draw public attention.

And the British public took notice, as evidenced by the many newspaper accounts of this new movement. Undoubtedly many conversations and arguments in pubs as well as West End drawing rooms centered around the Army, some sharply criticizing and caricaturing it, others defending it as a group of faithful women and men finally demonstrating what Christianity was always intended to be and thereby shining a light on an ineffective institutional church. Various denominations had opinions about The Salvation Army. Generally the Methodists were open

231

to what the Booths were doing, and some Methodist groups were even enthusiastic about their work.[32] And even Cardinal Manning of the Roman Catholic Church commented at length on The Salvation Army in an article in *The Contemporary Review*.[33]

Also among those who took notice of the Army was the Anglican Church. Reflecting one side of the public sentiment about the Army, some Anglican clergy soundly condemned it for bringing Christianity into disrepute by its outlandish methods. Others, however, defended the Army. In any case, the church realized that the Army was not some passing religious fancy. In fact, in the early 1880s the Army was often invited to attend Anglican worship services.

> Frequently they marched thereto in full force from open-air meetings, headed by clergymen and surpliced choirs, and usually followed by huge crowds which sometimes threw brickbats! The first recorded occasion was when on Sunday 21st March 1880 the Wednesbury corps went to St. John's Church. Among the most noteworthy of other similar instances were services at Nottingham (21st November 1881), Newcastle (January 1882), Bristol (Monday 11th April 1882), Coventry (Whit Monday 1882), Stoke Newington and Halifax (June 1882), Oldham (July 1882), and Bethnal Green (November 1882 and February 1884).[34]

The Bishop of Chichester perhaps summarized much Anglican opinion when in November 1882, in speaking of the Army, he warned his audience, "Let us beware of looking at them with indifference or contempt or dislike, lest haply we be found to fight against God."[35]

At Canterbury on Wednesday, May 10, 1882, the question of how Anglicanism was to relate to The Salvation Army was raised in the Lower House of Convocation, and the Lower House petitioned the Upper House "to ascertain the tenets and practices of the society and to consider how far it would be possible to attach it to the Church, and generally to advise the clergy as to their duty in reference to it."[36] The Archbishop, Dr. Tait, acted on this petition the next day, and "a committee was appointed to consider the matter."[37] The committee consisted of Dr. Benson, the Bishop of Truro, as chair; Dr. Lightfoot, Bishop of Durham; Canon West-cott of Westminster; Canon Wilkinson; and the chaplain to the Archbishop and Dean of Windsor, Dr. Randall Davidson.

Discussions were opened up with William Booth as to the questions raised by the Church of England, lengthy correspondence followed, and the committee visited various Salvation Army facilities, including the international headquarters and the training homes. The central issue, however, was this: Was there interest on either or both sides in The Salvation Army coming under the control of the Church of England? The delegation from the Church of England was concerned about such matters as Salvation Army theology, the ministry of women in The Salvation Army, the Army's sacramental position, and the hierarchical organization of the Army. Bramwell, the chief of the staff, also took part in some of these negotiations, but there is no record of the committee meeting with Catherine or soliciting her opinions, although Dr. Lightfoot expressed appreciation for Catherine's writings. Although Catherine was not present at the formal conversations, it would be wrong to assume, knowing what we do about her, that she did not have settled views about the matters under discussion as well as profound influence on both her husband and her eldest son as to the course and the outcome of the proceedings. Booth-Tucker does give one reference to her on this matter: "The General and Mrs. Booth were willing, on their part, to give the question their impartial and disinterested consideration."[38]

The discussions were marked on both sides with mutual respect and courteous attention to the concerns of the other in spite of the fact that many members of the committee really could not stomach the Army's methods. However, it soon became apparent that, while many issues were placed on the table for discussion, three problems in the end proved to be insurmountable, and all three were inextricably related. First, what would be the position of General Booth should the Army come under the control of the Church of England, and along with that, what would be the standing of Booth's officers? Bramwell Booth noted that

233

Dr. Davidson was adamant that William's powers be limited. He wrote:

> He struck me as a man who, while sincerely anxious to explore the ground and, if possible, to arrive at some means of linking The Salvation Army with his Church, and of helping forward its work, was yet fully determined, if this should be the issue, not to allow the Founder to continue in what was called his "autocratic" relationship. Evidently it was unthinkable to him that William Booth should ever become a high ecclesiastic in the Church of England, and for that reason alone he was careful to ensure that no power beyond what he could not help conceding should remain in the Founder's hands if the Army should come into alliance with his Church. Dr. Davidson was very urbane and considerate throughout the negotiations, and although he was the rigid—not to say narrow—ecclesiastic, he showed real ability in fastening upon essentials when in conference with the Founder.[39]

Davidson was, however, quite slow in realizing that William Booth "was not willing to relinquish his full control, no matter what advantages might be secured from the inclusion of himself and his Organization under the wing of the Church of England. So far as Dr. Davidson was concerned, this was . . . from the beginning, fatal to the project."[40] How Davidson, obviously a man of intelligence and ability, could have been so remarkably naive and uninformed in these negotiations is difficult to assess. It is likewise impossible to explain his lack of insight into the formation of religious organizations, as well as the strength of their continued life. In the words of St. John Ervine,

> Why Dr. Davidson, now that Booth had brought his forces to a high state of efficiency and popularity, should have expected him to yield them to other people, some of whom had striven, and were still striving, to destroy them, is hard to understand. Booth, though he might appear unimpressive to Dr. Davidson, had done what Dr. Davidson had not: made an Army where none had been, and had sent it fighting across the world. As the General sat and listened to the young Dean of Windsor and gazed round the room

at the distinguished ecclesiastics who had come to solicit his co-operation, he must have felt a glow of pride in his heart as he reflected that he had achieved what none of them had achieved, and that the once absurd evangelist who banged a Bible and waved an umbrella to attract attention on Mile End Waste, was now being entreated to help the Established Church to relate itself to the poor! And the young Chief-of-Staff, better aware than anyone of the trials that had been endured in the founding of that Army, grew hot with resentment as he heard Queen Victoria's favourite, the suave and urbane Dean of Windsor, blandly assume that if an arrangement could be made between Booth's forces and the Anglican Church, Booth would quietly drop into obscurity as an honorary canon or a prebendary of the metropolitan cathedral. Booth had not raised his Army to be spoil for the Church of England: he had raised it to make war on hell. And he, better than any of these bishops and canons and deans, knew how to lead it into battle. God helping him, he would die at its head.[41]

Davidson obviously did not know Catherine Booth either. For, although he admired her a great deal, he was clearly ignorant of the mind of this woman. Catherine had no doubt that God had raised up William and called him to a particular work. The evidence of such calling was daily before their eyes, and Catherine considered the organization of the Army providential. To limit now the power and godly influence of her husband was unthinkable.

The second insurmountable problem, related to the first, was the position of the church regarding women in ministry. It would take another hundred years before the Church of England would allow the ordination of women, and it was of course then unthinkable that the women officers of the Army could be recognized as clergy within the Church of England. This was, for the Anglican representatives, not negotiable. The most the Church would allow would be for some of the female officers to be appointed as deaconesses. Bramwell Booth wrote:

To the more straight-laced of the negotiators the accredited position which the women officers already occupied in the Army presented serious difficulty; and it was Wilkinson, again, who suggested that these comrades should be given an assured position and recognized as a body of deaconesses, but that any future additions to their number should be required to go through a certain examination following our Training. I think that Canon Wilkinson worked more arduously to bring about what they all desired than any of the others, and also that he had more faith than any of them for a practical outcome.[42]

For Catherine the relegation of her women officers to deaconesses and the subsequent limitation of their powers was out of the question. Any curtailing of the rights and privileges of women to preach the gospel would be debilitating to the privilege for which Catherine, and by now countless followers, had fought and suffered. Women were equal with men in ministry. That, to Catherine, was clear and nonnegotiable since, in her mind, the justification for it arose from the pages of the Bible itself.

This leads to the third crucial matter at stake in these discussions—that of the place of the sacraments. The Army had taken no final stand on the question of the sacraments, and naturally female as well as male officers were serving communion at least occasionally. "The Salvation Army initially instructed all officers, men and women, to offer communion monthly. Challenged to explain why women were permitted to perform this sacred ritual, George Scott Railton wrote, 'In this, as in everything else, the Lord's own principle there being "neither male nor female" in Christ Jesus is fully acted upon.'"[43] But should the Army unite with the Anglican Church, such duties and responsibilities of women officers would be completely eliminated, thus diminishing their role. Again, one can hardly imagine Catherine being silent on this matter! Her views were settled on every aspect of women in ministry. Union with the Church of England could hardly be desirable with such strictures placed on women.

The issue of the sacraments was still open and debatable among William, Catherine, Bramwell, and George Scott Railton, but all of this talk about union caused the Army finally to focus on resolving the question. Both Catherine and William were concerned about the questions regarding the sacraments that had fractured the church for centuries: How many sacraments? Who could administer the sacraments? Was Christ fully present at the Lord's Supper or only symbolically present? How often should the Lord's Supper be taken by the faithful? Should sinners be invited to the communion rail as John Wesley had done in the previous century? Such discussion seemed fruitless to the founders, and the practice of baptism and the Lord's Supper in The Christian Mission and the early Salvation Army took place with a Methodistic emphasis. Bramwell Booth recalled:

> I do not think that any of us were much troubled about the baptismal question, although for some years we followed the practice of many Churches and baptized infants. I have in some cases myself "sprinkled" as many as thirty in one service! And, by the way, such services were made both interesting and useful. We had a simple and yet very definite formula where by the parents engaged to give the children over to be the servants of God and to train them for Him. This practice, however, died down gradually, chiefly because it had no very strong conviction behind it; and in place of it The Army introduced a service of Dedication which has become much valued among many people in many lands.
>
> The case with regard to the Supper was on a different plane altogether. Here, as in some other matters, the Founder's early training in the Church of England and his later Church work influenced him. He was in some measure predisposed to attach importance to ceremonial of this nature, and while he never allowed that in itself it possessed any spiritual efficacy, or that it was in the least degree necessary to the Salvation of any man, yet he used it, though with increasing misgiving.
>
> When I came on the scene as a responsible official of the Mission in 1874, the Lord's Supper was administered monthly at all our stations to all members of the Mission and to such other Christian friends as were known to be in good standing and who desired to join with us. These services were in many cases really impressive. There was a simplicity and naturalness about them which made them very welcome, and whether the number partaking was

a score, or whether—as on special occasions—it ran up to six or seven hundred, the gatherings were in many respects remarkable. There was a total absence of display, but wonderful freedom. The faith of many was strengthened, former promises and vows were recalled and renewed, and not seldom the unsaved or irreligious who had been allowed to come into the buildings as spectators were there and then brought to Christ.[44]

But whether or not to administer the sacraments had remained a lingering question in the minds of Catherine and others ever since Christian Mission days, especially since Catherine had no desire of getting involved in the controversies of the church and less interest in creating new problems. These were secondary issues to Catherine. What became important to her was what she considered to be the central prevailing doctrine of Christianity—that of holiness of heart and life. Catherine was increasingly convinced that

> it must be self-evident . . . that it is *the most important question* that can possibly occupy the mind of man—how much like God can we be—how near to God can we come on earth preparatory to our being perfectly like Him, and living, as it were, in His very heart for ever and ever in Heaven. Anyone who has any measure of the Spirit of God, must perceive that this is the most important question on which we can concentrate our thoughts.[45]

Purity of heart issuing in sacramental living became the touchstone of her theology, and everything was weighed and measured in the light of that. For this she had the witness of the Quakers, but precisely how influential Quaker theology was in this matter is difficult to say. In any case, Catherine and William, supported by the iconoclastic Railton and the increasingly influential Bramwell, firmly believed that the full presence of Christ is realized in sanctification and that this realization is lived out in the world in sacramental living. Catherine feared that a great detriment to such holiness of heart and life was any reliance on the outward material forms of the church—on ceremonies or outward acts. These had the potential of being a substitution for the real experience of Christ in the life of the believer. Bramwell wrote of his mother,

A sense of misgiving, however, arose, and made itself more evident with the growing work. I think that this misgiving was experienced first of all by Catherine Booth. She had a deep horror of anything which might tend to substitute in the minds of the people some outward act or compliance for the fruits of practical Holiness. Her knowledge of the low tone of spiritual life in the Churches, gained as a result of her friendship with many religious people and their leaders, made her look with dread upon the possibility that our people, most of whom were very ignorant and simple, might come in time to lean upon some outward ceremonial instead of upon the work of the Holy Spirit as witnessed in a change of heart and life.[46]

Catherine herself wrote the following in *Popular Christianity:*

Furthermore, another mock salvation is presented in the shape of *ceremonies and sacraments*. These were only intended as outward signs of an inward spiritual reality, whereas men are taught that by going through them or partaking of them, they are to be saved. Amongst these may be classed Baptism, the last Supper, and the ceremonials of ancient or modern churches.

Oh, the thousands of souls who are resting their hopes of salvation on the fact that they have been baptized, not only such as believe in the palpable delusion of baptismal regeneration, but amongst ordinary church and chapel-going people. As I look at our Army congregations in the rinks, theaters, and other similar places, and note the signs of sin, debauchery, and crime on many of their faces, I say to myself, I suppose all these people have been baptized; but I do not think there are many thieves, or harlots, or drunkards, or openly immoral people who claim baptismal regeneration. Thank God! It is only genteel sinners who can bring themselves to believe in such a palpable sham, and yet, if baptism possesses any efficacy, it should be as effective in the one class of sinners as in the other.

What an inveterate tendency there is in the human heart to trust in outward forms, instead of seeking the inward grace! And where this is the case, what a hindrance, rather than a help, have these forms proved to the growth, nay, to the very existence, of the spiritual life which constitutes the real and only force of Christian experience.[47]

The Army's founders and their counselors were theologically aware enough to realize that it was that theology of sanctification that drove their mission to win the lost for Christ, along with their postmillennial vision that convinced them it was the duty of the Army to win the whole world for Christ before he returned in glory.

Finally, in the beginning of 1883, the Army took its non-sacramental position—more appropriately labeled its sacramental position—explained by the General in an officers' council in London on January 2, 1883, and published in *The War Cry* on January 17, 1883. In theological terms what took place is best summarized by David Rightmire:

> The emphasis on sacramental living by the early Army leaders was the result of a dialectic between their pragmatic theology and explicit pneumatological presuppositions. The abandonment of sacramental practice by no means implied a denial of the sacramental aspect of life. For the Army, the emphasis was upon the reality of new life in Christ, experienced spiritually. The sacraments, as memorial ritual, were not essential to spiritual religion. What was essential was the necessity of spiritual communion with Christ. This was possible only in the experience of entire sanctification.[48]

Walker noted that the decision "reinforced the Army's refusal to countenance distinctions between men's and women's relationship to the sacred. By rejecting material forms of receiving grace, the Army underscored the meaninglessness of outward, human physicality against the transforming grace of the Holy Spirit."[49]

The discussions with the Anglican Church did, after all, prove beneficial in two ways. It gave the Anglican Church a new appreciation for the work of aggressive evangelism as well as a renewed vision for the work of the church in seeking the salvation of people, although there continued to be grave reservations among some Anglicans about the means the Army used in winning the lost. There were four imitations of the Army within the Anglican Church. A Church Gospel Army had begun at Richmond, Surrey, and a Church Mission Army at Bristol. Late in 1882 a Church Salvation Army was formed in Berkshire. However, the Church Army, established by Wilson Carlisle and F. S. Webster at Walworth, "proved the strongest of the four and gradually received support from the Church authorities. Like its counterpart, the Church Army's open-air activities were often the subject of physical and verbal abuse and they were the butt of much amusement for the working-class."[50]

The discussions also forced the Army's leaders to consider precisely what it was that God had called into existence. The Army was now clearly positioned. It was obvious that it was not going to be incorporated into any ecclesiastical body—either Anglican or Methodist—and that it was a distinct part of the body of Christ regardless of whether it called itself a church or not. The Army mother was convinced that the Army was the embodiment of the New Testament church in the nineteenth century, and that was enough. Its doctrines were distinctly Methodistic in tone. And the central doctrine was that of holiness of heart and life. The sacramental life was the critical expression of that, and this was evidenced continually in the lives and ministries of women as well as men.

In addition, Catherine, by her writing and speaking, created a Salvationist ethos, a pattern of self-sacrificial, Christ-oriented living that attempted always to honor God, love the neighbor in distress, and express the compassion of Christ for a fallen world. Catherine's care for the animal world was still a part of her ministry, and it comes as no surprise that the *Orders and Regulations for Soldiers* included a section on how soldiers should treat animals. Catherine's hand is in evidence here.

A Salvation soldier should be kind-hearted, and deal lovingly with all those with whom he is associated. A soldier should manifest love and gentleness especially in his connection with . . . the animal world. To inflict or to witness cruelty should be impossible for a soldier in whom has been born a love to save men from any form of misery. Not only should he avoid causing any unnecessary hardship on animals but, as far as he has opportunity, he should ever be willing to lend a hand to aid or relieve any suffering creature.[51]

William later wrote this of Catherine: "Her sympathy for the sufferings of the animal world was constant. She never, within my knowledge, knew of any suffering but she sought to prevent it. It was nothing for her to stop in the street to deal with any who were beating donkeys or horses unmercifully, lashing cattle, or ill-treating dogs. I do not think any sufferer who appealed for help that she could render appealed in vain."[52]

With clarity of both doctrine and purpose, due in no small measure to Catherine, the Army continued its advances in 1883, Switzerland being its next mission field. In spite of early opposition and imprisonment of Army officers, the Army finally gained a foothold in that country. One of those put in prison was the leader of the officer contingent, young Catherine Booth. Hearing of her daughter's plight, Catherine wrote immediately to Katie and to the Prime Minister of England. Even in that letter to Mr. Gladstone, Catherine finds herself still defending the cause as well as coming out on the side of law and order in England. She wrote:

To the Right Honourable W. E. Gladstone:
    Sir:—Allow me to intrude on your valuable time for a moment in order to call your attention to the perils of my daughter, Miss Booth, and her companions in Switzerland, which may not have been fully presented to you. Six months ago, after this illegal and groundless persecution commenced, Earl Granville promised my husband that he would interfere, but, although we have made two or three applications to his Lordship through Parliamentary friends since then, so far as we can see, nothing has been *done!*

Now the authorities of Neufchatel are trying Miss Booth on a mere pretext, and we have reason to fear an entire miscarriage of justice. Miss Booth's imprisonment would probably help our cause more than anything else, and but for the very delicate state of her health, consequent on the very trying events of the last few months, I would not intrude on your much needed privacy; but fearing that even a short imprisonment would cause a serious illness, or even fatal consequences, and thus terminate her Christlike labours, I beg, with a mother's importunity, your timely interference.

You have probably seen Mrs. J. E. Butler's letter on this subject in this day's *Standard*. Allow me to introduce to your notice the small book sent herewith, which I would hope may convey to you a *true* idea of the genius and aim of the Salvation Army, which is simply a popular mode of attracting the attention of the masses to the claims of God and of goodness, so long forgotten by tens of thousands. Our measures *have succeeded* in reaching multitudes of the worst classes, and the grace of God has reclaimed thousands of them from lives of open debauchery to temperance, industry, and religion.

With deepest respect and unfeigned gratitude for all your hard service for humanity, I am, honoured sir,

Yours, on behalf of the lost,

Catherine Booth.[53]

The response from 10 Downing Street was cordial but not consoling. The Office of the Foreign Ministry would have to intervene in such matters, and the Prime Minister was satisfied that this was already being done. Fortunately correspondence from her daughter in prison assured Catherine that Katie was not in any physical danger, and although she might be expelled from Switzerland, the work of the Army would continue through the many officers and soldiers who had been raised up.

At the trial young Catherine defended the Army much as she had heard her mother do in the past. She spoke of the aim, the message, and the methods of the Army and claimed, under the law of the land, the right and the freedom to preach the gospel as she and her other Salvationists saw fit. She and her comrades were found not to have acted with culpable intention and so were

Catherine Booth

set free. Young Catherine returned to England, and a meeting of thanksgiving was held in Exeter Hall in London, both Catherines being present. This, of course, provided yet another opportunity for the elder Catherine to speak about the Army, which she claimed was bringing to life the goals and purposes and methods of both Jesus and the New Testament church. "The grand purpose of this movement," Catherine said on this occasion, "is to bring all men back to God and goodness."[54] For Catherine that included all people who are in rebellion against God by their sin, the rich and the poor, those living in lovely homes and those dwelling in the cellars of the back slums of English cities. The universality of sin was a favorite theme of hers, and she took delight, as on this occasion, of reminding all her hearers of that biblical fact. "Immorality is not confined to overcrowded dwellings, is it? Alas! alas! I question whether some of the darkest, and blackest, and most overcrowded dens of this city, and of many other cities, could outdo the debaucheries that are hidden away by crimson and gold, and smothered by smooth-tongued officials who are paid according to their adroitness in hiding the vices of their masters or their mistresses."[55]

The years 1883 to 1885 found Catherine continuing her work as the mother of an Army. Her addresses in the spring of 1883 delivered at the Cannon Street Hotel were later published under the title *The Salvation Army in Relation to Church and State*. There she took up the issue of how invaluable the Army's ministry was to both. Her book *Life and Death* was also published, dealing with, as Catherine wrote in the preface, "some more direct and pointed truth on the subject of personal Salvation."[56] *Popular Christianity* was published as a collection of addresses delivered in Prince's Hall, Piccadilly, in the autumn of 1884. Catherine did not allow these to be published immediately, "chiefly because I feared that in cold type they might produce an impression of censoriousness, which was not possible when, as I believe, assisted by the Spirit of God, I dealt with my hearers face to face on these burning topics."[57] Those addresses dealt with such topics as false Christs, mock salvation, sham compassion, and cowardly service. Catherine was characteristically forthright. Encouraged, however, by her friend Railton, she finally published the book in 1887.

One of her listeners at that time wrote of

the remarkable preaching powers of the woman who is . . . the soul of whatever is best in the movement—Mrs. Booth. Her real eloquence, with all its quaint and even grotesque forms of pronunciation and grammar, and amazing fabrication of words (such, for example, as "Jumbleization" occurring in a very solemn argument), is a powerful engine of persuasion; but she possesses more than mere rhetoric, however varied and vivifying. She has an immense store of sound sense and practical experience, combined with a genuinely high ideal of life and duty. After listening to her many times for hours together, I have found myself bringing away more fresh and sound ideas, and less "padding," than from any series of discourses it has been my fate to hear for many a day.[58]

By the end of 1883 the Army had moved into New Zealand and South Africa, and between 1883 and 1885 the Army's work was strengthened and secured in many of the countries where it had undertaken its work. As far as Catherine was concerned, by the mid-1880s the Army was well advancing, blessed by God, endowed with power from on high, and faithful to a sacred trust and a gospel message. Catherine, William, and the Army were now seen as agencies of Evangelical Protestant Christianity, just as Caughey and Finney had been a few years previously. Catherine had more than fulfilled her role as the first among the Booths to defend the Army's work, and many people, including some wealthy benefactors, were mightily impressed by the preaching of this woman. These remarks of the Army mother, delivered in 1882, best summarize her religious convictions as well as her hopes for the Army during this time.

Amidst many weaknesses and shortcomings we have been wholehearted in our devotion to Him and His service. This is why He

245

has blessed us during the past, and why we dare to believe He will bless us even more during the years that are to come.

This is but the beginning of our days of triumph. If we are only faithful, if we take heed where others have fallen, if we are careful to keep close to God, not regarding the criticisms of our neighbours, the opposition of our enemies, nor even what religious people say or do, but simply being guided by what GOD SAYS and what humanity wants—while taking hold of God with one hand, and stooping with the other to the poorest, most fallen, and abject of our race, and bringing them together by our mighty prayer, faith, and effort—nothing can hurt us. All the legions of earth and hell combined cannot hinder our progress; because we trust not in human strength, and with Shadrach, Meshach and Abednego we can say, "Our God whom we serve is able to deliver us, and HE WILL DELIVER US." Nothing can stop us![59]

Catherine's human sensitivities were soon to be greatly moved, however, and her religious convictions heightened. She began to learn about and understand, through her thorough knowledge of the ministry of the Army in cities throughout England and in many urban slums, the abuse of many of the weakest of her own sex in the streets, the brothels, and the homes in England. The Army had access to the lives of the working class. She was repulsed, indignant, and angry at what she learned; and in 1885 she was poised for one of the greatest moral and religious battles of her life against those debaucheries often hidden by proper English respectability. This was a battle she was determined to win regardless of consequences to herself, her family, or her Army. This was the Purity Crusade.

9

A National Crusade

*Truth Fallen in the Street**

The organized social ministry of The Salvation Army had not yet begun. Various services in The Christian Mission stations were strategically suited to meet the needs of the people to whom each station was ministering. And there had been a systematic feeding program in The Christian Mission from 1870 to 1874 in the manner of soup kitchens set up to feed the poor, called "Food for the Millions." This was not free food but was designed to provide inexpensive and nourishing meals for the poor. The feeding stations were placed under the administration of Bramwell Booth, who was ably assisted by James Flawn. Eventually, however, these soup kitchens had to be closed for lack of funds, the last of the stations being closed in 1874.

*"Truth Fallen in the Street" is the descriptive title of the chapter Frederick Coutts wrote to provide an account of this aspect of the Army's history and its work in *Bread for My Neighbour: The Social Influence of William Booth* (London: Hodder and Stoughton, 1978).

It is important to remember that Catherine was well acquainted with the plight and conditions of the poor. She first began to minister to alcoholics and their families during William's appointment at Gateshead and continued that ministry on a larger scale after the founding of The Christian Mission and The Salvation Army. After the establishment of the Army, many in the corps found themselves attending to the physical as well as the spiritual needs of people. Such work was understood as being a natural consequence of their salvation in Christ, their involvement in every aspect of the lives of people, and a faithful witness to such biblical passages as Matthew 25. This ministry had many faces, depending on local need—the establishment of a halfway home for released prisoners in Melbourne, Australia, in December 1883, or an institution for alcoholic women in Toronto, Canada, in 1886. Frederick Coutts has rightly stated, "The Army's social services were not born out of any doctrinaire theory but out of the involvement of the Salvationist himself in situations of human need."[1]

It was The Salvation Army's work with prostitutes in London that captured Catherine's heart and set her on a fighting crusade from which she refused to retreat until she had won. This part of her story is a complicated one, involving many characters—some noble and some scandalous. It begins with one of the most remarkable women of early Salvation Army history, Mrs. Elizabeth Cottrill.

Prostitution was common in Victorian society, and many girls as young as twelve years of age were sold into that trade by poor parents in need of money.[2] Salvationists were accustomed to dealing with prostitutes in their street as well as indoor meetings. But an organized attempt to help these girls did not begin until February 1881 at the instigation of Mrs. Cottrill, the Converts' Sergeant at the Whitechapel Corps in the East End. During an indoor meeting at the corps, a young girl from the country knelt at the Army's mercy seat, a place of prayer for the confession of sins. She divulged her story—she had come to London in search of work and, "lured by a false address, found herself in a brothel."[3]

Mrs. Cottrill was determined not to send her back to the brothel. She took her into her own home located near the corps at 102 Christian Street. "Already three families of 16 people lived under the roof . . . but room was found for yet another. In this way began the rescue work of Booth's Army, and many a girl found refuge in Christian Street."[4] Where there was one girl in such trouble, there were bound to be others. Mrs. Cottrill continued to make room in her house until other quarters could be found. *The War Cry* told of her initial endeavors three years later:

> Some years ago a devoted soldier of the Whitechapel corps became very interested in the poor, fallen girls who sometimes came to the penitent-form there. When she found they often had no home she took them to her own house and, although mother of a large family, shared her food with them, and toiled all her spare time to get them into situations, sometimes walking many miles a day. She would often give them her own clothes in order to start them respectably. The Lord has blessed her efforts, and many of the girls she thus sheltered are today in superior situations, gaining the respect of all around them. One, after being two years in a situation, is now an officer in The Salvation Army.[5]

Eventually in 1884 in nearby Hanbury Street, a house was rented for the purpose of providing for what Victorian England labeled "fallen women." Bramwell's wife, Florence Soper Booth, was placed in charge of this home. At the time she was put in charge of this work, she was only twenty-two. Ann R. Higginbotham has written:

> Despite her youth and retiring nature . . . Florence Booth succeeded in establishing and expanding Salvationist rescue work. During the nearly thirty years that she headed the Women's Social Services, its operations grew from one rescue home in Whitechapel to 117 homes for women in Britain and around the world. Under the direction of Florence Booth and her assistant Adelaide Cox, a vicar's daughter who joined The Salvation Army in 1881, the Women's Social Services earned a reputation as one of the largest,

most effective, and, to some extent, most innovative rescue organizations in Britain.[6]

Catherine herself took a great interest in the home on Hanbury Street and helped to furnish it.[7]

The age of consent, that is "the age up to which it shall be an offence to have or attempt to have carnal knowledge of, or to indecently assault a girl"[8] was set at the age of thirteen in 1875, and three times between 1875 and 1885 the House of Lords passed a bill recommending the raising of the age of consent, all three recommendations failing in the House of Commons. In the meantime, the stories the Army heard from the girls under their care, first at Christian Street and then at Hanbury Street, enraged the moral conscience of Catherine Booth and others, and they determined to enter the battle against vicious evils lurking on the streets of London, especially child prostitution and enforced prostitution. Many protested that these things happened on the Continent but not in England, but the Army knew firsthand that such practices were contaminating English life as well.

Catherine's primary allies in this war were three: Josephine Butler, W. T. Stead, and Bramwell Booth. Butler had made known her support of the Army since her letter to Catherine in 1882 and had been a champion of the Army during young Catherine's persecution in Switzerland, having written a letter on the subject to the *Standard*. She had long been a defender of children who were trapped in the European white slave market. The elder Catherine was well aware of her efforts in these matters, and the two of them would become colaborers in this cause, often speaking at the same rallies. W. T. Stead, whose affection for Catherine and The Salvation Army had begun in earlier years and continued still, had moved to London in 1880 as an associate editor of the *Pall Mall Gazette* and became the acting editor succeeding John Morley in 1883. This son of a Congregationalist minister had been furious that Parliament did not pass the Criminal Law Amendment Act raising the age of consent. Bramwell Booth was particularly generous about Stead's motivations. He wrote,

"Stead always impressed me in that early association as a man intensely anxious to seek the guidance of God. The deepest passion which moved him was for the victory of a righteous cause. He was a journalist, but he always subordinated his journalism to what he believed to be right. Religion with him was service. He set out, heart and soul, to serve his generation. The world was cleaner and sweeter for his eloquent voice."[9]

Bramwell was the third ally. He was, to say the least, shocked by what he heard from his wife in the course of her daily work at Hanbury Street. It was beyond question that a vicious white slave trade operated in England, that many victims were as young as twelve years of age, and that Victorian society refused to discuss sexual ethics openly while some of London's upstanding gentlemen were engaging in what was actually, if not legally, child prostitution without fear of legal or moral recrimination. Bramwell, while at first disbelieving the stories that came out of Hanbury Street, was finally and fully convinced of their truth.

He consulted with his mother, with Josephine Butler, and with his friend W. T. Stead. Stead was at first doubtful of the evidence Bramwell presented to him, believing it to be grossly exaggerated. But finally, after meeting with Benjamin Scott, the City Chamberlain, "who was especially familiar with the details of one branch of this iniquity—the Continental traffic,"[10] he was persuaded. Catherine was incensed by the mounting evidence of crimes against England's most defenseless victims. She corresponded with Josephine Butler and received a warm reply from her friend who had been fighting in this war for years. Catherine knew that it was time for this crime to be brought to the bar of public opinion. And she was determined to be the prosecutor.

Stead was also resolved to bring this to the attention of the Victorian public, the delicacy of the matter notwithstanding. It was time, he believed, for English gentlemen and ladies to face up to what was happening to some of the youngest and most vulnerable victims of English law and English hypocrisy. But a battle plan had to be set in place with which he could expose the white slave trade in his newspaper and thus force a change in the law through the tide of public opinion.

By now Stead had heard the personal accounts of several young girls who had been entrapped and he proposed a plan devised by a secret commission of the *Pall Mall Gazette* that he believed would shine a light on the immoral practices of child prostitution in England as well as expose the gentlemen and ladies who either directly or indirectly were supporting the white slave trade. Bramwell wrote, "We then decided . . . to make an experiment with an actual case, and to carry it through in such a way that we could call evidence from people of repute with regard to what had happened. We thought out the plan most carefully, and it was put into execution on the Derby day of 1885."[11] Stead wisely informed the Archbishop of Canterbury; Frederick Temple, the recently appointed Bishop of London; Cardinal Manning; and Charles Spurgeon of his plan and its desired results and found support from these gentlemen. How many of the details of this plan were known by Catherine and William is impossible to say. It is highly unlikely, however, that Bramwell did not inform his mother and father of such details.

For the plan to succeed, someone with inside knowledge of the business was needed. Stead contacted Rebecca Jarrett, a former prostitute and brothel keeper who happily came under the influence of The Salvation Army first in Northampton and then at Hanbury Street and, through Catherine's personal intervention, went to Josephine Butler's refuge in Winchester to get away from the old evil influences of her former friends in London. Rebecca Jarrett was approached by Stead and told of the plan to expose this crime. Understandably, Jarrett was at first reluctant to take part in this scheme but she finally convinced of its ultimate worth.

She reentered her old world and, through some unsavory contacts, was finally able to purchase Eliza Armstrong, then thirteen years of age, from her mother. It was understood that the procurement of this young girl was for immoral purposes, and Eliza's mother, as far as she knew, gave up her own daughter to a life of prostitution in a London brothel. Eliza was then taken to

Madame Mourez, a midwife and a professional procuress, where she was certified to be a virgin. From there she was taken to a brothel where Stead himself had rented a room. Stead spent about an hour in the room with Eliza, and then Eliza was taken from the brothel by a trusted Salvation Army officer, Mrs. Major Reynolds, who herself had posed as a woman desiring to enter a brothel so that she could report on the criminal behavior from the inside. Eliza was taken to a specialist who again pronounced her to be a virgin.

Bramwell then arranged for Eliza, in the company of Rebecca Jarrett, to leave the country, and they did so accompanied by Madame Combe, a soldier of the Geneva, Switzerland, corps and a "widow of independent means who was in the Army's service at Clapton."[12] They went to Paris. Both Bramwell and W. T. Stead believed that a strong case had been made. They demonstrated that "although this particular girl had received no whit of harm, it was shown to be possible for a procuress to buy a child for money, to certificate her, bring her to a house of ill fame, leave her with a man she had never seen before, and sent [sic] her off to the Continent so that nothing further need be known of her."[13]

All that was left now was for Stead to expose such criminal behavior to the British public. The first of ten articles titled "The Maiden Tribute of Modern Babylon" appeared in the *Pall Mall Gazette* on Monday, July 6, 1884, and, as Coutts wrote, "The run on the paper beggared description."[14] "The circulation of the paper rose from twelve thousand to over a million."[15] Stead's articles found their way to both Europe and America. The offices of the *Gazette* were besieged, many people offended by the content of Stead's article. W. H. Smith's bookstalls refused to sell the *Gazette* because of the indecency of the article, so William Booth opened up International Headquarters as a distribution center, with cadets from the officers' training homes distributing the newspapers on the streets. "George Bernard Shaw offered to take as many copies as he could carry and peddle them in the streets."[16] W. T. Stead was either much maligned, some of that coming from competitor newspapers jealous of the instant popularity of his paper, or hotly defended. In any case, for better or for worse here was the beginning of investigative journalism.

Catherine entered the battle publicly after the story was out. Mass meetings were conducted to increase the pressure of public attention on this cancer within Christian England. On one occasion, addressing a meeting at Exeter Hall, Catherine attacked the members of Parliament for their lack of will and was especially indignant against one member of Parliament who wanted to reduce the age of consent to ten! Catherine said:

> I read some paragraphs from the report of a debate in the House of Commons which made me doubt my eyesight . . . I did not think we were so low as this—that one member should suggest that the age of these innocents . . . should be reduced to ten and, Oh! my God, pleaded that it was hard for a man—HARD—<u>for a man</u>—having a charge brought against him, not to be able to plead the consent of a child like that. . . .
>
> <u>Well</u> may the higher classes take care of <u>their</u> little girls! Well may they be so careful never to let them go out without efficient protectors. But what is to become of the little girls of unprotected widows? Of the little girls of the working classes of this country? . . . I could not have believed that in this country such a discussion amongst so-called gentlemen could have taken place.[17]

Once again, Catherine was vigilant for the rights of the poor, those unable to protect themselves, those who found themselves at the mercy of unscrupulous men and women. She was on the side of the victim. She was further convinced that had the wealthy experienced what the poor and working classes had with the sale of their daughters, this crime would long ago have been exposed and eradicated.

But Catherine was not content with speaking at mass meetings. She wanted other pressures to be brought to bear in this battle, so she wrote to Prime Minister Gladstone and twice to Queen Victoria, pleading her majesty's intervention in this matter. The first letter, written on June 3, 1885, read as follows:

May it please your Majesty:—

My heart has been so filled with distress and apprehension on account of the rejection by the House of Commons of the Bill for the Protection of Young Girls from the consequences of male profligacy, that, on behalf of tens of thousands of the most pitiable and helpless of your Majesty's subjects, I venture to address you.

First, I would pray that your Majesty will cause the bill to be re-introduced during the present session of Parliament; and

Second, I would pray that your Majesty will be graciously pleased to insist on the limit of age being fixed at sixteen.

I feel sure that if your Majesty could only be made acquainted with the awful sacrifice of infant purity, health, and happiness, to the vices of the evil-minded men who oppose the raising of the age, your mother's heart would bleed with pity.

The investigation in connection with our operations throughout the kingdom of cases continually transpiring, brings to our knowledge appalling evidence of the enormity of the crimes daily perpetrated, crimes such as must, ere long, if something is not done, undermine our whole social fabric and bring down the judgment of God upon our nation.

If I could only convey to your Majesty an idea of the tenth part of the demoralization, shame, and suffering entailed on thousands of the children of the poor by the present state of the law on this subject, I feel sure that your womanly feelings would be roused to indignation, and that your Majesty would make the remaining years of your glorious reign (which I fervently pray may be many) even more illustrious than those that are past, by going off merely conventional lines in order to save the female children of your people from a fate worse than that of slaves or savages.

May He who is the Avenger of the oppressed, incline the heart of your Majesty to come to His help in this matter, prays Yours, on behalf of the innocents,

  Catherine Booth[18]

Catherine's appeal to the queen centered on the issue of the children of the poor being the primary victims of this crime. Catherine directly and consciously took the side of the poor in the hope that her request to the queen would produce results. From Balmoral Castle on June 6, 1885, Queen Victoria sent the following message to Catherine through the Dowager Duchess Roxburgh:

> The Dowager Duchess Roxburgh presents her compliments to Mrs. Booth, and is desired by the Queen to acknowledge Mrs. Booth's letter of the 3rd instant, and to say that Her Majesty, fully sympathizing with Mrs. Booth on the painful subject to which it refers, has already had communication thereon with a lady closely connected with the Government, to whom Mrs. Booth's letter will be immediately forwarded.[19]

Public pressure was continuing on this issue, largely through Catherine's speeches as well as others. Catherine took it upon herself once again to write to Queen Victoria, praying that her majesty would render a word of encouragement for this moral battle being waged in her land. Catherine wrote this on July 14, 1885:

> To Her Most Gracious Majesty The Queen,
>
> Your Majesty will be aware that since your last communication to me some heart-rending disclosures have been made with respect to the painful subject on which I ventured to address you. It seems probable that some effective legislation will be the result, for which multitudes of your Majesty's subjects in the Salvation Army will be deeply grateful.
>
> Nevertheless, legislation will not effect what requires to be done. Nothing but the most desperate, sympathetic, and determined effort, moral and spiritual, can meet the case, and it would be a great encouragement to thousands of those engaged in this struggle if your Majesty would at this juncture graciously send us a word of sympathy and encouragement to be read at our mass meetings in different parts of the kingdom, the first of which takes place on Thursday evening next at Exeter Hall.
>
> Allow me to add that it would cheer your Majesty to hear the responses of immense audiences in different parts of the land, when it has been intimated that the heart of your Majesty beats in sympathy with this effort to protect and rescue the juvenile daughters of your people.
>
> Praying for your Majesty's highest peace and prosperity,

I have the honour to be, Your Majesty's loyal and devoted servant,
Catherine Booth[20]

To this the Dowager Marchioness of Ely replied on July 22, 1885:

The Dowager Marchioness of Ely presents her compliments to Mrs. Booth and begs leave to assure her that her letter, addressed to the Queen, has received Her Majesty's careful consideration. Lady Ely need scarcely tell Mrs. Booth that the Queen feels very deeply on the subject to which her letter refers, but Her Majesty has been advised that it would not be desirable for the Queen to express any opinion upon a matter which forms at present the object of a Measure before Parliament.[21]

Catherine's reply two days later to the Dowager Marchioness of Ely is critical. Catherine wrote:

To the Dowager Marchioness of Ely:
Madam,
I am in receipt of the communication which Her Majesty has done me the honour to forward through your Grace, and I am deeply grateful for the expression it contains of Her Majesty's continued interest in the question to which it refers. I fully appreciate the delicacy of Her Majesty's position at the present juncture. At the same time, may I suggest that this is not a political question, and all the impression I wish to be allowed to convey to the people of England is that Her Majesty is fully with us in abhorrence of the iniquities referred to, and of opinion that every effort should be made to bring them to an end.

I am led to write this feeling that the comparative silence of the press is calculated to render it extremely difficult for Her Majesty to appreciate the intense and growing anxiety of the masses of the people on the subject.

I am proposing therefore to read the note which Her Majesty has been pleased to send me by your Grace at a meeting of 5,000 people on Monday night in London, and also at large meetings

257

in Yorkshire unless you have reason to believe that Her Majesty would object to such a course.

This, however, I cannot fear, seeing that it simply assures the nation that the interests of the children of her people are still dear to Her Majesty's heart.

If your Grace could arrange to send a line by the bearer; or, if this is impracticable, to telegraph if Her Majesty objects to my proposition, I should be grateful if you would do so. Otherwise, I will conclude that I may use the letter in the manner I have indicated.

Catherine Booth[22]

With no response forthcoming, Catherine assured people in her public addresses that the heart of the queen was with them in this cause!

A third letter to the queen requesting an interview with the Prince of Wales may have gone unanswered.[23] Clearly, Catherine wanted to press home the problem of vice in England. However, the strategy for winning this battle by letter writing and appealing to the government for immediate action was now over for Catherine and others. It was time to take this case to the public—and it was time for political action by the people. Catherine and William organized mass meetings in the provinces and in London to bring the battle directly to the people. Catherine was, as she wrote on the day previous to the publication of the first issue of "The Maiden Tribute Campaign," "determined to have the law altered."[24] She was gravely concerned because "the rascals who are in this iniquity are raging, and our one fear is that it may make it worse for our poor people; however, we see no way to mend the evil but by fighting it out."[25]

Catherine took to the platforms of Prince's Hall, St. James's Hall, and Exeter Hall, all now familiar venues for her, supported by those veterans in the fight—William, Bramwell, Mrs. Bramwell Booth, Stead, Josephine Butler, Samuel Morley, Professor Stuart, and others. Catherine readily admitted that "I felt as though I must go and walk the streets and besiege the dens where these hellish iniquities are going on. To keep quiet seemed like being a traitor to humanity."[26] In her many speeches she made this an issue of human rights for the poor, speaking not only of the protection of young women but the equal protection of young men from exposure to vice and corruption.

The Booths wrote a petition to the House which, in the course of seventeen days, received 393,000 signatures.[27] The petition was nearly two miles in length and was coiled up into an immense roll bound and draped with Salvation Army colors—yellow, red, and blue. The petition was then

> conveyed through London to Trafalgar Square, accompanied by an escort of mothers and the men cadets' band. To comply with the law that no procession should approach within a mile of Westminster when the House was in session, the petition was then carried down Whitehall on the shoulders of eight cadets and laid on the floor of the House because there was not sufficient room on the customary commons table.[28]

Here is the reading of the final petition:

  I. The age of responsibility for young girls must be raised to eighteen.

  II. The procuration of young people for seduction or immoral purposes must be made a criminal offence, having attached to it a severe penalty.

  III. The right of search, by which a magistrate shall have power to issue an order for the search of any house wherein there is reason to believe that girls under that age are detained for immoral purposes, or where women of any age are so detained against their will.

  IV. The equality of women and men before the law; seeing that whereas it is now a criminal act for a woman to solicit a man to immorality, it shall be made equally criminal for a man to solicit a woman to immorality.[29]

The Home Secretary decided to resume debate on the Criminal Law Amendment Act, and on August 14, 1885, after a third reading, the bill carried and the age of consent was raised to sixteen. Frederick Coutts simply wrote, "A thanksgiving meeting was held in the Exeter Hall."[30] That is understating the case. Thousands of Salvationists and other English citizens throughout England rejoiced over what many perceived to be a grand moral victory. And the Army was now prepared to set up homes to care for the young girls who would be out on the streets as a result of this ruling.

All went well, so everyone thought. There was, unfortunately, a fatal flaw in this whole scheme. When Rebecca Jarrett made arrangements for the purchase of Eliza from her mother, she assumed—as did all who took part in the plot—that the father's consent had also been given. This was not the case, or so it seemed. The mother was acting alone in this matter, and Rebecca Jarrett had dealt only with the mother and had never spoken to the father, Charles Armstrong.

Problems began when Mrs. Armstrong began to search for her missing daughter, prompted undoubtedly by greed and by reporters from *Lloyd's Newspaper*—"a Sunday rival of the *Gazette*"[31]—who were looking for a good story. Mrs. Armstrong, accompanied by a police inspector from Marylebone, went to 101 Queen Victoria Street to ascertain the whereabouts of her daughter. Eliza and Mrs. Armstrong were reunited, Eliza having been brought home from Paris where she had been staying with Rebecca Jarrett and Madame Combe. She may have been reluctant to be reunited with her mother, who did, after all, sell her into what was apparently going to be a life of prostitution. Eliza was fully paid for all her troubles, and everyone thought the episode was now at an end. However, to everyone's amazement, on September 8, 1885,

W. T. Stead, Rebecca Jarrett, Bramwell Booth, Madame Combe, Jacques (one of Stead's assistants), and Madame Mourez (the midwife) were charged at Bow Street under . . . an Act of 1861 entitled Offenses Against the Person, with the abduction of Eliza Armstrong from the care of her father. When proceedings began, however, the Attorney General announced that he had now

decided to proceed under section 55 which made it a misde-
meanour to abduct an unmarried girl under sixteen. To this was
added the charge of "aiding and abetting an indecent assault on
Eliza Armstrong."[32]

Public opinion was polarized. Stead and the Army had their
defenders, while others were sure that there was duplicity to be
accounted for. Motives were suspected. Intentions were questioned. In spite of such public disgrace, Bramwell later affirmed
that "the mistakes never made me regret in the least the plan that
we pursued."[33] And in a letter to his mother from the dock, he
wrote, convinced that he was going to be convicted:

> As to the case I have no regrets as to what I did. The mistakes and
> accidents all through have only been such as are usually attached
> to all human enterprises. I regret them, but I could not prevent
> them, glad as I would have been to do so. It is painful to have all
> regard for motive shut out of what they think it well to shut it out
> from, and yet to imply all sorts of bad motives in connexion with
> the smallest incidents of the affair. But I do beg you not to be dis-
> tressed in any way about me personally. God will take care of me![34]

Stead was of the same opinion, and in an article titled "Why
I Went to Prison" stated that "for one-tenth of the result then
achieved I would gladly go to gaol again today."[35] In that same
article he said, "When I die I wish for no other epitaph upon my
tomb than this: 'Here lies the man who wrote "The Maiden Tribute of Modern Babylon."'"[36]

Lawyers were hired, and a defense fund of six thousand pounds
was quickly raised. Among those subpoenaed for the defense
were the Archbishop of Canterbury, Cardinal Manning, Bishop
Temple, Samuel Morley, and Mrs. Butler. *The War Cry* kept the
case before the public and Salvationists, and the defendants were
viewed as heroes.[37] Bramwell explained his role in this case to
his fellow Salvationists in an open letter published on the front
page of *The War Cry*.[38] Needless to say, Catherine did not sit
idly by while her friend, W. T. Stead, and her eldest son were

unjustly accused while criminals were still engaging in grievous evils against women and children throughout the empire.

Catherine was on a preaching campaign with William in the provinces when they received a telegram informing them of the government prosecution of Stead and Bramwell. They were shocked. Catherine was indignant. The government should be pursuing those who already were breaking the Criminal Law Amendment Act rather than those who brought the evil to light, she thought to herself and expressed to others.

Catherine twice wrote to the Home Secretary, Sir Richard Cross, the first time pleading the case of Rebecca Jarrett. She wrote:

> This woman was herself a victim of male criminality at the age of fifteen, and lived an immoral life for fourteen years, the greater part of which time she kept a brothel and was allowed to prosecute her vile trade without the interference of the law. Nine months ago this woman was rescued by The Salvation Army, and has since lived an entirely changed life. . . .
>
> She is now in solitary confinement in a stone cell, with only a mat to lie on, without bed or pillow, her own warm clothing having been taken away, leaving her shivering with cold by day and night, notwithstanding that she is suffering from incurable hip disease, having left the hospital only a few months.
>
> Jarrett gave herself up voluntarily twenty-four hours after she knew that a warrant had been issued for her arrest; nevertheless she was not allowed bail, although a brothel keeper charged with keeping a disorderly house was granted that privilege the day before. . . .
>
> I cannot believe, Sir Richard, that you will allow such an injustice to continue.[39]

And, as she had done during the Maiden Tribute Campaign, she wrote to the queen:

> To Her Most Gracious Majesty the Queen:
> May it please Your Majesty to allow me to state that I know W. T. Stead, whose prosecution has been instigated by the hate and revenge of bad men, to be one of the bravest and most righ-

teous men in Your Majesty's dominions and if tomorrow he should be sentenced to imprisonment it will shock and arouse millions of your best and most loyal subjects to the highest indignation. I pray by all the love I bear Your Majesty and by all the pity I feel for your outraged infant subjects that you will if possible interfere to avert such a national calamity. May God endue Your Majesty with wisdom and strength to ignore all evil counselors and to exert your royal prerogative for the deliverance of those who are persecuted only for righteousness sake prays your loyal and devoted servant in Jesus,

Catherine Booth[40]

The return telegram to Catherine simply read:

Following from Balmoral the Queen has received your telegram. It is well understood that Her Majesty cannot interfere in the proceedings of any trial while it is going on. If necessary an appeal through the Secretary of State can be made to the Queen for a remission of sentence.[41]

Catherine, undaunted and single-minded in this, perhaps did not realize the full extent of the queen's revulsion against Stead and the *Pall Mall Gazette*. While Her Majesty sympathized with the victims in her realm, she saw as quite unorthodox the methods used to expose this crime as well as the rescue work of the Army and others. She could not stomach such extreme forms of exhibitionism. Moreover, she felt compelled to safeguard at least the appearance of virtue in England and really had no idea of the depths of depravity practiced by those around her, including, no doubt, some within her own court.

Catherine, however, persevered. Taking the advice of Her Majesty in the recent telegram, she wrote to Sir Richard Cross once again, asking this time directly for the release of the prisoners:

Sir:—Having appealed to Her Majesty the Queen on behalf of Mr. Stead and Rebecca Jarrett, prior to the passing of their sentences, Her Majesty graciously wired me in reply, stating that she could not interfere while the trial was going on, but instructing me to appeal through the Secretary of State for a remission of sentence if desired; accordingly I pray, on behalf of The Salvation Army, and also of thousands of the most virtuous, loyal, and religious of Her Majesty's subjects, that you will present our most humble and earnest appeal to Her Majesty for the immediate release of these prisoners, who, although they may have been guilty of a technical breach of the law, have been actuated by the highest and most patriotic motives, and have by their action procured an unspeakable and lasting boon to the most helpless and pitiable of the subjects of this realm, in the passing of the Criminal Law Amendment Bill.

I have the honour to be,
Yours faithfully,
Catherine Booth[42]

The result of the legal deliberations was cause for sadness, but not regret, for the defendants. Stead had evidently been able to maintain a sense of humor. Bramwell wrote, "I remember that when I was in the witness-box at the Old Bailey, answering, I hope, with some effectiveness the cross-examining counsel, Stead sent me a slip of paper on which he had written, 'Hallelujah! The Court feels like a Salvation Army prayer meeting.' That was the spirit in which the whole of that dreadful business was carried through."[43] Frederick Coutts has well summarized the complex legal proceedings in this way:

At the Old Bailey hearing which opened on October 23rd a single major ruling by Mr. Justice Lopes virtually determined the course of events. He supported the judgment of the lower court that any evidence as to the motives which had governed Stead's actions was inadmissible. So the Archbishop of Canterbury waited in vain to speak, nor were either Lord Dalhousie or Samuel Morley called to testify. It was enough for the judge that Eliza Armstrong had been taken away without her father's consent, and consent gained by fraud was no consent at all. When the jury, in considering their verdict, wished to distinguish between abduction for criminal purposes and the technical offence which Stead and Rebecca Jarrett had committed, Mr. Lopes repeated that no motive, however high-minded, justified the taking away of a child from her parents without their consent. With the case narrowed down to this one point, the acquittal of Bramwell Booth was virtually assured but the fate of Stead and the others was sealed.[44]

When all was finished the verdicts were read: Bramwell Booth and Madame Combe were acquitted; Stead received a sentence of three months; Sampson Jacques, one month; Rebecca Jarrett, six months but without hard labor—she had to serve that time herself in spite of the fact that a female Salvation Army Captain offered to take her place; and Madame Mourez, six months with hard labor for having assaulted Eliza. She died in prison. Bramwell recorded that The Salvation Army continued to assist Eliza and that Rebecca Jarrett "has done well. Her subsequent life has amply proved the sincerity of her repentance. She is still with the Army, enjoying a happy old age, free from the bondage of the past, and trying to serve God in the sphere in which He has in His mercy placed her."[45]

As for Stead, he was gladly welcomed by Salvationists at the Congress Hall following his release from prison. He claimed, "I do not suppose there is one man in England who has done you more harm than I myself. . . . I most distinctly say that I received no more than my deserts, if it was only for the trouble and expense which I brought upon The Salvation Army."[46]

Of course, the audience would have none of that. They believed he had acted for the cause of biblical righteousness, and for that he was lauded that night. He was probably carrying a shilling in his pocket, for after the passage of the Criminal Law Amendment Bill "a girl of thirteen, dying in hospital from venereal disease, sent Stead a shilling in gratitude for his work. He kept this with him all his life."[47] To commemorate his incarceration for the sake of justice, every year on November 4 Stead wore his prison uniform all day, "wearing it even on the train to and from work."[48] For the rest of his life, until his death on the *Titanic,* he was a friend of The Salvation Army.

Two postscripts to this whole affair lend irony to its telling. Before the completion of the trial, Stead had a suspicion as to why Eliza's father had played such a minor role in this drama. Stead suspected that he was not really her father, and, had that been proved to be true, the prosecution would have been left without a case. Stead did not pursue this, but ten years later it was proved that Charles Armstrong was indeed not Eliza's father! The second irony was that Mrs. Armstrong's home on Charles Street was eventually owned by The Salvation Army, and the ministry from that home continued to reach out to poor women and children. A day-care center was established for the children of working mothers—both single and married. The first child to be admitted was Eliza Armstrong's own niece. Such Salvation Army homes would continue to become a familiar sight on the religious and social scene of England. Furthermore, they provided opportunities for yet another aspect of ministry for women and thereby increased the Army's recruitment of women as well as their authority in ministry. "For Salvationist women, the Rescue Work was particularly important because it developed the justification for women's religious activities by extending it to social service work. These women did not undertake the work in a submissive, passive spirit but rather went into a sinful world, empowered by the Holy Spirit to make it anew."[49] Ann R. Higginbotham wrote:

> Although female street-corner evangelists remained the most enduring image of Salvationist women, their work for the Army had another, more conventional side. The Women's Social Services, begun nearly seven years before General Booth published his scheme for social regeneration, *In Darkest England and the Way Out* (1890), became one of the largest rescue organizations in Victorian and Edwardian Britain. It had responsibility for the Army's work with children and with fallen, homeless, or alcoholic women, but by the end of the nineteenth century the Women's Social Services were particularly noted for their work with a special class of fallen women—unmarried mothers. Salvationist women raised and administered the necessary funds for the Women's Social Services, which operated independently

from other branches of the Army. One observer described the Army's rescue workers as "ladies by birth and instinct." Rescue work may well have appealed to Salvationist women who would have hesitated to lead a brass band or harangue a crowd in the slums of Whitechapel. Vicars' wives and squires' daughters participated in the work to reclaim fallen women throughout the Victorian period without any loss of respectability. The more respectable, or less adventurous, of The Salvation Army's female converts could have found an acceptable outlet for their energies in the homes and missions established by the Women's Social Services.[50]

The Army was expanding its social ministries by the end of 1885—though not yet in a completely organized fashion. The organization of its increasing social work would come in 1890, with the inauguration of the Social Wing of the Army and the publication of William Booth's *In Darkest England and the Way Out*. W. T. Stead was influential in the writing of that work.[51] But there was no question that the Purity Crusade increased the reputation of The Salvation Army. As one author has noted, "The Army was now firmly established."[52]

The question must be asked, though, if Catherine Booth intended the Purity Crusade to set the stage for the social work of the Army. Did she eventually see this crusade as a precursor to organized social ministry, and if so, what form of social ministry did she envision at the time? Some have suggested, "The fact is that Catherine was deeply involved in the preparation of the social blueprint which incorporated many of her concerns that previously had been abandoned for lack of funds or personnel by the fledgling movement."[53]

Support for this idea is given in some of William's own reflections after Catherine's death, as well as by W. T. Stead, who wrote a tribute to Catherine in *The War Cry* following her death. Stead wrote:

That The Salvation Army is entering upon a new development is probably due more to her than to any single human being, and in its new social work we see the best and most enduring monument to the memory of the saintly woman who has at last been released from her sufferings. But that may also be said to be true of The Salvation Army itself. The Army could no more have come into existence without Mrs. Booth than could the family of sons and daughters who are now carrying on the movement. No one outside can ever know how much all that is most distinctive of The Army is due directly to the shaping and inspiring impulse of Mrs. Booth. But even outsiders like myself can see that but for her it would either never have been, or else it would have been merely one more of the many small but narrow sects which carry on mission work in the nooks and corners of the land.[54]

Stead's words should not be taken at face value, however. He was a man of sympathy with social reformation and without doubt was one of the prevailing influences on William for the full inauguration of social work in the Army. Viewing Catherine as the chief protagonist for the use of social ministry is a way of simply trying to justify a program with which Stead himself was in sympathy—and which was completely organized and publicized coincidentally at the time of Catherine's death. It furthermore demonstrates Stead's genuine affection for Catherine—which caused him to write about her without the objective eye of the trained journalist and which explains his occasional antagonism toward William. The General and W. T. Stead were often in conflict; as a matter of fact, William was much more reticent about the Purity Crusade than was Catherine partly because he feared that Stead, in his enthusiasm, was taking the Army along a path that should not be trod. In his correspondence with Catherine during the campaign and trial, William is often critical of Stead and his measures.

Obviously, the question of Catherine Booth and social ministry is more complicated than Stead would have people believe. In this case, Booth-Tucker may well express more clearly the conflict in Catherine's mind that was not yet settled after the Purity

Crusade. He wrote that after the Criminal Law Amendment Act
was passed, Catherine

> left London with the General for the provinces, eager to use the
> widespread interest of the hour in awakening universal attention
> to the one great theme: the salvation of the world. The General,
> in particular, was anxious to remind his followers that the subject
> which had lately engrossed the public mind was but a single man-
> ifestation of the all-prevailing sin which, in a thousand different
> forms, was the source of the miseries of mankind. Nothing has
> perhaps more emphatically contributed to the success of the Army
> than the persistency with which its leaders have ever kept the one
> main object in view.[55]

The author further states:

> As has already been remarked, *the spiritual work of The Salva-
> tion Army was not allowed to be interrupted during the year.*
> Indeed it was a time of special progress. The foreign corps had
> increased from 273 to 520, being an addition of 247. Those in
> Great Britain had risen from 637 to 802, making an increase of
> 165. The total number of corps had thus multiplied from 910 to
> 1,322, an increase of 412. There had been proportionate progress
> in regard to officers. The year 1884 had closed with a grand total
> of 2,164. At Christmas, 1885, there were no less than 3,076, being
> an increase of close upon 1,000 for the year [italics mine].[56]

In Catherine's mind, though, was there a clear distinction
between the cause for which she had fought in 1885 and the spiritual work of the Army? Should social ministry be thought of as
separate from spiritual ministry, as Booth-Tucker implied? He
clearly thought of the spiritual work of the Army only in terms
of the ministry of the corps, which was still largely evangelistic—
street meetings and indoor meetings in which sinners were saved
and saints sanctified. There was very little of what might be called
social work taking place in the corps in 1885.

Catherine, even at age fifty-six, was still the product of her
strict Methodistic rearing. She continued undoubtedly to think

269

of spiritual work as that of winning souls for Christ, while social ministry might be helpful as a prelude to such a task. As one who read the manuscript for *In Darkest England and the Way Out,* Catherine was certainly in agreement with William's thesis stated so carefully in the preface:

> My only hope for the permanent deliverance of mankind from misery, either in this world or the next, is the regeneration or remaking of the individual by the power of the Holy Ghost through Jesus Christ. But in providing for the relief of temporal misery I reckon that I am only making it easy where it is now difficult, and possible where it is now all but impossible, for men and women to find their way to the Cross of Our Lord Jesus Christ.[57]

At the wedding of her daughter Emma in 1888, Catherine said:

> There are plenty of other people about all other kinds of work, and I am always glad to hear of anybody doing anything good and kind and true and helpful to humanity; whether it is feeding little boys and girls or the poor, or enlightening the ignorant, or building hospitals, or anything else whatever so long as they are doing more good than harm, I say "Amen, God bless you!" *But that is not the particular work Jesus Christ has set His people to do.* There are plenty of people to do all that kind of work, but there are few for the peculiar work which Christ has set His people to do. The great characteristic of His people in the world was that they were to be saviours of men—Salvationists. Their work was to be to enlighten men with respect to God's claims upon them, and enlighten them with respect to what God is willing to do for them, and enlighten them with respect to what God wants to do by them in the salvation of others; therefore, I ask you to help us. If you won't be Salvationists yourselves, do the next best thing—help us. Help us save the world. Amen [italics mine].[58]

On the other hand, there were times when Catherine was remarkably insightful, and her vision of the sacramental life and of every common act as being a means of grace would certainly give rise to the logical conclusion that social ministry was of itself sacramental and therefore spiritual. It needed no further justification but was itself a full expression of God's grace and a means of such grace—if done in a redemptive context and carried out as a sign both to the ministers and the recipients that God's ultimate desire was to save people for the present as well as for eternity.

There is no clear resolution in Catherine's thinking concerning this theological matter as there was, for example, in her theology of women in ministry. It is likely nearer the truth that at times she felt conflicted and fretful about the relationship of social work and spiritual work, while at other times she had a calm settled view as to their perfect harmony and unity. It is better to leave as a moot point precisely and exactly what Catherine's thinking would have been about the social ministry of the Army once she saw that ministry fully inaugurated after the development of the Social Wing and the publication of *In Darkest England and the Way Out*.

She may have given clearer theological expression to the relationship of the Army's social ministry and spiritual ministry. She may have had some serious reservations about the fully developed social ministry, as did her friend and ally George Scott Railton, which he finally and clearly expressed in 1894.[59] Or she may have seen the Darkest England Scheme, which outlined the social ministry of the Army, as subordinate to the Army's corps and spiritual work and as a means of expressing the soldiers' and officers' life of salvation and holiness. This apparently was the position of her son Bramwell, articulated when he became the second General of The Salvation Army, succeeding his father in 1912. A reporter from the *Daily News and Leader* asked Bramwell to "take your mind back nearly twenty years to the writing of 'Darkest England and the Way Out,' and tell me how, in the light of that book, you regard The Salvation Army's social achievements today." The second General responded:

My answer . . . is that I have always looked on the Darkest England scheme and what came out of it as a comparatively small, though essential, part of the work of The Salvation Army—as a link rather than the main body of the thing. I say essential because

271

it was, and is, an expression of the passion at the heart of the organism itself, but as such it takes a subordinate place in my own conception of the history—and, shall I say the hopes?—of the Army.[60]

Whatever case one is prepared to make in this matter, the kind of national crusade Catherine waged with Stead, Josephine Butler, and Bramwell was not repeated by Catherine in her lifetime. The exhausting work associated with the Purity Crusade along with the spiritual and moral energy mustered to wage that war proved detrimental to Catherine's already delicate health. As one writer noted, the crusade "was Catherine Booth's last battle to reform England and it had probably done something towards ending her life."[61]

Following the crusade and the trials, Catherine stayed home for many months to convalesce and did not take part in the Army's public meetings until the next year. She did use this occasion to continue her correspondence, though. She also dedicated the *Victory,* the first of many Salvation Army "cavalry forts"— large vans that carried cadets from the training homes to small villages, which otherwise would never hear the preaching of Salvationists. Also, it was during this time that the first *Order and Regulations for Field Officers* was published, and the Army's first missionary publication, *All The World,* was issued. This was edited by Susie F. Swift, a graduate of Vassar College, who first met the Army in Edinburgh during a visit to Great Britain. She then journeyed to London to question General and Mrs. Booth about their Army in the early 1880s. She decided to become a Salvation Army officer, and her writing and editorial skills were used in the service of *All the World.*

After the prolonged time of convalescence, Catherine resumed a demanding preaching schedule that took her throughout much of England as well as London. She was, by all accounts, extremely popular and an important Christian voice in England. Her meetings were crowded, which was remarkable when one considers that she was ever ready to deliver the hard news of the gospel as well as the good news. She continued to preach about sin and judgment as readily as she preached about grace and salvation. Indeed, it might be said that she had learned even more about both sin and grace during the Purity Crusade. In her thinking, these themes were all part of God's Word and therefore inseparable.

She did not demur when preaching to the wealthy but condemned them for the sins attendant with their wealth—greed, selfishness, pride, or lack of concern for the poor and dispossessed of the world. She knew the power of the visual in people's minds, and she had the gift of drawing verbal pictures of the biblical stories and narratives. She was a gifted preacher, and it was her preaching for which she should best be remembered. There was an authority in her preaching that she attributed to the Spirit of the Lord alone. She possessed no earthly authority—she was never ordained by any denomination or commissioned as a Salvation Army officer. But she was convinced that she had a heavenly authority, and that was enough. She was her own best example when giving advice on how to preach. Here is Catherine on preaching:

We need men and women who are trained for the fight, not only people who have experienced a change of heart, but who are drilled in knowing how to use the weapons of the Spirit—knowing how to handle God's truth. You would think, if you heard some people's representation of the truth of God, that it was all honey and soap; you would not think there was any cut in it—any dividing asunder. A great deal of the truth preached nowadays would not cut the wings off a fly, much less pierce asunder the soul and spirit.

You must preach God's justice and vengeance against sin as well as His love for the sinner. You must preach hell as well as heaven. You must let your Gospel match the intuitions of humanity, or you may as well throw it into the sea, and thus save both trouble and money. A Gospel of love never matched anybody's soul. The great want in this day is truth that cuts—convicting truth—truth that convinces and convicts the sinner and pulls off the bandages from his eyes. The Lord knew the order in which His truth ought to be preached better than we do. Hence His commission to Paul, to go and "open the eyes" of sinners to their danger, and turn them round from the power of Satan unto God. This was to be done before they were converted. "Oh!" says someone, "don't talk to them about hell, death, and judgment; show them the love of Christ." But we always get wrong when we reverse God's order. Tear the bandages off. Open their eyes, turn them round from the desire, embrace and choice of evil to the embrace and choice of God, that they may receive forgiveness of sins.

Tell them *the truth;* tell a man the truth about himself. First, begin with himself. Drive in the red-hot, convicting truth of God on to his conscience, and make him realize that he is a sinner. Never mind how he howls, even if he groans as loud as the Psalmist did when the pains of hell got hold of him. Until he has been made to feel himself a sinner he will never make anything of a saint. Then give him the Gospel. Say to him: "Have you had enough of the devil? Will you give up your drink? Will you renounce that idol, or that unholy affection?" Herod would have been saved if it could have been done without his giving up his idol.

Tell a man the truth about himself, then the truth about God, then the truth about his obligation to others. That is, if the things I have been saying are true. If they are not, I would not go to chapel, I would not have the Bible. I would throw the whole thing over-board and live at peace; that is, as far as a man can, living a mere nominal existence. I would give the whole thing up. If it is not true, be done with it; if it is true, act upon it. Oh, may God help us! [62]

On another occasion, Catherine made these remarks about preaching:

One great qualification for successful labour is power to get the truth home to the heart.

Not to *deliver* it. I wish the word had never been coined in con-nexion with Christian work. "Deliver" it, indeed—*that* is not in the Bible. No, no; not deliver it; but drive it home—send it in—make it *felt.* That is your work; not merely to say it—not quietly and gen-teelly to put it before the people. Here is just the difference between a self-consuming, soul-burdened, Holy Ghost, successful ministry, and a careless, happy-go-lucky, easy sort of thing, that just rolls it out like a lesson, and goes home, holding itself in no way responsi-ble for the consequences. Here is *all* the difference, either in public or individual labour. God has made you responsible, not for deliv-ering the truth, but for GETTING IT IN—getting it home, fixing it in the conscience as a red-hot iron, as a bolt, straight from His throne; and He has placed at your disposal the *power to do it,* and if you do not do it, *blood* will be on your skirts. Oh, this genteel way of putting the truth! How God hates it! "If you please, dear friends, will you listen? If you please will you be converted? Will you come to Jesus? Shall we read just like this, that and the other?" No more like apostolic preaching than darkness is like light.[63]

On September 17, 1886, Ballington was married to Maud Charlesworth, a vicar's daughter and young Catherine's lieutenant during her ministry in Switzerland. Then on February 8, 1887, Catherine Booth's namesake and eldest daughter was married to Colonel Arthur S. Clibborn, formerly a Quaker and one who had worked with the Army in France and Switzerland. The Salvation Army's Clapton Congress Hall was the venue for the Salvationist weddings.

Like the other Booth sons-in-law who followed him, Colonel Clibborn took on the Booth name, so the married couple were henceforth Colonels Catherine and Arthur Booth-Clibborn. They were later promoted to the rank of Commissioner. Finally, on April 10, 1888, on William's fifty-ninth birthday, Emma, the Booths' second daughter, was married to Commissioner Tucker, who had served in the Indian civil service and had joined The Salvation Army in England years earlier. For the wedding he wore the Indian dress and turban of a beggar. He was barefooted and his begging bowl was on the platform during the ceremony. He had gone back to India to commence the work of the Army there in 1882, and now, he and Emma, Mrs. Booth-Tucker, would return to India to continue the work together.

Catherine preached at this wedding, but she would have to give up her public ministry soon after this occasion. This makes her sermon interesting for many reasons, but primarily because the Army mother reflected on her own personal Christian pilgrimage and the sacramental life in a poignant way.

Before I was fifteen years of age, God had, in an especial manner, taught me what I consider the first and fundamental and all-com-

275

prehensive principle of Christ's salvation—of real Christianity—
that every act of our lives, every relationship into which we enter,
every object at which we aim, every purpose that inspires our souls,
should be centered and bounded by God and His glory, and that,
whether we eat or drink, or whatsoever we do—whether we marry
or are given in marriage, do business, or become Salvation Army
officers or whatever we do—we should do all to the glory of God.[64]

Catherine was able to continue in ministry for about three
months, while William was in America and Canada. She held
meetings and opened corps, often having to travel by train alone.
She was frequently astonished by what she witnessed. For example, when she dedicated the new Salvation Army hall in Oldham,
she found there four hundred soldiers, even though the Army
had been at work in that town for only three years and had
encountered great difficulty in building the hall. She constantly
attributed such miracles to God's good grace and providence.

She also continued as a forthright apologist for the Army's
doctrines, methods, and language, which were still being attacked
in some quarters, although much of the public was now getting
quite used to the Army. In answer to one critic of the language
used by the Army, Catherine wrote, "You see, we are aiming at
the rough, untutored, undisciplined multitudes, and we find as
a matter of fact that the further we can keep away from religious
phraseology and old-fashioned modes the better we can reach
them and influence them."[65] She was fond of saying that it was
the Spirit who gave life to the Army and not the Army's means
and methods. These were only an expression of that life. Speaking for herself and William, she once wrote: "We have no ambition for this work to live any longer than He desires, therefore if
it ever loses its spirit and life we are content for it to die."[66] And
she constantly warned that each Army corps was "a place where
real soldiers were to be fed, taught, and equipped for war, not a
place to settle down in as a comfortable snuggery in which to
enjoy themselves."[67] In speaking apparently at the opening of a
new corps, Catherine said that she "hoped if ever they did settle
down God would burn their new Barracks over their head."[68]

Even now, when her health was poor, she at times appeared vigorous in her activities. Indeed, she speaks of this time in her life in a letter to a generous benefactor as "a hurricane of work and confusion."[69] But insurmountable physical problems were about to come to the surface. Her concern about her health had abated in recent years, undoubtedly because of the intensity of work and the single-minded purpose with which she pursued her tasks. Now, however, there was a genuine physical threat to her life. Catherine was about to learn lessons of suffering and dying that could be learned in no other way. Here was a turning point, a defining, trying time in her life. To understand Catherine Booth during this time is to appreciate her for the person she was. She lived a sacramental life by God's grace even, and perhaps especially, in time of suffering.

10

On Dying and Death

Promotion to Glory

The time was approaching for Catherine Booth to fight her last battle. She received fearful news from her physician in February 1888, shortly after returning from meetings at the Free Trade Hall in Manchester and the Colston Hall in Bristol. Both Catherine and William had preached at those meetings. Catherine's physician, Dr. Heywood Smith, had arranged for consultation with Sir James Paget, who diagnosed a small tumor on Catherine's breast to be cancerous. An immediate operation was advised to remove the tumor. Catherine, ever suspicious of surgical advances and medications, refused, knowing she would probably have fewer than three years to live. William later described his hearing this news.

> After hearing the verdict of the doctors she drove home alone. That journey can better be imagined than described. She afterwards told me how as she looked upon the various scenes through the cab window it seemed that the sentence of death had been

passed upon everything; how she had knelt upon the cab floor and wrestled in prayer with God; of the unutterable yearnings over me and the children that filled her heart; how the realisation of our grief swept over her, and the uncertainties of the near future, when she would be no longer with us.

I shall never forget in this world, or the next, that meeting. I had been watching for the cab and had run out to meet and help her up the steps. She tried to smile upon me through her tears, but drawing me into the room she unfolded gradually to me the result of the interviews. I sat down speechless. She rose from her seat and came and knelt beside me, saying, "Do you know what was my first thought? That I should not be there to nurse you at your last hour."

I was stunned. I felt as if the whole world were coming to a standstill. Opposite me on the wall was a picture of Christ on the cross. I thought I could understand it then as never before. She talked like a heroine, like an angel, to me: she talked as she had never talked before. I could say little or nothing. It seemed as though a hand were laid upon my very heart-strings. I could only kneel with her and try to pray.

I was due in Holland for some large meetings. I had arranged to travel that very night. She would not hear of my remaining at home for her sake. Never shall I forget starting out that evening, with the mournful tidings weighing like lead upon my heart. Oh, the conflict of that night journey! I faced two large congregations, and did my best, although it seemed I spoke as one in a dream. Leaving the meetings to be continued by others I returned to London the following evening.

Then followed conferences and controversies interminable as to the course of treatment which it might be wisest to pursue. Her objections to an operation finally triumphed.

And then followed for me the most painful experience of my life. To go home was anguish. To be away was worse. Life became a burden, almost too heavy to be borne, until God in a very definite manner visited me in a measure, and comforted my heart.[1]

The family, of course, was devastated by the news. In so many ways Catherine had been the center of family life in spite of her countless preaching engagements. Family members tried to dissuade her from her determination not to allow the operation, but she would have none of it. She was determined to not undergo surgery and to suffer through the consequences of her decision. Another remedy, suggested by W. T. Stead, was tried, but to no avail.

This mother of an Army would have to give up her public ministry. Her last address, save for speaking briefly to Salvationists in a subsequent meeting, was in the City Temple in London on Thursday, June 21, 1888, at the invitation of Dr. Joseph Parker. She had preached at her daughter Emma's wedding on April 10, 1888, the date for the wedding being arranged as early as possible for Catherine's sake. During the wedding sermon she publicly acknowledged her illness. She said, "I have, as you know, been wounded and worsted in the fight, and I have felt it hard, sometimes, not to be able to answer the bugle's call and jump to the front, as has been my custom for the last twenty-six years, when there has been need for me."[2]

On finishing her sermon at the City Temple she sat, exhausted, for nearly an hour. The congregation dispersed, and Catherine was gently led to her cab and taken home. Her preaching ministry of nearly thirty years concluded with that sermon.

Even during her illness, however, she still thought about ministry. She continued to advise William on all matters both personal and professional and continued as well to dictate letters, unable herself to write any longer. In one letter, written to a Salvation Army officer imprisoned in Switzerland, Catherine was likely speaking to herself as well as to the recipient. She addressed the letter as "One Prisoner to Another":

I would especially warn you against allowing your present depressing circumstances to cast you down, or lead you to fear that this event has happened outside the Divine programme. I know how cunningly Satan can misrepresent our very highest blessings and honours, making them to appear as misfortunes or curses, and leading us, if we yield to unbelief, to exclaim, "All these things are against me!" Remember, "whom the Lord *loveth* He chasteneth," and to those who endure His chastening the promise is, "If we suffer, we shall also reign with Him."[3]

Nevertheless, the inactivity now imposed on Catherine troubled her greatly. She had for so many years been active, and indeed energized, by the ministry to which she felt singularly called. "Although not able to be at the front of the battle," she wrote, "my heart is there; and the greatest pain I suffer arises from my realisation of the vast opportunities of the hour, and of the desperate pressure to which many of my comrades are subject, while I am deprived of the ability to assist them as in days gone by."[4]

She was able to appear only briefly at subsequent Salvation Army events. She attended for a short time a celebration at the Alexandria Palace in Wood Green in 1888, and on April 10, 1889, she managed to go to the sixtieth birthday celebration for William held at Clapton Congress Hall. "Immediately after the banquet Mrs. Booth, extremely weak and bearing the traces of much suffering on her face, was tenderly led on to the platform for 'The feasting of souls.'"[5] Aware of the seriousness of her affliction, she said, "Having the prospect of the fight soon ending in my own case except God should intervene, I cannot help but feel deeply moved."[6]

She was unable to be present for The Salvation Army twenty-fifth anniversary celebration in 1890 at the Crystal Palace. But she did send her last word to her assembled Salvationists, and to make her message available to the largest audience possible, it "was written in large letters on a sheet of calico coiled on a roller. As this was unwound—to be wound on another roller on the other side of the platform—the audience could read it, sentence by sentence, from the farthest corner."[7] This was her message:

My Dear Children and Friends,

My place is empty, but my heart is with you. You are my joy and crown. Your battles, sufferings, and victories have been the chief interest of my life these past twenty-five years. They are so still. Go forward! Live holy lives. Be true to the Army. God is your strength. Love and seek the lost; bring them to the Blood. Make the people good; inspire them with the Spirit of Jesus Christ. Love one another; help your comrades in dark hours. I am dying under the Army Flag; it is yours to live and fight under. God is my Salvation and Refuge in the storm. I send you my love and blessing—Catherine Booth.[8]

Catherine loved the sea. For a brief period in the fall of 1888, she went to Clacton-on-Sea for a time of recuperation. Perhaps her stay there reminded her of her visit to Brighton as a young girl, where she also spent a period of recuperation. After returning to London, further remedies were tried but without any lasting success. The cancer was progressing, and the attendant hemorrhaging and nausea continued to weaken her. In August 1889 Catherine once again returned to Clacton-on-Sea, perhaps intuitively knowing that she would never see London again. "On her way from her home in Barnet to Liverpool Street Station she had expressed a conviction that she would never return. She spoke frequently and in the most touching manner regarding her memories of the great city, east and west, its rich and poor, its evil and its good."[9]

The home at Clacton was set up as a kind of miniheadquarters. Some rooms were turned into offices while other rooms were retained as living quarters for a nurse, secretaries, visitors, and members of the Booth family. Catherine was unable to escape, even in her final days, the accoutrements of the salvation war. And perhaps she desired no such escape. She insisted on being kept constantly apprised of the furtherance of the war. Never one to waste a moment, she often dictated letters, even as she walked with William and other members of the family. At first she attempted to maintain a daily routine of carriage rides or walks, but that became increasingly impossible as her disease progressed and she got weaker.

William was ever watchful when home and attended lovingly to the needs of his wife. But his Army duties often removed him from Clacton. Catherine was always in the capable hands of her daughters and of Staff-Captain Carr, who was assigned as Cather-

283

ine's private nurse and ministered compassionately to her until her death.

Catherine was held in high esteem and almost reverence by many who had served with her, and now her battle with cancer and her long, lingering suffering seemed to bestow on the Army mother an almost saintly presence. Many officers, soldiers, and friends made a pilgrimage to visit her. Her bedroom often became a place for a Salvation Army meeting—complete with songs, Scripture readings, and prayers offered on behalf of Mrs. Booth. There were times of reminiscing about the struggles and victories of the war in the early days of The Christian Mission and The Salvation Army. And Catherine was still not at a loss for words; her messages to the visitors were often recorded. To one delegation, headed by such early Army leaders as Commissioner Howard and Colonels Dowdle and Higgins, Catherine reflected, "I thank God that, notwithstanding all the defects and imperfections I see in my life and work as I look back upon them from this bed, I can say that by His grace I have ever kept the interests of His Kingdom first, and have never withheld anything He required of me in order to help forward the salvation of the world. And my prayer for all of you is that you may be able, when you come as near the end, to say the same."[10]

There was a particularly difficult time for Catherine in late December 1889, when it seemed certain she would die at any moment. As many of the family as possible came to her side, including her trusted friend and ally, George Scott Railton. Catherine elicited promises from all those present that they would be true and faithful to the Army and its principles. She reflected with them on their service in years past, her words being recorded all the time by a stenographer. There were many such deathbed scenes following this one that were excruciatingly prolonged. As W. T. Stead wrote, "Like Charles II, she was an unconscionably long time dying, but never was a deathbed turned to better account."[11] Such deathbed scenes were not uncommon to the life and culture of the Methodism Catherine knew so well. One author has noted the following:

Almost as important for the early Methodists as a life well lived was a death well died, and indeed a number of the short accounts of Methodist worthies in the *Magazine* were simply extended deathbed scenes with little else; blow by blow accounts of the last scenes were a prominent feature of all biographies. This kind of account has a long pedigree in Christian hagiography, and once again the old Puritans provide the closest parallel to the Methodist variety. . . . The histories of holy dyings were valued, as a later Nonconformist said, "to perfume the name of the deceased; to console surviving mourners; to gratify descendants; and to instruct and edify the church." They were also a proof of the truths taught by the dying saint: an important part of Methodist apologetic.[12]

During these times when the family felt certain that Catherine was about to leave this world, all were called to the bedside and final farewells were made. The grief of the family, other officers, and servants was at times overwhelming as they looked on Catherine on the threshold.[13] They all wished for her suffering to cease. She sent this message to her Salvationists on December 19, 1889, which she certainly believed would be her last: "1:18 p.m.—The waters are rising, but so am I. I am not going under, but over. Don't be concerned about your dying; only go on living well, and the dying will be all right."[14]

But Catherine recovered. She passed through this time of turmoil in late December 1889, only to repeat several other similar trials for nearly a year. Constant bedside vigils were kept. However, her stubborn constitution was evident, and Catherine lingered. In the meantime the visitations continued, as did Catherine's reflections on the past and her defense of the Army's measures and methods and her warnings about the priorities of Army service. To members of a visiting Salvation Army brass band, now central to the Army's life, culture, and worship, especially in the British context, Catherine said:

I did not expect to see your faces any more. It is very kind of you to come and play to me. I only wish I were stronger, that I might say more of what is in my heart, but I rejoice in one or two points

285

expressed in your letter very much; in one especially: and that is, that you see the importance of keeping your music *spiritual,* and of using it only for the one great end.

We had a great deal of argument regarding the first introduction of bands into the Army, and a great many fears.

I had always considered music as belonging to God. Perhaps some of you have heard me say in public that there will not be a note of music in hell; that it will all be in heaven, and that God ought to have it all here. But, unfortunately, God has not His rights here, and the Church has strangely lost sight of the value of music as a religious agency. I think God has used the Army to resuscitate and awaken that agency, and while the bandsmen of the Salvation Army realise it to be as much their service to blow an instrument as it is to sing or pray or speak, and while they do the one in the same spirit as they would do the other, I am persuaded it will become an ever-increasing power amongst us. But the moment you, or any other bandsmen, begin to glory in the excellency of the music alone, apart from spiritual results, you will begin at once to lose your power. It is the same with everything else—meetings, testifying, singing, marching, or praying. It is a combination of the human and the divine. And when you separate the human from the divine it ceases to have any power over souls. Don't forget that.[15]

One of her visitors was her friend, W. T. Stead. He went to Clacton-on-Sea twice to visit Catherine and kneel by her bedside. In spite of their theological differences over such issues as spiritualism and mediums or the inspiration of the Bible, which Catherine defended in the face of Stead's broader views, they were kindred souls. The Army mother had by far a higher appreciation of Stead than did William, and Stead's appraisal of Catherine in his biography and in other writings is, naturally, quite flattering. Stead recorded his last visit to Catherine before her death. It was on Sunday afternoon,

one of those glorious summer days which, in 1890, made September a belated substitute for July. The sun had just set, but from the window of the sick room you could still see the crimson splendour along the western horizon. The air was filled with stillness, in which the lapping of the rippling waves on the beach below was hardly audible. In pain that ever and anon increased to anguish, in weakness so great that her voice could hardly make itself heard, she spoke to me for the last time.[16]

By January 1890 it was obvious that Catherine Booth had no hope of recovery. Army publications began keeping both Salvationists and the broader public informed of the state of her health. *All The World,* the Army's missionary journal with a wide international outreach, began publishing accounts of "Mrs. Booth's Condition." The January 1890 record of Catherine's illness read:

During the past month there has been a serious change in Mrs. Booth's condition. Her suffering has greatly increased, and the usual methods of giving relief have more or less failed in her case. To this has been added other complications of an alarming character; among them severe hemorrhage, and consequent prostration.

The change took place on Sunday, December 8th, and since that day, up to the date of going to press, December 13th, the beloved sufferer has been lying in the utmost weakness, and passing through the most terrible anguish. Mrs. Booth-Tucker is constantly with her.

Our dear leader is thus drawing near to her last great battle with the enemy, attended by weakness and suffering, but her heart does not fail. The messages of love and faith which slip out of the sick chamber ever and anon, assure us that in holy confidence and blessed resignation to His will, she is going forth to meet her Lord and join the throng of those who have fought the fight of righteousness and truth, and triumphed by the word of their testimony and the blood of the Lamb.

For the General and every member of his family, we bespeak the earnest faith and prayers of our readers. To them this is indeed a moment of uttermost sorrow and loss—loss equally terrible whether viewed as a personal one, or as that of the great work, whose one first need is workers and leaders who will not flinch.[17]

Catherine lingered on, and in March 1890 she had rallied enough to receive a delegation of officers who were stationed overseas. "The interview with Mrs. Booth lasted nearly an hour and she was able to speak with them at some length."[18] To these officers Catherine said, "They tell me that this illness has been used to increase the spirit of union and love in the Army and to lead members to a deeper consecration and a stronger determination than ever to fight for the salvation of the world. If so, then I don't regret it, though it is hard to bear—very hard. If this is the result, I shall be quite satisfied—quite."[19]

In spite of some slight recuperation, Catherine quickly relapsed, suffering many serious hemorrhages. Easter Monday, April 6, 1890, was another close call; but she rallied remarkably and lived until October of that year.

In her lucid moments, she was still single-minded, still had some fight left. She continued to think a great deal about the Army's work and especially about its women. She cared deeply about "those women who are so dear to me and to my principles—our female officers all over the world."[20] She had presence of mind enough to dictate a letter to the first woman divisional commander, Polly Ashton.

My Dear Captain:

In my sick chamber I have heard of your promotion to the command of a Division with great interest, and with good hope that it may help forward that honorable and useful employment of my own sex in the Master's service, which I have so strongly desired and labored for, and of which I have been enabled in some measure, by the mercy of God, to be an example.

I lie here in a corner of the battlefield, helpless to do more than send out a counsel or two, and give my blessing, and cry to my Father that His presence may be with those who are in the thick of the fight.

I am sure He will be with you and make you a great power for good.

Never forget that He is almighty to save and to keep in the darkest hour. He keeps me through my suffering hours and when the battle is over and the everlasting morning breaks I will meet you at His feet.

Yours forever in His love, Catherine Booth[21]

Later that year Catherine was also concerned about the October Self-Denial week, a time of raising funds from the soldiers and friends of the Army to help support the Army's missionary work. To further that cause, Catherine dictated a letter for Army publications. Titled "Have You Been a Self-Denier?" her letter was published in *The War Cry* on Saturday, October 4, 1890—the day Catherine Booth was promoted to glory. "My Dear Children and Friends," Catherine wrote, "I have loved you much, and in God's strength have helped you a little. Now at His call I am going away from you. The war must go on. *Self denial* will prove your love to Christ. All must do something. I send you my blessing. Fight on and God will be with you. Victory comes at last. I will meet you in heaven."[22]

Catherine had recuperated well enough for the doctors to believe that she might live into the new year. In fact, engagements had been arranged for William, and Catherine was in the good hands of her daughter Emma and her private nurse. However, the hemorrhaging resumed, and this time all knew that the end was quite near. William and other members of the family were hastily summoned to Clacton. That was Wednesday, October 1, 1890.

Catherine slept throughout Thursday evening but was awake with much pain on Friday. The family kept vigil throughout the day and evening as a violent storm raged outside, symbolic to the family of the final battle Catherine was fighting. To comfort her, the family continued to sing some of her favorite hymns, and every once in a while she mustered strength to say a few words.

Catherine had a fitful sleep on Friday night but seemed rather calm and resigned on Saturday. The members of the family one by one said good-bye to her and stayed by her side with William until, at half-past three on Saturday afternoon, October 4, 1890, Catherine Booth went to be with her Lord. A Salvationist in later years wrote a poem about passing from this world into the next, which could well be applied to Catherine.

I would go silently, Lord, when I come to Thee;
Glide as some gallant barque into the mighty dark.

Softly and gently ride o'er the receding tide;
Steer from the shores of time t'ward an eternal clime.
Lord, on a quiet sea, let me sail home to Thee.[23]

The vacant chair in the first-floor parlor was a reminder to everyone of the emptiness in their lives with Catherine's passing. The family was for a time inconsolable. Booth-Tucker wrote, "The anguish of bereavement is the necessary penalty of love."[24] News of Catherine's death was released to the public. *The War Cry* contained not only a detailed account of her last hours by Booth-Tucker but a letter from William Booth, in which he wrote:

> The Army will mourn her loss and has reasons for it; but she will live on, and on, and on in the hearts and lives of thousands and thousands of her daughters. Never before, perhaps, save in the case of one, and that one the most "blessed among women," the mother of our Lord, has there lived a saint who has had the privilege during her lifetime of seeing so many of her own sex encouraged and emboldened by her example, working out her principles, and walking in her steps.[25]

Telegrams and letters, words of condolence as well as of praise, poured into London when news of Catherine's death was out. The article in the *Manchester Guardian* said, "It would be difficult to say whether Mrs. Booth has been more remarkable as a preacher and organizer or as a mother. In the first capacity her eloquence has been recognized by large audiences which have flocked to hear her in every large city. She has probably done more in her own person to establish the right of women to preach the Gospel than anyone else who has ever lived."[26] *The Methodist Times* cited Catherine Booth as "the greatest Methodist woman of this generation."[27] And from the pulpit of the City Temple on the morning after Catherine's death, Dr. Joseph Parker said:

> Since I came to the church this morning I have heard of a very solemn incident, yet one that has been almost daily expected for many months. Mrs. Booth, of The Salvation Army, died yester-

day afternoon. She has ceased to fight; she is with God's angels. Mrs. Booth has not gone into the unseen world on the strength of a new religious fancy, a new-fangled theory, a startling speculation. She threw her arms around the Cross, and went into the unseen sanctuary trusting to the all-saving and all-cleansing blood of Christ.

She was a valiant soldier of the Cross, eloquent, clear-sighted, firm to soldierliness, yet gentle to motherliness. She fought a good fight and died like a warrior who had won a crown of glory. We sympathise with General Booth and his whole family; we pray that they may triumph here also, to show that they can suffer patiently as well as fight strenuously and heroically. Everyone bears loving witness to the ability and zeal of the deceased. She won all hearts. She has left us the legacy and the responsibility of a great example. Who will take up her work, or take up any little portion of it? She does not ask to be admired, she asks to be replaced.[28]

It had been decided to take Catherine's body to London. She was placed in a plain oak coffin with a glass cover so that mourners could see her one last time. The Army flag was draped over the coffin lid, and a brass plate was affixed to the coffin that read, "Catherine Booth. The Mother of The Salvation Army. Born 17th January, 1829. Died 4th October, 1890. More than Conqueror."[29] The General and others who had been at Clacton went to London to prepare for the memorial service and the funeral. The trusted family friend, George Scott Railton, was put in charge of the funeral arrangements.

Clapton Congress Hall, the large Salvation Army Corps seating five thousand, and a place Catherine knew so well, was used for the viewing. The glass-covered casket was placed at the northern end of the hall, and the seats in the center of the hall were cleared away so that people could more easily file by the casket. Cadets assisted with keeping the crowds moving, and—typical of the breadth of Catherine's ministry—both the poor and the rich came to pay tribute. The viewing lasted five days, and it was estimated that fifty thousand people filed past.

On Monday, October 13, Catherine's body was taken from Clapton to the Olympia for the funeral service. The Olympia was an exhibition center in the northern part of Hammersmith opened only a few years earlier. The journey was a reminder of Catherine's ministry in both the East End and the West End. The cavernous structure could accommodate thirty-six thousand people when all the galleries and center of the building were used. Every seat was taken, and countless people had to be turned away. *The War Cry* reported that "Olympia is now used as a skating rink, and is profusely decorated with Chinese lanterns, Japanese umbrellas, and the like. None of these had been disturbed. We met the world on its own ground that night, in one supreme engagement to manifest the faith which overcomes it and annihilates death!"[30]

The funeral—or the promotion to glory service, as Catherine would have it—was scheduled for 6:00 P.M., and at that time the congregation rose to sing Isaac Watts's "When I Survey the Wondrous Cross." Because it was impossible for everyone in that large auditorium to hear the announcements, instructions were printed in large letters on posters that were lifted up at certain intervals, telling the congregation to "Rise and Sing" or "Pray."

The War Cry reported the funeral in great detail, taking note especially of the procession down the center aisle of the flag-covered casket carried on the shoulders of several officers. Booth-Tucker has described the scene this way:

> Slowly and sorrowfully, yet with an air of mingled hope and triumph, the advance-guard of men and women officers filed their way, bearing the flags of various nations, together with those of some of the oldest corps presented in early days by Mrs. Booth. Others carried many-coloured bannerettes. White badges on the left arm and white streamers from the flag-pole took the place of customary crepe, and taught that they who mourned mourned not as those who had no hope; that heaven was a reality, and that they believed the Army Mother to be there.
>
> And when, borne on the shoulders of a band of officers, Mrs. Booth's mortal remains entered and passed slowly down the hall,

preceded by her faithful nurse, who carried the flag under which she had breathed her last, few could restrain their tears, and it seemed as if a visible wave of sympathetic sorrow swept over the hearts of the entire audience.[31]

The singing, praying, and preaching proceeded according to plan in the midst of great grief. But in traditional Salvation Army style, and in conformity with Catherine's custom at the conclusion of her preaching services, an invitation was extended to the congregation to consecrate themselves to God. Hundreds responded to this appeal by rising to their feet, and at the conclusion of the memorial service, there was a recessional and the crowds dispersed.

All that was left was the burial service. British pageantry and the Booth flair for the dramatic were instrumental in planning this. It had been determined that on Tuesday morning, October 14, Catherine's body would be borne on an open hearse from International Headquarters on Queen Victoria Street to the Abney Park Cemetery at Stoke Newington, a distance of about four miles. Three thousand Salvation Army officers were the only ones allowed to march with the Booth family in the funeral procession; the thousands of other officers and soldiers who would have liked to have such an honor formed only part of those viewing the procession. The entire Booth family followed the casket save only Ballington and Maud, who were then The Salvation Army national commanders in America and were unable to be present.

Admission to the cemetery had been limited to ten thousand persons, and the platform that had been erected for the occasion sat fifteen hundred. After the march through the streets of London and the cemetery, the coffin was placed on the platform. Around it sat William, his children, other members of the Booth family, and some officers. Commissioner George Scott Railton led the service. Songs were sung, prayers offered, Scripture read, tributes given, and then William rose to speak. The love between Catherine and William was genuine and indeed one of the great love relationships of that Victorian world. William was inconsolable but nevertheless knew that he had an obligation to speak at this moment as a last tribute to his departed wife and the leader of an international Army whose followers were awaiting his words. William Booth said:

My beloved Comrades and Friends:

You will readily understand that I find it a difficulty to talk to you this afternoon. To begin with, I could not be willing to talk without an attempt to make you hear, and sorrow doesn't feel like shouting.

Yet I cannot resist the opportunity of looking you in the face and blessing you in the name of the Lord, and in the name of our beloved one, who is looking down upon us, if she is not actually with us in this throng today.

As I have come riding through these, I suppose, hundreds of thousands of people this afternoon, who have bared their heads and who have blessed me in the name of the Lord at almost every revolution of the carriage wheels, my mind has been full of two feelings, which alternate—one is uppermost one moment, and the other the next—and yet which blend and amalgamate with each other; and these are the feeling of sorrow and the feeling of gratitude.

Those who know me—and I don't think I am very difficult to understand—and those who knew my darling, my beloved, will, I am sure, understand how it is that my heart should be rent with sorrow.

If you had a tree that had grown up in your garden, under your window, which for forty years had been your shadow from the burning sun, whose flowers had been the adornment and beauty of your life, whose fruit had been almost the very stay of your existence, and the gardener had come along and swung his glittering axe and cut it down before your eyes, I think you would feel as though you had a blank—it might not be a big one—but a little blank in your life!

If you had had a servant who, for all this long time, had served you without fee or reward, who had administered, for very love, to your health and comfort, and who had suddenly passed away, you would miss that servant!

If you had had a counsellor who, in hours—continually occurring—of perplexity and amazement, had ever advised you, and
seldom advised wrong; whose advice you had followed and seldom had reason to regret it; and the counsellor, while you are in
the same intricate mazes of your existence, had passed away, you
would miss that counsellor.

If you had had a friend who had understood your very nature,
the rise and fall of your feelings, the bent of your thoughts, and
the purpose of your existence; a friend whose communion had
ever been pleasant—the most pleasant of all other friends, to
whom you had ever turned with satisfaction—and your friend
had been taken away, you would feel some sorrow at the loss!

If you had had a mother for your children who had cradled
and nursed and trained them for the service of the living God, in
which you most delighted; a mother indeed—who had never
ceased to bear their fortunes on her heart and who afterwards
was willing to pour forth that heart's blood in order to nourish
them—and that darling mother had been taken from your side,
you would feel it a sorrow!

If you had had a wife, a sweet love of a wife, who for forty
years had never given you real cause for grief; a wife who had
stood with you side by side in the battle's front, who had been a
comrade to you, ever willing to interpose herself between you and
the enemy and ever the strongest when the battle was fiercest, and
your beloved one had fallen before your eyes, I am sure there
would be some excuse for your sorrow!

Well, my comrades, you can roll all these qualities into one personality and what would be lost in each I have lost in all. There
has been taken away from me the delight of my eyes, the inspiration of my soul, and we are about to lay all that remains of her
in the grave. I have been looking right at the bottom of it here,
and calculating how soon they may bring and lay me alongside
of her, and my cry to God has been that every remaining hour of
my life may make me readier to come and join her in death, to go
and embrace her in life in the Eternal City!

And yet, my comrades (for I won't detain you), my heart is full
of gratitude, too, that swells and makes me forget my sorrow, that
the long valley of the shadow of death has been trodden, and that
out of the dark tunnel she has emerged into the light of day. Death

came to her with all his terrors, brandishing his heart before her for two long years and nine months. Again and again she went down to the river's edge to receive his last thrust, as she thought, but ever coming back to life again. Thank God, she will see him no more—she is more than conqueror over the last enemy!

Death came to take her away from her loved employment. She loved the fight! Her great sorrow to the last moment was: "I cannot be with you when the clouds lower, when friends turn and leave you, and sorrows come sweeping over you; I shall no longer be there to put my arms round you and cheer you on!"

But she went away to help us! She promised me many a time that what she could do for us in the Eternal City should be done! The valley to her was a dark one in having to tear her heart away from so many whom she loved so well. Again and again she said, "The roots of my affections are very deep." But they had to be torn up. One after another she gave us up; she made the surrender with many loving words of counsel, and left us to her Lord.

This afternoon my heart has been full of gratitude because her soul is now with Jesus. She had a great capacity for suffering and a great capacity for joy, and her heart is full of joy this afternoon.

My heart has also been full of gratitude because God lent me for so long a season such a treasure. I have been thinking, if I had to point out her three great qualities to you here, they would be: First, she was *good*. She was washed in the Blood of the Lamb. To the last moment her cry was, "A sinner saved by grace." She was a thorough hater of shams, hypocrisies, and make-believes.

Second, she was *love*. Her whole soul was full of tender, deep compassion. I was thinking this morning that she suffered more in her lifetime through her compassion for poor dumb animals than some doctors of divinity let out for the wide, wide world of suffering mortals! Oh, how she loved, how she compassioned, how she pitied the suffering poor! How she longed to put her arms round the sorrowful and help them!

Lastly, she was a *warrior*. She liked the fight. She was not one who said to others, "Go!" but, "Here, let *me* go!" And when there was the necessity she cried, "I *will* go." I never knew her flinch until her poor body compelled her to lie aside.

Another thought fills my soul with praise—that she has inspired so many to follow in her track.

My comrades, I am going to meet her again. I have never turned from her these forty years for any journeyings on my mission of mercy but I have longed to get back, and have counted the weeks, days, and hours which should take me again to her side. When she has gone away from me it has been just the same. And now she has gone away for the last time. What, then, is there left for me to do? Not to count the weeks, the days, and the hours which shall bring me again into her sweet company, seeing that I know not what will be on the morrow, nor what an hour may bring forth. My work plainly is to fill up the weeks, the days, and the hours, and cheer my poor heart as I go along with the thought that, when I have served my Christ and my generation according to the will of God—which I vow this afternoon I will, to the last drop of my blood—then I trust that she will bid me welcome to the skies, as He bade her.

God bless you all. Amen![32]

Following William's tribute, Catherine's body was lowered into an awaiting grave while the congregation sang one verse of a song by Herbert Booth:

Blessed Lord, in Thee is refuge, Safety for my trembling soul,
Power to lift my head when drooping "Midst the angry bil-
    lows" roll!
I will trust Thee! All my life Thou shalt control![33]

Commissioner Railton then pronounced the words of The Salvation Army burial service. Bramwell Booth led the audience in the covenant that, followed by the benediction, concluded the service. The covenant read:

Blessed Lord—We do solemnly promise—Here by the side of this open grave—And before each other—That we will be true to our cause—And valiant in Thy service—That we will devote ourselves to the great end of saving souls—That we will be faithful to Thee— Faithful to one another—and faithful to a dying world—Till we meet our beloved mother in the morning. Amen.[34]

The service was ended.

At an officers' meeting on the night after Catherine's funeral, William said, "She called me up at four one morning in the week she died, to give me a solemn message. It was that she feared the women of The Salvation Army were not going to rise up to take the place she wished for them."[35] Catherine, being dead, yet spoke, and her influence lingered long beyond her death, especially throughout the lengthy ministry of William, who was not promoted to glory until 1912. He spoke often of her in public, and as the years passed she became a figure larger than life to Salvationists.[36]

To be sure, her leaving at this time in Salvation Army history was difficult. The Army was ready to launch a newly organized social ministry, made known to the British public with the publication of William's book *In Darkest England and the Way Out*. Also, the Army was still expanding its missionary work, and the second generation had not yet begun to take over the Army's leadership. However, Catherine interpreted the events of life as providential. All was known to God, and in Catherine's thinking, all was ultimately to the glory of God.

In her leaving she entrusted a legacy of ministry for women as well as men, serving the kingdom of Christ with all the gifts available to them, through the agency of an Army she helped create. The religion of the Bible and of Jesus was nothing to Catherine if not practical. It had to do with everyday life, and the heart as well as the mind had to be brought to the service of religion completely—without deceit or hypocrisy—if one were to be a true follower of the Christ. This is what she sought for herself, and this is what she wished for all who joined the Army or were in sympathy with its methods and message. She was pleased to be remembered for many things—wife, mother, preacher, teacher, writer—but what delighted her most was that she would be remembered for being the mother of an Army.

Notes

Introduction

1. W. T. Stead, *Mrs. Booth of The Salvation Army* (London: James Nisbet and Co., 1900), 168. As will be mentioned in this biography, W. T. Stead was a great admirer of Catherine Booth and attributed the founding of The Salvation Army primarily to Catherine. Indeed, one of the early titles of this book by Stead was *Life of Mrs. Booth: The Founder of The Salvation Army*.

Chapter 1: *Beginnings*

1. Owen Chadwick, *The Victorian Church*, vol. 2 (London: SCM Press, 1987), 106. See also Kenneth Slack, *The City Temple—A Hundred Years* (London: Albert Clark and Company, 1974).

2. "Mrs. Booth at the City Temple," *The War Cry* (June 30, 1888), 9. Note that unless otherwise indicated, references to *The War Cry* in this book refer to the English *War Cry*. Catherine Booth did speak subsequently to Salvationists, but this address at the City Temple was her last full public sermon. See "Mrs. Booth's Welcome and Address," *The War Cry* (April 20, 1889), 3.

3. "Mrs. Booth's Last Public Address," *The War Cry* (October 18, 1890), 1.

4. Ibid., 2.

5. Ibid.

6. Ibid.

7. Ibid.

8. "Mrs. Booth's Last Public Address," *The War Cry* (October 25, 1890), 10.

9. Catherine Bramwell-Booth, *Catherine Booth* (London: Hodder and Stoughton, 1970), 423.

10. Booth Papers, Mss. 64806, The British Library. See also Stead, *Mrs. Booth*, 22.

11. Frederick De Latour Booth-Tucker, *The Life of Catherine Booth, The Mother of The Salvation Army*, vol. 1 (New York: Revell, 1892), 13.

12. Stead, *Mrs. Booth*, 19.

13. See, for example, her chapter "The Training of Children—An Address to Parents" in her book *Papers on Practical Religion* (London: International Headquarters, 1891), 3–32. She concludes this chapter by stating the following:

I cannot close these remarks without lifting up my voice against the practice now so prevalent amongst respectable families, of sending children to boarding schools before their principles are formed or their characters developed. Parents are led away by the professedly religious character of schools, forgetting that, even supposing the master or governess may be all that can be desired, a school is a little *world* where all the elements of unrenewed human nature are at work with as great variety, sub-tlety, and power as in the great world outside. You would shrink from exposing your child to the temptation and danger of association with unconverted worldly men and women, why should you expose them to the influence of children of the *same* character, who are not unfrequently sent to these schools because they have become utterly vitiated and unmanageable at home? I have listened to many a sad story of the consequences of these school associations, and early made up my mind to keep my children under *my own influence,* at least until they had attained that maturity in grace and principle which would be an effectual safeguard against ungodly associations. To this end I have rejected several very tempting offers in the way of educational advantage, and every day I am increasingly thankful for having been enabled to do so. God has laid on *you,* parents, the *responsibility* of training your children, and you cannot possibly *delegate* that responsibility to another with-out endangering their highest interests for *time and for eternity*.

14. Bramwell-Booth, *Catherine Booth,* 53.

15. Ibid., 120.

16. Stead, *Mrs. Booth,* 19.

17. Booth-Tucker, *The Life of Catherine Booth,* 1:16.

18. Ibid., 17–18.

19. Chadwick, *The Victorian Church,* 1:378.

20. "As a quite young girl, I early made up my mind as to certain qualifications, which I regarded as indispensable to the forming of any engagement.... Another resolution that I made was that I would never marry a man who was not a total abstainer, and this from conviction, and not merely to gratify me" (Stead, *Mrs. Booth,* 57, 59).

21. See Harold Begbie, *The Life of General William Booth,* vol. 1 (New York: Macmil-lan, 1920), 232–33.

22. For two examples of this, see William Booth, *Religion for Every Day* (London: The Salvationist Publishing and Supplies, n.d.), 106: "Animal food should not be taken, at most, more than once a day. There are multitudes of men and women who would be wiser, healthier, happier, and holier without meat altogether. I recommend everybody who has not made the experiment of total abstinence from flesh meat in every form to do so at once. Give it a month's trial." See also Bramwell Booth, "The Advantages of a Vege-tarian Diet" (London: The London Vegetarian Society, n.d.).

23. *The Orders and Regulations for Soldiers of The Salvation Army* (1943), chapter IV, section 8 reads: "A salvation soldier should be kind-hearted, and deal lovingly with all those with whom he is associated. A soldier should manifest love and gentleness espe-cially in connection with . . . the animal world. To inflict or to witness cruelty should be impossible for a soldier in whom has been born a love to save men from any form of mis-ery. Not only should he avoid causing any unnecessary hardship on animals but, as far as he has opportunity, he should be ever willing to lend a hand to aid or relieve any suf-fering creature." See Bramwell-Booth, *Catherine Booth,* 21–22.

24. See Stead, *Mrs. Booth,* 195–96.

25. Booth-Tucker, *The Life of Catherine Booth,* 1:25. A brief biography of Catherine Booth written by S. Carvosso Gauntlett was titled *Queen of Protests,* and the cover of the biography depicted a horse being whipped and young Catherine interfering with that cruel act.

26. Booth-Tucker, *The Life of Catherine Booth,* 1:26.

27. Ibid.

28. Henry D. Rack, *Reasonable Enthusiast: John Wesley and the Rise of Methodism* (Philadelphia: Trinity Press International, 1989), 241.

29. Booth-Tucker, *The Life of Catherine Booth,* 1:47.

30. It is evident that by this time in her life Catherine Booth had read Finney's *Lec-tures on Revivals of Religion* and that this one book, above all others, would be the one

she continually encouraged those around her to read. The *Lectures* were widely read in England. "The twenty-two lectures which make up the volume, *Lectures on Revivals of Religion*, were delivered on successive Friday evenings at the Chatham Street Chapel and recorded by Joshua Leavitt, editor of the *New York Evangelist*. After they were edited by Finney himself, they were published as a series in the *New York Evangelist* to boost a sagging circulation brought on by Leavitt's strongly abolitionist editorial policy. Later, in 1835, they were published as a book. The volume was revised and reissued in 1868" (Garth M. Rosell, "Charles Grandison Finney and the Rise of the Benevolence Empire" [Ph.D. diss. University of Minnesota, 1971], 181 n. 2). See also John Stanley Mattson, "Charles Grandison Finney and the Emerging Tradition of 'New Measure' Revivalism" (Ph.D. diss. University of North Carolina at Chapel Hill, 1970).

31. Booth-Tucker, *The Life of Catherine Booth,* 1:50–51.

32. Rack, *Reasonable Enthusiast,* 393.

33. Stead, *Mrs. Booth,* 35.

34. Ibid., 36.

35. Ibid., 37.

36. Ibid., 38–39.

37. Ibid., 43.

38. Bramwell-Booth, *Catherine Booth,* 47.

39. This is found in Catherine's earliest extant letter written to her mother. Catherine is writing about the servant, Maria: "Her church holds Calvinistic doctrines. I went to her chapel once, but could not receive all I heard, though I believe the minister was a true Christian. I am sorry she has received these opinions, and am endeavoring by simple Scripture, which is the best weapon, to show her the true extent of the blessed Atonement. She says I have thrown much light upon her mind, and she desires to be led into all truth. If so, the Spirit will guide her. May it be so. Amen!" (Booth Papers, Mss. 64803, The British Library).

40. Ibid.

41. Begbie, *The Life of General William Booth,* 1:9.

42. Chadwick, *The Victorian Church,* 1:379.

43. Booth-Tucker, *The Life of Catherine Booth,* 1:66–67. For a more balanced view of James Caughey and a brief description of his methods and influence on Catherine and William, see Norman H. Murdoch, *Origins of The Salvation Army* (Knoxville: University of Tennessee Press, 1994), 7–12. For an excellent treatment of Caughey see chapter 4 as well as other references in Richard Carwardine, *Transatlantic Revivalism: Popular Evangelicalism in Britain and America, 1790–1865* (Westport, Conn.: Greenwood Press, 1978), and John Kent, *Holding the Fort: Studies in Victorian Revivalism* (London: Epworth Press, 1978), 77–87. For a treatment of Finney, see Carwardine, chapter 5 and various references in Kent.

44. Carwardine, *Transatlantic Revivalism,* 131.

45. Booth-Tucker, *The Life of Catherine Booth,* 1:70.

Chapter 2: *Providential Meeting*

1. Begbie, *The Life of General William Booth,* 1:27.

2. See the copy of the baptismal certificate for William Booth in The Salvation Army International Heritage Centre. In 1855 the marriage certificate for William and Catherine mentioned both Samuel Booth (deceased) and John Mumford as "Gentleman." A copy of the marriage certificate is also held at The Salvation Army International Heritage Centre.

3. St. John Ervine, *God's Soldier: General William Booth,* vol. 1 (New York: Macmillan, 1935), 11.

4. See Begbie, *The Life of General William Booth,* 1:42. St. John Ervine gives the date of Samuel Booth's death as September 23, 1843, and disputes Begbie's date. See Ervine, *God's Soldier,* 1:31.

5. Begbie, *The Life of General William Booth*, 1:89.

6. St. John Ervine in *God's Soldier*, 1:47, incorrectly states that James Caughey had been banished from Nottingham in 1851 during this purge of the Connexion. Caughey had been sent out of England in 1847 and did not return until 1857. See Murdoch, *Origins of The Salvation Army*, 11, and Carwardine, *Transatlantic Revivalism*, 102, 175.

7. Begbie in *The Life of General William Booth* gives the name as Mr. E. J. Rabbits (1:111), and Booth-Tucker consistently misspells the name as Rabbitts.

8. Bramwell-Booth, *Catherine Booth*, 53.

9. Begbie, *The Life of General William Booth*, 1:112.

10. Booth-Tucker, *The Life of Catherine Booth*, 1:81.

11. See the many references to temperance in Keith J. Hardman, *Charles Grandison Finney 1792–1875: Revivalist and Reformer* (Grand Rapids: Baker, 1987).

12. Begbie, *The Life of General William Booth*, 1:113.

13. Ibid. See "The Army Mother. An Interview with the General," *The War Cry* (October 8, 1910), 8, in which William incorrectly gives April 10, 1852, as the day he met Catherine Mumford.

14. Begbie, *The Life of General William Booth*, 1:125–26.

15. Ibid., 125.

16. Booth Papers, Mss. 64799, The British Library.

17. It is clear that this is the date of their engagement. At least twice Catherine provides the wrong date in later letters. A year after their engagement she wrote: "We are one in all things; it will be twelve months on the 13th May since, bowed together at this sofa, we solemnly gave ourselves to each other and to God." And in 1857 she wrote the following to her parents: "It was Good Friday, April 10, the anniversary of our engagement. . . ." (Bramwell-Booth, *Catherine Booth*, 69, 164). Murdoch in his dissertation titled "The Salvation Army: An Anglo-American Revivalist Social Mission" (Ph.D. diss., University of Cincinnati, 1985) 96, n. 22, discusses this date. Murdoch is in error when in that endnote he states that "Ervine, 1, 57, for some reason cited May 5." A correction sheet inserted in Ervine clarifies that this was a misprint in the book and should have read May 15 instead of May 5. Ervine was correct in the date of the engagement. Murdoch did not include this discussion in his *Origins of The Salvation Army*.

18. Bramwell-Booth, *Catherine Booth*, 47.

19. Booth Papers, Mss. 64799.

20. Booth-Tucker, *The Life of Catherine Booth*, 1:98.

21. Bramwell-Booth, *Catherine Booth*, 73.

22. Begbie, *The Life of General William Booth*, 1:131–32. Begbie was quoting from "some autobiographical notes of a more or less fragmentary nature which were never published," (1:130).

23. For Wesley's most polemic stance against the Calvinist doctrine of election as taught by Whitefield and others, see Wesley's sermon "Free Grace," first published in 1739, in Frank Baker, *The Works of John Wesley*, vol. 3 (Nashville: Abingdon Press, 1986), 542–63.

24. Begbie, *The Life of General William Booth*, 1:133.

25. Booth-Tucker, *The Life of Catherine Booth*, 2:151.

26. Rack, *Reasonable Enthusiast*, 313.

27. Booth-Tucker, *The Life of Catherine Booth*, 1:105.

28. Booth Papers, Mss. 64800, The British Library, letter written March 20, 1853.

29. Ibid.

30. Booth Papers, Mss. 64799.

31. Ibid.

32. Begbie, *The Life of General William Booth*, 1:169.

33. Booth Papers, Mss. 64799.

34. Ibid. See also Booth-Tucker, *The Life of Catherine Booth*, 1:114–15, where this letter is quoted, although with some slight inaccuracies. See also Catherine's later remarks on this subject in Catherine Booth, "Christianity and the Drink Traffic," in *The Highway*

of Our God (London: The Salvation Army, n.d.), 88–94; and Catherine Booth, "Strong Drink Versus Christianity" in *Papers on Practical Religion,* 35–50.

35. Booth-Tucker, *The Life of Catherine Booth,* 1:133.

36. Catherine Booth, "Courtship by Principle," in *The Highway of Our God,* 74–75. See also Booth-Tucker, *The Life of Catherine Booth,* 1:134, who is quoting perhaps from the original manuscript of this material before it was edited by Catherine for inclusion in *The Highway of Our God.* The wording in the third paragraph is a bit stronger:

> In the first place, each of the parties ought to be satisfied that there are to be found in the other such qualities as would make them friends if they were of the same sex. In other words, there should be a congeniality and compatibility of temperament. For instance, it must be a fatal error, fraught with perpetual misery, for a man who has mental gifts and high aspirations to marry a woman who is only fit to be a mere drudge; or for a woman of refinement and ability to marry a man who is good for nothing better than to follow the plough, or look after a machine. And yet, how many seek for a mere bread-winner, or a housekeeper, rather than for a friend, a counsellor and companion. Unhappy marriages are usually the consequences of too great a disparity of mind, age, temperament, training, or antecedents.

37. Catherine Booth, *The Highway of Our God,* 75.

38. Ibid.

39. Ibid., 76.

40. Ibid.

41. Ibid.

42. Ibid., 77. Note an example of Catherine and William's trying to resolve a difference of opinion through their correspondence, even during their engagement, in Bramwell-Booth, *Catherine Booth,* 102–4.

43. Booth Papers, Mss. 64800.

44. Booth Papers, Mss. 64801, The British Library.

45. See W. J. Townsend, *Life of Alexander Kilham* (London: J. C. Watts, n.d.).

46. Booth-Tucker, *The Life of Catherine Booth,* 1:145–46.

47. Ibid., 1:149.

48. Chadwick, *The Victorian Church,* 2:288.

49. Booth Papers, Mss. 64801.

50. Begbie, *The Life of General William Booth,* 1:206–7.

51. Booth-Tucker, *The Life of Catherine Booth,* 1:162.

52. Ibid., 171. Booth-Tucker quotes this article at length but does not give the precise reference. Robert Sandall gives the date as June 1855 in *The History of The Salvation Army,* 7 vols. (Robert Sandall, vols. 1, 2, and 3; Arch Wiggins, vols. 4 and 5; Frederick Coutts, vols. 6 and 7), (London: Thomas Nelson, 1947–1986), 1:66. I have as yet been unable to find this article in the *Methodist New Connexion Magazine,* although I have no reason to discount Booth-Tucker's or Sandall's references to it. The article was reprinted many years later in *Harbor Lights* (September 1898), 264–66.

53. Booth-Tucker, *The Life of Catherine Booth,* 1:176.

54. Ibid., 176–77.

55. See references to this in a letter from William to Catherine from Holbeach dated January 1854 in Ibid., 153.

56. Ibid., 187.

57. Ibid.

58. Booth Papers, Mss. 64799, letter dated March 17, 1853.

59. Quoted in Bramwell-Booth, *Catherine Booth,* 65. In later life William would say this of Catherine's mother: "She was a very superior woman, possessing a remarkable character, notable for its simplicity, nobility, strength, and religion" ("The Army Mother," 9).

Chapter 3: *The Gathering Storm*

1. Booth-Tucker, *The Life of Catherine Booth,* 1:196.
2. Booth Papers, Mss. 64803, The British Library.
3. Bramwell-Booth, *Catherine Booth,* 108, 162.
4. Booth Papers, Mss. 64803.
5. Ibid.
6. Ibid.
7. Booth-Tucker, *The Life of Catherine Booth,* 1:237.
8. Booth Papers, Mss. 64803.
9. Booth-Tucker, *The Life of Catherine Booth,* 1:240.
10. Stead, *Mrs. Booth,* 50.
11. Murdoch, *Origins of The Salvation Army,* 8.
12. Booth-Tucker, *The Life of Catherine Booth,* 1:247.
13. Bramwell-Booth, *Catherine Booth,* 162.
14. Booth-Tucker, *The Life of Catherine Booth,* 1:247.
15. Murdoch, *Origins of The Salvation Army,* 8–9.
16. Booth-Tucker, *The Life of Catherine Booth,* 1:271.
17. Ibid., 1:273.
18. See David Luker, "Revivalism in Theory and Practice: The Case of Cornish Methodism," *Journal of Ecclesiastical History,* 37, no. 4 (October 1986): 603–19.
19. Rack, *Reasonable Enthusiast,* 172.
20. Ibid., 493.
21. Ervine, *God's Soldier,* 1:211.
22. Booth-Tucker, *The Life of Catherine Booth,* 1:285.
23. Rack, *Reasonable Enthusiast,* 353.
24. Catherine Booth, "The Training of Children—An Address to Parents," in *Papers on Practical Religion,* 11–12.
25. Murdoch, *Origins of The Salvation Army,* 11.
26. Booth-Tucker, *The Life of Catherine Booth,* 1:291.
27. Booth Papers, Mss. 64804, The British Library.
28. Booth-Tucker, *The Life of Catherine Booth,* 1:298.
29. Ervine, *God's Soldier,* 1:212.
30. Booth Papers, Mss. 64804.
31. Ibid.
32. Ibid.
33. Ibid.
34. Ibid.
35. Ibid.
36. Ibid.
37. Ibid., Catherine to her mother in a letter dated June 17, 1858.

Chapter 4: *Gateshead*

1. Booth Papers, Mss. 64804.
2. Booth-Tucker, *The Life of Catherine Booth,* 1:324.
3. Ibid.
4. Ibid., 326.
5. Booth Papers, Mss. 64804.
6. Booth-Tucker, *The Life of Catherine Booth,* 1:337. See also Catherine's letter to her parents written sometime in September 1860, where she describes her work with alcoholics in Booth Papers, Mss. 64805, The British Library.
7. Booth-Tucker, *The Life of Catherine Booth,* 1:337.

8. Ibid., 338.

9. William Booth, "What Is The Salvation Army?" *The Contemporary Review* (August 1882), 181.

10. Booth-Tucker, *The Life of Catherine Booth*, 1:371.

11. Ervine, *God's Soldier*, 1:227.

12. Booth Papers, Mss. 64805.

13. Ibid.

14. Baker, *The Works of John Wesley*, 2:275. See also Wesley's sermon "On Dress," in 3:247–61.

15. Booth Papers, Mss. 64805.

16. Booth-Tucker, *The Life of Catherine Booth*, 1:376.

17. Ibid., 379.

18. John Wesley, *A Plain Account of Christian Perfection* (Kansas City, Mo.: Beacon Hill Press, 1966), 114. This was Wesley's account of his teaching of holiness from the years 1725 to 1777.

19. Ibid., 115.

20. John R. Tyson, ed., *Charles Wesley: A Reader* (New York: Oxford University Press, 1989), 39.

21. Wesley, "Original Sin," first preached in 1759, in Baker, *The Works of John Wesley*, 2:185. Albert Outler, the editor of John Wesley's sermons in these *Works*, writes this in a footnote on that page: "The recovery of the defaced image of God is the axial theme of Wesley's soteriology."

22. Rack, *Reasonable Enthusiast*, 156–57.

23. Ibid., 389.

24. Baker, *The Works of John Wesley*, 1:263.

25. Booth Papers, Mss. 64806.

26. Wesley, "On Working Out Our Own Salvation," in Baker, *The Works of John Wesley*, 3:204.

27. Booth Papers, Mss. 64805.

28. Chick Yuill, "Restoring the Image (Catherine Booth's Holiness Teaching)" in Clifford W. Kew, ed., *Catherine Booth—Her Continuing Relevance* (London: The Salvation Army International Headquarters, 1990), 62.

29. Booth-Tucker, *The Life of Catherine Booth*, 1:382–83.

30. Ibid., 384.

31. Booth Papers, Mss. 64805. Booth-Tucker quotes from this important letter in his biography but inexplicably omits the beginning of the sentence: "In reading that precious book 'The Higher Life'. . . . " Such a reference is important in order to understand the rest of what Catherine wrote. Her reference was to William Edwin Boardman's book *The Higher Christian Life*, and Catherine followed with what she learned from that important source. Boardman was an American holiness evangelist, and one author notes that "though all but forgotten today, it is one of the most influential books on the subject of holiness in the latter half of the nineteenth century and underwent numerous reprints both in Britain and America." Yuill, "Restoring the Image," 68.

32. For an example of Catherine Booth's writings on holiness, see her three-part series "The Perfect Heart" in these issues of *The War Cry* (English): May 19, 1881, 4; May 26, 1881, 2; and June 2, 1881, 4. See also the reprint of these articles in Catherine's book *Godliness* (Boston: McDonald and Gill Co., 1883), 97–103. In that same book see Catherine's articles titled "Enthusiasm and Full Salvation" (124–27); "Hindrances to Holiness" (128–32); and "Addresses on Holiness" (133–58). The importance of this doctrine to Catherine will again be discussed in chapters dealing with her role in the founding of The Christian Mission and The Salvation Army.

33. There is some difficulty knowing the precise date of this letter. Booth-Tucker gives the date as March 5, 1861. Ervine gives the date as March 15, 1861. Begbie does not make reference to this letter or to Stacey, strange omissions from a biography which was considered to be a definitive biography of William Booth.

34. Booth-Tucker, *The Life of Catherine Booth,* 1:393.

35. Booth-Tucker wrote that Booth received a rather curt answer to his letter, not from Stacey himself, who was ill, but from members of the Annual Committee. "Not a word of counsel, nor a symptom of approval was conveyed, and it was manifest that the proposal would encounter from certain parties as vigorous an opposition as ever" (1:396). St. John Ervine was characteristically critical of Booth-Tucker on this point, and wrote that "Booth-Tucker, incurably sentimental and addicted to discovering the worst in the minds of those who do not instantly agree with him, complains that this letter contained 'not a word of counsel, nor a symptom of approval,' but was manifestly antipathetic to Booth's appeal. As, however, he does not publish the letter, his readers are not able to agree or disagree with his interpretation" (1:234). As mentioned, Harold Begbie publishes neither the letter nor the response, which is inexplicable in that the letter to Stacey is such an important one and is preserved in its entirety in Booth-Tucker.

36. Booth Papers, Mss. 64805.

37. Ervine, *God's Soldier,* 1:238–39.

38. Booth-Tucker, *The Life of Catherine Booth,* 1:412.

39. Ervine, *God's Soldier,* 1:240.

40. Ibid., 243.

41. Ibid., 242.

42. Ibid., 240–41.

43. Ibid., 243.

44. Begbie, *The Life of General William Booth,* 1:287.

45. Bramwell-Booth, *Catherine Booth,* 207.

46. Ervine, *God's Soldier,* 1:243.

47. Booth Papers, Mss. 64805. See Booth-Tucker, *The Life of Catherine Booth,* 1:417–18; Bramwell-Booth, *Catherine Booth,* 208; and Begbie, *The Life of General William Booth,* 1:287. All three authors quote from parts of the letter but omit Catherine's disdain for New Connexion Methodism.

48. Booth Papers, Mss. 64805.

49. Ervine, *God's Soldier,* 1:243.

50. Booth Papers, Mss. 64805, letter written in July 1861.

Chapter 5: *Settled Views*

1. Catherine frequented this church during a time when William was considering entering the Congregational ministry, being discouraged by the doctrinal and organizational controversies within Methodism. Catherine's disagreement with Thomas about the equality of women with men did not, however, sever their personal friendship, as evidenced by Thomas's officiating at Catherine's wedding in 1855. See Booth-Tucker, *The Life of Catherine Booth,* 1:191; Bramwell-Booth, *Catherine Booth,* 145; Begbie, *The Life of General William Booth,* 1:251; Ervine, *God's Soldier,* 1:64.

Bramwell-Booth erroneously attributed Catherine's attendance at Thomas's church to a matter of convenience when she stated, "The Reform Chapel was at rather a distance, and walking there was often beyond Catherine's strength, especially in the bad weather. This led to attendance at a nearby Congregational Church where there was an exceptionally good preacher, Dr. David Thomas" (49). The reason for her attendance, however, was theological and doctrinal, as Booth-Tucker hinted (1:99), and as Ervine stated outright when he noted that Catherine attended the church "in search for a church in which she could find satisfaction." (1:64). This view was supported by Murdoch in "Female Ministry in the Thought and Work of Catherine Booth," *Church History* 53 (Fall 1984): 349. I am likewise convinced that this was the reason and stated so in my article "Settled Views: Catherine Booth and Female Ministry," *Methodist History* 31 (April 1993): 131–47.

2. See Booth Papers, Mss. 64806. See also Booth-Tucker, *The Life of Catherine Booth,* 1:117–23; Bramwell-Booth, *Catherine Booth,* 49–53; Stead, *Mrs. Booth,* 89–90. The date of the writing of this letter is certainly under question. Inexplicably in blue ink at the top of the manuscript in The British Library is the date 1855. This is an error. Pamela Jane Walker refers to this letter in her doctoral dissertation "Pulling the Devil's Kingdom Down: Gender and Popular Culture in The Salvation Army, 1865–1895" (Rutgers The State University of New Jersey, New Brunswick, 1992), 22. See also 61 footnote 14. Walker also gives the date 1855 based on Catherine's words in the letter, "I had the privilege of hearing you preach on April 22nd—55." However, Catherine was mistaken about other dates and may have been in error here. Murdoch is in error in his article "Female Ministry in the Thought and Work of Catherine Booth," where he gives the date of the letter as 1850. The date of this letter is most probably 1853, the date given by Booth-Tucker in *The Life of Catherine Booth,* 1:117. Ervine refers to this dispute over the dating of the letter in *God's Soldier,* 1:125.

3. Booth Papers, Mss. 64806.

4. Ibid.

5. Ibid.

6. Ibid.

7. London University would not admit women to degrees until 1878. Oxford finally followed in 1920 and Cambridge in 1948.

8. Booth Papers, Mss. 64806.

9. Ibid.

10. Catherine Booth, "Courtship by Principle," in *The Highway of Our God,* 76. See also Booth-Tucker, *The Life of Catherine Booth,* 1:135–36, and Stead, *Mrs. Booth,* 57–60. See also Nancy A. Hardesty, *Great Women of Faith* (Grand Rapids: Baker, 1980), 104, and Ruth A. Tucker and Walter Liefeld, *Daughters of the Church* (Grand Rapids: Zondervan, 1987), 265.

11. Stead, *Mrs. Booth,* 94. See also Booth-Tucker, *The Life of Catherine Booth,* 1:125, from whom Stead is quoting without giving the reference.

12. Booth Papers, Mss. 64802, The British Library. Note the similarity of the language in Catherine's article published a year earlier in the *Methodist New Connexion Magazine.* See Booth-Tucker, *The Life of Catherine Booth,* 1:176–77.

13. Begbie, *The Life of General William Booth,* 1:236.

14. William Booth, "Mrs. Booth as a Woman and a Wife," *All The World* (October 1910), 508.

15. Booth-Tucker, *The Life of Catherine Booth,* 1:116–17.

16. Stead, *Mrs. Booth,* 92. His use of "Mrs. Booth" is of course anachronistic here.

17. Bramwell-Booth, *Catherine Booth,* 143.

18. Stead, *Mrs. Booth,* 93. See also W. T. Stead, *General Booth, A Biographical Sketch* (London: Isbister and Company, 1891), 94.

19. See "Phoebe Palmer, 1807–1874" in Hardesty, *Great Women of Faith,* 87–91; the section on Phoebe Palmer in chapter 7, "Trans-Atlantic Reform and Revivalism: Social Workers and Lay Evangelists," 261–64 in Tucker and Liefeld, *Daughters of the Church.* See also Harold E. Raser, *Phoebe Palmer: Her Life and Thought* (Lewiston, N.Y.: Edwin Mellon Press, 1987). For two specific articles on the influence of Phoebe Palmer on Catherine Booth see Lucille Sider Dayton and Donald W. Dayton, "'Your Daughters Shall Prophesy': Feminism in the Holiness Movement," *Methodist History* 14 (January 1976):

67–92; and Margaret McFadden, "The Ironies of Pentecostalism: Phoebe Palmer, World Evangelism, and Female Networks," *Methodist History* 31 (January 1993): 63–75. See also Kate P. Crawford Galea, "'Anchored Behind the Veil': Mystical Vision as a Possible Source of Authority in the Ministry of Phoebe Palmer," *Methodist History* 31 (July 1993): 236–47.

20. Murdoch, *Origins of The Salvation Army,* 18.

21. Booth Papers, Mss. 64805. See also Bramwell-Booth, *Catherine Booth,* 181, and Murdoch, "Female Ministry in the Thought and Work of Catherine Booth," 352. The Booths had something else in common with Phoebe Palmer beyond the issue of female ministry. They also embraced the biblical and Wesleyan doctrine of holiness. There was a later official connection between Phoebe Palmer and The Salvation Army when Mrs. Palmer donated her home on East 15th Street in New York City to The Salvation Army, which became the Army's first home for unwed mothers in America. For further information on the relationship between Phoebe Palmer and the Booths, see Murdoch, *Origins of The Salvation Army,* 16–20.

22. This pamphlet, thirty-two pages in length, was first published in 1859 as *Female Teaching: or the Rev. A. A. Rees versus Mrs. Palmer, Being a Reply to a Pamphlet by the Above Named Gentleman on the Sunderland Revival,* and I have never been able to discover a copy of this original pamphlet. It was republished in London by C. J. Stevenson in 1861. In a letter dated October 18, 1861, Catherine refers to the emendations for a new edition of her pamphlet and felt that it was much improved (Booth Papers, Mss. 64805). The third edition was published by Morgan and Chase in London in 1870. It was with this edition that the title was changed to *Female Ministry; or Women's Right to Preach the Gospel.* Catherine wrote the following in the preface:

> The principle arguments contained in the following pages were published in a pamphlet entitled *Female Teaching,* which, I have reason to know, has been rendered very useful.
>
> In this edition all the controversial portions have been expunged, some new material added, and the whole produced in a cheaper form, and thus, I trust, rendered better adapted for general circulation.
>
> Our only object in this issue is the elicitation of the truth. We hold that error can in the end be profitable to no cause, and least of all to the cause of Christ. If therefore we were not fully satisfied as to the correctness of the views herein set forth, we should fear to subject them to the light; and if we did not deem them of vast importance to the interests of Christ's kingdom, we should prefer to hold them in silence. Believing however that they will bear the strictest investigation, and that their importance cannot easily be over-estimated, we feel bound to propagate them to the utmost of our ability.
>
> In this paper we shall endeavour to meet the most common objections to female ministry, and to present, as far as our space will permit, a thorough examination of the texts generally produced in support of these objections. May the great Head of the Church grant the light of His Holy Spirit to both writer and reader.

This was reprinted in 1891 in London by The Salvation Army Printing and Publishing Offices, in 1909 by The Salvation Army Book Department in London, and in 1975 in New York by The Salvation Army Supplies, Printing, and Publishing Department. Most of the article is reproduced in Catherine Booth, *The Highway of Our God,* 94–105, and in Catherine Booth, *Papers on Practical Religion,* 131–67. See also Booth-Tucker, *The Life of Catherine Booth,* 1:344–49; Bramwell-Booth, *Catherine Booth,* 182–84; Stead, *Mrs. Booth,* 97–103. See also Douglas Clarke, "Female Ministry in The Salvation Army," *The Expository Times* 95 (May 1984): 232–35; Green, "Settled Views," 135–40; Murdoch, "Female Ministry in the Thought and Work of Catherine Booth," 351–54; Murdoch,

Origins of The Salvation Army, 33; and "Female Ministry and the New Revision of the Bible," *The War Cry* (London), July 15, 1885, 1.

The third edition of this pamphlet has been reprinted recently in Donald Dayton, ed., *Holiness Tracts Defending the Ministry of Women* (N. Y.: Garland Publishing, 1985), and Dale Johnson, ed., *Women in English Religion* (Lewiston, N.Y.: Edwin Mellon Press, 1983). One of the finest analyses of this pamphlet was done in Walker, "Pulling the Devil's Kingdom Down," 33–43.

My analysis of the pamphlet is done based on the second edition as well as the third edition, which is very significant for Catherine's more developed views on the subject of women in ministry and the one she chose to include in two of her books in later years.

23. Booth Papers, Mss. 64805, letter written from Catherine to her parents on December 25, 1859.

24. See Catherine's lengthy letter to her parents written on December 25, 1859, describing the pamphlet in Booth Papers, Mss. 64805.

25. Bramwell-Booth, *Catherine Booth,* 183.

26. Catherine Booth, *Female Teaching,* 3. Note that all quotations from this source will be taken from the 1861 edition.

27. Ibid., 3–4.

28. Ibid., 3.

29. Walker, "Pulling the Devil's Kingdom Down," 43.

30. Murdoch, "Female Ministry in the Thought and Work of Catherine Booth," 348. See also Janette Hassey, *No Time for Silence* (Grand Rapids: Zondervan, 1986), 99–100, where Hassey asserts the same thing and compares Catherine Booth's pamphlet with Phoebe Palmer's *Promise of the Father,* written also in 1859. Walker states the same thing in "Pulling the Devil's Kingdom Down," 41, where she writes that "Catherine's pamphlet was not hermeneutically original."

31. Walker, "Pulling the Devil's Kingdom Down," 41.

32. Catherine Booth, *Female Teaching,* 10.

33. Ibid., 16.

34. Ibid.

35. Ibid., 14–15.

36. Catherine Booth, *Female Ministry,* 17. Her arguments from the Galatians passage are more cogently presented in her pamphlets written under the title *Female Ministry.*

37. Ibid., 20.

38. Ibid., 13.

39. Booth-Tucker, *The Life of Catherine Booth,* 1:352.

40. Booth Papers, Mss. 64806.

41. Booth-Tucker, *The Life of Catherine Booth,* 1:353.

42. Booth Papers, Mss. 64806.

43. Ervine, *God's Soldier,* 1:212.

44. Booth-Tucker, *The Life of Catherine Booth,* 1:303.

45. Booth Papers, Mss. 64804.

46. Ibid.

47. Ibid.

48. Stead in his *Mrs. Booth,* 156, incorrectly gives January 1860 as the beginning of her preaching ministry. The American *War Cry* (January 19, 1980) inexplicably gives 1880 as the beginning of Catherine's preaching, and the article stated, "It was the beginning of a great ministry, brief but blessed beyond all human expectation. The full impact of those eight years (1880–1888) may never be known."

49. Booth-Tucker, *The Life of Catherine Booth,* 1:358.

50. "Our Army Mother's First Sermon," *All The World* (June 1897), 245. See also

"Our Army Mother's First Sermon," *Harbor Light* (July 1899), 223; Booth-Tucker, *The Life of Catherine Booth*, 1:358–63; Bramwell-Booth, *Catherine Booth*, 184–87; Stead, *Mrs. Booth*, 156–59.

51. Stead, *Mrs. Booth*, 42.

52. Booth-Tucker, *The Life of Catherine Booth*, 1:359.

53. "Our Army Mother's First Sermon," *All The World*, 245.

54. Ibid.

55. Booth-Tucker, *The Life of Catherine Booth*, 1:362.

56. Booth Papers, Mss. 64802.

57. Booth Papers, Mss. 64805. Booth-Tucker in his biography of Catherine Booth incorrectly dates this letter as September 24, 1860.

58. Ibid.

59. Booth-Tucker, *The Life of Catherine Booth*, 1:436.

60. Ibid., 453–55.

61. Booth Papers, Mss. 64805.

62. Booth-Tucker, *The Life of Catherine Booth*, 1:474.

63. Ibid., 503–4. Although, from Catherine's letters during this time, we know that the Booths also occasionally preached in Wesleyan, Free Methodist, and Baptist chapels in Wales.

64. Booth Papers, Mss. 64806, letter written from Catherine to her parents on April 1, 1863.

65. Booth-Tucker, *The Life of Catherine Booth*, 1:522.

66. See the chapter "A Neighborhood Religion: The Salvation Army and Working-Class Communities" in Walker, "Pulling the Devil's Kingdom Down," 167–219.

67. Booth-Tucker gives this date. St. John Ervine gives May 19 as the date in *God's Soldier*, 1:269.

68. Ervine, *God's Soldier*, 1:269.

69. P. W. Wilson, *General Evangeline Booth of The Salvation Army* (New York: Charles Scribner's Sons, 1948), 44.

70. Begbie, *The Life of General William Booth*, 1:307.

71. Ervine, *God's Soldier*, 1:270.

72. Ibid., 269.

Chapter 6: *The Beginning of a Mission*

1. Ervine, *God's Soldier*, 1:276.

2. Ibid., 277.

3. Ibid.

4. Booth-Tucker, *The Life of Catherine Booth*, 1:547.

5. Murdoch, "The Salvation Army: An Anglo-American Revivalist Social Mission," 88–89.

6. Ervine, *God's Soldier*, 1:282.

7. Booth had proposed the establishment of a Christian Revival Association in *The Revival*. The East London Christian Revival Union was evidently the first name of that association, as attested in a ticket of membership for September 1865 within a month of the opening of the work in the Dancing Academy. The name was changed from these two early names to the East London Christian Revival Society, The East London Christian Mission, and finally in 1870 to The Christian Mission, reflecting the establishment of Christian Mission preaching stations beyond East London. The Christian Mission became The Salvation Army in 1878.

8. Stead, *Mrs. Booth*, 195–96.

9. George Scott Railton, *The Authoritative Life of General William Booth Founder of The Salvation Army* (New York: Reliance Trading Co., 1912), 56.

10. Wilson in *General Evangeline Booth* states this about the names for Eva:
Naturally there arose the question what the child should be called. General Evangeline Booth remembers how Evangeline was the name chosen for her by her mother. But, it has to be added, that Catherine Booth had been reading Uncle Tom's Cabin and she decided that there should be another Little Eva, a joy in the home. Instructions to this effect were given to a proud father but on the register, for some reason, appeared the name, Evelyne, and apparently he really meant it for there is Evelyne in letters that he wrote many years later. However, Evelyne was never other than Eva in the home and on a day that she dimly remembers she was presented to a mouselike lady called Harriet Beecher Stowe, who unwittingly had been created her patron saint. For many years she remained Eva but in due course she came to the United States where she met the veteran, Frances Elizabeth Willard, founder of the Women's Christian Temperance Union, who had learned by experience that prestige is essential to a woman of responsibility if she is to hold her allotted place in the world. Frances Willard advised Eva Booth that she would be wise to assume the use of the full name, Evangeline, to which she was entitled. The suggestion was accepted (26).

11. Ervine, *God's Soldier,* 1:296.

12. Booth-Tucker, *The Life of Catherine Booth,* 1:585–86. Spurgeon's church, the Metropolitan Tabernacle, had been built in 1861 and had a seating capacity of 6,000.

13. The date of the birth of this child is disputed. Both Booth-Tucker and Begbie date the birth as 1867. St. John Ervine gives 1868 as the date and states this in a footnote: "The date of her birth is misstated by Booth-Tucker, who gives the year as 1867. Begbie follows him. Phillimore, in *County Pedigrees,* gives both the day and the year incorrectly. According to him, Lucy was born on April 26, 1867" (1:294). Inexplicably Booth-Tucker in a family tree on page 678 of volume 2 of his *The Life of Catherine Booth* gives 1868 as the date of birth. Bramwell-Booth gives April 28, 1868.

14. Booth-Tucker, *The Life of Catherine Booth,* 1:586.

15. See *The Christian Mission Magazine* (July 1877), 175, and *The Christian Mission Magazine* (November 1878), 305. In the first reference William referred to their nine children, and in the second reference Catherine did the same. See also Arch R. Wiggins, *T. H. K.: A Biography* (London: Salvationist Publishing and Supplies, 1956), 22–23, and Jenty Fairbank, *Booth's Boots: The Beginnings of Salvation Army Social Work* (London: The Salvation Army, 1987), 49–51 for the circumstances surrounding Georgie's coming into the Booth family.

16. See Sandall, *The History of The Salvation Army,* 1:265–66; and Roger J. Green, *War on Two Fronts: The Redemptive Theology of William Booth* (Atlanta: The Salvation Army, 1989), 78–79.

17. The name was changed in 1870 to *The Christian Mission Magazine,* in 1879 to *The Salvationist,* and in 1880 to *The War Cry,* the name that is presently retained internationally by The Salvation Army.

18. Booth-Tucker, *The Life of Catherine Booth,* 1:626. See Jenty Fairbank, "The Power of the Army's Press," *The War Cry* (American) (April 29, 1995), 16–19.

19. Catherine Booth and William Booth, "Dedication," *The East London Evangelist* (October 1868): 1.

20. Begbie, *The Life of General William Booth,* 1:324–25. See Ervine, *God's Soldier,* 1:307, footnote: "There is an odd error in Mrs. Mumford's death certificate. She is described as a widow. Her husband, however, outlived her by ten years. He died on April 10, 1879. The cause of this error is not known, but it may be supposed that Mumford, because of his drunken habits, had not been living in the same house with his wife, although there was no formal separation, and that the person who gave notice of Mrs. Mumford's

death, one Emma Drain, was a stranger to the family, a nurse, perhaps, who concluded, because she had never seen Mr. Mumford, that her patient was a widow." See also Walker, "Pulling the Devil's Kingdom Down," 47. Neither Ervine nor Walker take into account that Mr. Mumford had been converted earlier under his daughter's ministry. His absence at this time is, however, inexplicable.

21. Booth-Tucker in *The Life of Catherine Booth* is careful to note the following about the proposed feeding program for this Mission station: "Connected with the People's Market was all the material for a large soup kitchen. This led to the first experiment in the direction of establishing depots for the sale of cheap food for the poor. Not having, however, the necessary capital with which to commence, nor a sufficient staff of workers to superintend the effort, and finding, moreover, that it interfered considerably with the ever-increasing claims of the spiritual operations of the Mission, it became evident that the hour had not yet come, and the attempt was accordingly abandoned. Nevertheless much valuable experience was gained, which was turned to good account in the subsequent inauguration of the Social Scheme upon a sound and promising basis" (1:658–59).

22. Glenn K. Horridge, *The Salvation Army: Origins and Early Days: 1865–1900* (Godalming, England: Ammonite Books, 1993), 18.

23. Catherine Booth, "The Uses of Trial," in *Papers on Practical Religion,* 201.

24. Booth-Tucker, *The Life of Catherine Booth,* 2:3.

25. Ibid.

26. Ervine, *God's Soldier,* 1:317.

27. "William Booth patterned the Annual Conferences of The Christian Mission from 1870 through 1878 after the Methodist model which had so frustrated him just a decade earlier. The Annual Conference was at the top of a hierarchy pyramid which moved downward to Quarterly Conferences in Circuits and Elders Meetings at Stations. The General Superintendent presided at the Annual Conference of the Mission, Circuit Superintendents at Quarterly Conferences, and Station Evangelists at the local Station. Annual Conference normally met the second Monday in June at 11:00 A.M. and was composed of the Headquarters staff, full-time evangelists (also known as the superintendents of Circuits), and two lay members from each Circuit. After the Conference approved the credentials of the delegates, it settled issues of organizational or doctrinal importance and voted on disciplinary rules" (Murdoch, "The Salvation Army: An Anglo-American Revivalist Social Mission," 182–83).

The first Conference was recorded as being held at The People's Mission Hall, 272 Whitechapel Road, London, from June 15–18, 1870. However, The Foundation Deed of 1875 is correct in listing November as the month when the first Conference was held. See Sandall, *The History of The Salvation Army,* 1:180.

28. Chadwick, *The Victorian Church,* 2:289.

29. Horridge, *The Salvation Army,* 27–28.

30. Sandall, *The History of The Salvation Army,* 1:181.

31. Minutes, First Conference of The Christian Mission, held at People's Mission Hall, 272 Whitechapel Road, London, June 15–17, 1870, microfilm collection, The Salvation Army Archives and Research Center, Alexandria, Virginia.

32. Sandall, *The History of The Salvation Army,* 1:271.

33. Horridge, *The Salvation Army,* 23.

34. Walker, "Pulling the Devil's Kingdom Down," 119. Walker notes the following in an endnote: "The pamphlet was published by Messrs. Morgan and Chase, editors of *The Revival.* Their decision to publish her pamphlet indicates that support for women's preaching was gaining ground among English evangelicals. In 1862, *The Revival* argued that nature and scripture forbade the practice and a reviewer commented that her 'caustic tone' did not dispose him to her. . . . By 1866 *The Revival* declared that women were

'bound by God' to preach and in 1870 Morgan and Chase published the pamphlet once deemed 'caustic'" (158).

35. Booth-Tucker, *The Life of Catherine Booth*, 2:143.

36. Begbie, *The Life of General William Booth*, 1:384.

37. For two biographies of Railton see Eileen Douglas and Mildred Duff, *Commissioner Railton* (London: The Salvationist Publishing and Supplies, 1920), and Bernard Watson, *Soldier Saint: George Scott Railton, William Booth's First Lieutenant* (London: Hodder and Stoughton, 1970). See also John D. Waldron, *G. S. R.: Selections from the Published and Unpublished Writings of George Scott Railton* (Oakville, Ontario, Canada: Triumph Press, 1981).

38. This is generally referred to as William's work. However, Booth-Tucker, in *The Life of Catherine Booth*, referring to this book speaks of "its authors" (2:14).

39. Watson, *Soldier Saint*, 33.

40. Ibid., 13.

41. Bramwell Booth, *Echoes and Memories* (London: Hodder and Stoughton, 1925), 178.

42. Sandall, *The History of The Salvation Army*, 1:168–69.

43. Booth-Tucker, *The Life of Catherine Booth*, 2:65.

44. Ibid., 81.

45. Ibid., 88.

46. Sandall, *The History of The Salvation Army*, 1:181.

47. Booth-Tucker, *The Life of Catherine Booth*, 2:146.

48. Ibid., 147.

49. Sandall, *The History of The Salvation Army*, 1:197.

50. Booth-Tucker, *The Life of Catherine Booth*, 1:326.

51. Ibid., 2:142.

52. Ibid., 2:151–52.

53. Horridge, *The Salvation Army*, 3.

54. Walker, "Pulling the Devil's Kingdom Down," 173–74.

55. Horridge, *The Salvation Army*, 20.

Chapter 7: *Mother of an Army*

1. Begbie, *The Life of General William Booth*, 1:367–68.

2. Booth-Tucker, *The Life of Catherine Booth*, 1:74.

3. See Stead, *General Booth*, 87–88. This is also Rack's assessment in *Reasonable Enthusiast*, 552.

4. Stead, *General Booth*, 13. For further consideration of this matter see the following: Begbie, *The Life of General William Booth*, 1:367–68; 2:74, 141, 170, 305; Booth-Tucker, *The Life of Catherine Booth*, 2:138, 164–68; Ervine, *God's Soldier*, 1:165; Norman H. Murdoch, "Wesleyan Influence on William and Catherine Booth," *Wesleyan Theological Journal* 20 (Fall 1985): 97–103; G. M. Trevelyan, *English Social History* (New York: David McKay Co., 1965), 569; and Wiggins, *The History of The Salvation Army*, 4:219.

5. Rack, *Reasonable Enthusiast*, 248.

6. Booth-Tucker, *The Life of Catherine Booth*, 2:139.

7. Ibid., 168.

8. Horridge, *The Salvation Army*, 33.

9. J. Hampson, *Memoirs of John Wesley*, 3 vols. (London: 1791), vol. 3, 200–1. Quoted in Rack, *Reasonable Enthusiast*, 541.

10. Watson, *Soldier Saint*, 39–40.

11. Sandall, *The History of The Salvation Army*, 1:202.

12. Booth-Tucker, *The Life of Catherine Booth*, 2:173.

13. George Scott Railton, *Heathen England* (London: The Salvation Army, 1891), 28–29.

14. Horridge, *The Salvation Army*, 36.

15. Ibid., 37.

16. Booth-Tucker, *The Life of Catherine Booth*, 2:175–76.

17. See Wesley's sermon "Causes of the Inefficacy of Christianity," in Baker, *The Works of John Wesley*, 4:93.

18. Booth-Tucker, *The Life of Catherine Booth*, 2:179.

19. Minutes, Eighth Conference of The Christian Mission, held at People's Mission Hall, 272 Whitechapel Road, London, August 3–8, 1878.

20. See John Wesley's sermon "On Working Out Our Own Salvation" in Baker, *The Works of John Wesley*, 3:204.

21. William Booth, "Holiness: An Address at the Conference," *The Christian Mission Magazine* (August 1877), 1. See John Kent's analysis of the relationship of American revivalists to the Booths' thinking about the doctrine of holiness in *Holding the Fort*, 325–40.

22. Sandall, *The History of The Salvation Army*, 2:16.

23. Booth-Tucker, *The Life of Catherine Booth*, 2:217.

24. Ibid., 184.

25. Walker, "Pulling the Devil's Kingdom Down," 123.

26. Ibid., 135–36.

27. Booth-Tucker, *The Life of Catherine Booth*, 2:227.

28. Sandall, *The History of The Salvation Army*, 2:338. See also Horridge, *The Salvation Army*, 38.

29. Booth-Tucker, *The Life of Catherine Booth*, 2:248.

30. Ibid., 249–50.

31. Ibid., 253–54.

32. Ibid., 254.

33. Ervine, *God's Soldier*, 1:486.

34. Booth-Tucker, *The Life of Catherine Booth*, 2:261.

35. Quoted in Sandall, *The History of The Salvation Army*, 2:9–10.

36. For Catherine Booth on spiritualism, see Booth-Tucker, *The Life of Catherine Booth*, 2:510–13. In an introduction to the American edition of Stead's biography of Catherine Booth, Frederick Booth-Tucker, at the time in charge of the work of The Salvation Army in America along with his wife Emma, wrote the following: "Mr. Stead has written freely and from his own view-point. While heartily recognizing the general faithfulness of the story, it will not be expected that we accept every deduction from the experiences of so eventful a life. With the author's views in regard to psychic phenomena we are bound to differ, but this in no way detracts from our appreciation of his brilliant and effective narrative."

37. In his biography of Catherine Booth, Stead mentions visiting Catherine in Clacton where she was dying. "I was down there helping General Booth as a kind of voluntary secretary and amanuensis in getting the MSS. of 'Darkest England' into shape" (Stead, *Mrs. Booth*, 211).

38. Victor Pierce Jones, *Saint or Sensationalist? The Story of W. T. Stead* (East Wittering, West Sussex, England: Gooday Publishers, 1988), 81.

Chapter 8: *An Army Advances*

1. Edward H. McKinley, *Marching to Glory: The History of The Salvation Army in the United States of America*, 1880–1980 (San Francisco: Harper and Row, 1980), 17.

2. Booth-Tucker, *The Life of Catherine Booth*, 2:274.

3. Sandall, *The History of The Salvation Army,* 2:245.

4. Ibid., 248.

5. Ibid., 29.

6. Ibid., 30.

7. Booth-Tucker, *The Life of Catherine Booth,* 2:299.

8. William Booth, "What Is The Salvation Army?" *The Contemporary Review* (August 1882), 180.

9. Horridge, *The Salvation Army,* 76.

10. Booth-Tucker, *The Life of Catherine Booth,* 2:300.

11. Ibid.

12. Ibid., 301. See also Catherine's chapter "Religious Indifference" in her book *Life and Death* (London: Salvationist Publishing and Supplies, 1883), 3–14.

13. Catherine Booth, "The Salvation Army and the Bishop of Carlisle," *The War Cry* (October 9, 1880), 1.

14. Catherine Booth, "The Salvation Army and the Bishop of Carlisle," *The War Cry* (October 16, 1880), 2.

15. Catherine Booth, "The Salvation Army and the Bishop of Carlisle," *The War Cry* (October 23, 1880), 1.

16. Catherine Booth, *Aggressive Christianity* (Boston: McDonald and Gill, 1883), 59–60.

17. David Rightmire, *Sacraments and The Salvation Army: Pneumatological Foundations* (Metuchen, N.J.: Scarecrow Press, 1990), 72–73.

18. Booth-Tucker, *The Life of Catherine Booth,* 2:314–15.

19. James Strahan, *The Marechale: Founder of The Salvation Army in France and Switzerland* (London: Jas Clarke and Co., 1924), 47–48. See also Carolyn Scott, *The Heavenly Witch: The Story of the Marechale* (London: Hamish Hamilton, 1981) for an interesting, if not always accurate, account of the life of young Catherine.

20. Booth-Tucker, *The Life of Catherine Booth,* 2:334.

21. Ibid., 361–62.

22. Sandall, *The History of The Salvation Army,* 2:264. See also "France: Mrs. Booth's Visit," *The War Cry* (November 16, 1882), 1; and "Mrs. Booth in Paris," *The War Cry* (November 16, 1882), 4.

23. Booth-Tucker, *The Life of Catherine Booth,* 2:405–6.

24. Ibid., 404–5.

25. Horridge, *The Salvation Army,* 178. Horridge inadvertently omitted from his list one of the Manchester corps with a seating capacity of 600.

26. This is Booth-Tucker's account of the beginning of the work in Sweden. Sandall tends to place more of the drive for opening the work in Sweden on Bramwell and William, while Booth-Tucker gives more credit to Catherine. Bramwell Booth relates primarily his own efforts in beginning the work in Scandinavia in *Echoes and Memories,* 96–103. Unfortunately the official biographies of William Booth give little attention to this important chapter in early Army history and to the role and the influence of women, including Catherine, in opening fire in Sweden.

27. Bramwell-Booth, *Catherine Booth,* 370–71.

28. Ibid., 371.

29. Ibid., 373.

30. John D. Waldron, *The Quakers and the Salvationists* (Atlanta: The Salvation Army, 1990), 46. See also "Mrs. Booth at the Friends' Yearly Meeting," *The War Cry* (July 13, 1882), 4; "Mrs. Booth at the Friends' Yearly Meeting," *The War Cry* (July 20, 1882), 2; and "Mrs. Booth at the Friends' Yearly Meeting," *The War Cry* (July 27, 1882), 4.

31. Booth-Tucker, *The Life of Catherine Booth,* 2:410–11.

32. See Carolyn Ocheltree, "Wesleyan Methodist Perceptions of William Booth," *Methodist History* 28 (July 1990): 262–76.

33. See Henry Edward Manning, "The Salvation Army," *The Contemporary Review* 41 (August 1882): 335–42. See also "Why Cardinal Manning Thinks the Army Valuable and Hopes for Good from It," *The War Cry* (September 7, 1882), 4.

34. Sandall, *The History of The Salvation Army,* 2:137.

35. Ibid., 139.

36. Ibid., 146.

37. Ibid.

38. Booth-Tucker, *The Life of Catherine Booth,* 2:427.

39. Bramwell Booth, *Echoes and Memories,* 74–75.

40. Ibid., 75.

41. Ervine, *God's Soldier,* 1:610–11.

42. Bramwell Booth, *Echoes and Memories,* 77.

43. Walker, "Pulling the Devil's Kingdom Down," 122–23.

44. Bramwell Booth, *Echoes and Memories,* 201–2.

45. Catherine Booth, *Godliness,* 133.

46. Bramwell Booth, *Echoes and Memories,* 202.

47. Catherine Booth, *Popular Christianity* (Chicago: The Christian Witness Co., 1887), 48–49. Here Catherine parts company with her beloved John Wesley who taught "The Duty of Constant Communion." See Wesley's sermon by that title in Baker, *The Works of John Wesley,* 3:427–39.

48. Rightmire, *Sacraments and The Salvation Army,* 196.

49. Walker, "Pulling the Devil's Kingdom Down," 123–24.

50. Horridge, *The Salvation Army,* 115–16.

51. *Order and Regulations for Soldiers of The Salvation Army* (1943), chapter IV, section 8.

52. William Booth, "Mrs. Booth," 506.

53. Booth-Tucker, *The Life of Catherine Booth,* 2:438–39.

54. Ibid., 451.

55. Ibid.

56. Catherine Booth, *Life and Death,* preface written from London in November 1883.

57. Catherine Booth, *Popular Christianity,* preface, 7, written from London in July 1887.

58. Frances Power Cobbe, "The Last Revival," *The Contemporary Review* (August 1882): 184–85.

59. Booth-Tucker, *The Life of Catherine Booth,* 2:407.

Chapter 9: *A National Crusade*

1. Frederick Coutts, *No Discharge in This War* (London: Hodder and Stoughton, 1974), 102.

2. For details of the intricacies of prostitution in Victorian England, and for some accounting of the Army's work with prostitutes, see Edward J. Bristow, *Vice and Vigilance: Purity Movements in England since 1700* (Dublin: Gill and Macmillan, 1977), and Judith R. Walkowitz, *Prostitution and Victorian Society: Women, Class, and the State* (Cambridge: Cambridge University Press, 1980).

3. Frederick Coutts, *Bread for My Neighbour: The Social Influence of William Booth* (London: Hodder and Stoughton, 1987), 46.

4. Cyril Barnes, *With Booth in London* (London: The Salvation Army, 1986), 31.

5. *The War Cry* (August 9, 1884), 5.

6. Ann R. Higginbotham, "Respectable Sinners: Salvation Army Rescue Work with

Unmarried Mothers, 1884–1914," in Gail Malmgreen, ed., *Religion in the Lives of English Women, 1760–1930* (Bloomington: Indiana University Press, 1986), 218. See also Walker, "Pulling the Devil's Kingdom Down," 149.

7. See Sandall, *The History of The Salvation Army,* 3:16. See also Higginbotham, "Respectable Sinners," 219–20 for a comparison of the work of the Army with other rescue groups working in London at this time. Higginbotham concludes that "few other organizations worked on the scale of The Salvation Army."

8. Coutts, *Bread for My Neighbour,* 47.

9. Bramwell Booth, *Echoes and Memories,* 151.

10. Booth-Tucker, *The Life of Catherine Booth,* 2:471.

11. Bramwell Booth, *Echoes and Memories,* 134.

12. Coutts, *Bread for My Neighbour,* 56.

13. Bramwell Booth, *Echoes and Memories,* 134.

14. Coutts, *Bread for My Neighbour,* 51.

15. Jones, *Saint or Sensationalist?,* 26.

16. Coutts, *No Discharge in This War,* 108. George Bernard Shaw would have a continued interest in this case, and he used the Eliza Armstrong case "as the basis for his play *Pygmalion,* later the musical *My Fair Lady.* Liza Armstrong and Liza Dolittle both came from Lisson Grove" (Jones, *Saint or Sensationalist?,* 43).

17. Catherine Booth, *The Iniquity of State Regulated Vice,* published in London in 1884. Typed copy only in British Museum Catalogue 3275–AA2 (26) 6 (4), 10–11.

18. A transcript of the letter from Catherine Booth to Queen Victoria, Thursday, June 3, 1885, is in The Salvation Army International Heritage Centre, London, England. A copy of this letter as well as the queen's reply were printed in *The War Cry* (July 22, 1885), 1. The two lead articles on the front page of that edition of *The War Cry* were titled "Modern Babylon. The Protection of Young Girls. Salvation Army Meeting in the Prince's Hall, Piccadilly," and "The Horrible Immorality of London. Salvation Army Indignation Mass Meeting at Exeter Hall. A Solemn Appeal to the Country. Great Britain's Appeal to the Queen."

19. The Dowager Duchess of Roxburgh to Catherine Booth, June 6, 1885, in The Salvation Army International Heritage Centre.

20. A transcript of the letter from Catherine Booth to Queen Victoria, July 14, 1885, is in The Salvation Army International Heritage Centre. See also *The War Cry* (August 5, 1885), 1. Again, the titles of the lead stories of that edition on the first page indicate the continuation of the battle on the part of the Army. The articles were titled "The Tragedy of Modern Babylon," and "Protection of Young Girls."

21. The Dowager Marchioness of Ely to Catherine Booth, July 22, 1885, in The Salvation Army International Heritage Centre. See also *The War Cry* (August 5, 1885), 1.

22. Catherine Booth to the Dowager Marchioness of Ely, July 22, 1885, in The Salvation Army International Heritage Centre.

23. This letter is in The Salvation Army International Heritage Centre, dated simply July [1885].

24. Booth-Tucker, *The Life of Catherine Booth,* 2:479.

25. Ibid., 480.

26. Ibid., 481. These meetings were well publicized and reported in *The War Cry.* See "Mrs. Booth on the Revelations Made by the 'Pall Mall Gazette.' A Meeting Convened by The Salvation Army at Prince's Hall," *The War Cry* (July 18, 1885), 1. That issue also contained a letter from William Booth on the same subject titled "Giant Killing—Where Are the Davids?" See also "Modern Babylon. The Protection of Young Girls. Salvation Army Meeting in the Prince's Hall, Piccadilly. Samuel Morley, Esq., M.P. in the Chair. Speeches by Mrs. Booth, Mrs. Josephine Butler, and Professor Stuart, M.P.," *The War*

Cry (July 22, 1885), 1; "The Horrible Immorality of London. Salvation Army Indignation Mass Meeting at Exeter Hall," *The War Cry* (July 22, 1885), 1; "Immorality: The Recent Disclosures. Great Agitation Demonstration in the Free Trade Hall, Manchester," *The War Cry* (July 25, 1885), 1; the General's letter in this same edition titled "Misery-Strippers," 1; "Protection of Young Girls. Great Mass Meeting of Women in Exeter Hall. Held by Mrs. Booth," *The War Cry* (July 29, 1885), 1; "The Recent Revelations. The General at the Albert Hall, Sheffield," *The War Cry* (July 29, 1885), 1; "Mrs. Josephine Butler on the Protection of Young Girls," *The War Cry* (July 29, 1885), 1; "The Horrible Immorality of London. Mass Meeting of Women at Exeter Hall. Speech by Mrs. Booth," *The War Cry* (August 1, 1885), 1; "The Tragedy of Modern Babylon. Great Meeting at Clapton Congress Hall. Second Letter from the Queen. Speeches by the General, Prof. Stuart, M.P., and Mrs. Booth," *The War Cry* (August 5, 1885), 1; "New National Scheme for the Deliverance of Unprotected Girls and the Rescue of the Fallen," *The War Cry* (August 8, 1885), 1–2; and "Protection of Young Girls. Mrs. Booth at Portsmouth," in that same issue, 2. There were similar accounts in following *War Crys* as well as speeches by William Booth in Leeds, Portsmouth, and Newcastle-Upon-Tyne.

27. The petition was first announced in *The War Cry* (July 18, 1885), 1: "Special Notice! Protection of Young Girls." The notice read, "A PETITION to the HOUSE OF COMMONS for the above purpose will lie for Signature at the various Corps throughout the country, for the next few days. All Officers and Soldiers are earnestly desired to sign it and obtain as large a number of Signatures as possible, and forward the sheets, when full, to Headquarters, 101 Queen Victoria Street, E. C."

28. Coutts, *Bread for My Neighbour,* 54–55. See also *The War Cry* (August 8, 1885), 1–2, for a full account of this event.

29. "The Salvation Army's Petition to the Government," *The War Cry* (July 25, 1885), 1.

30. Coutts, *No Discharge in This War,* 110.

31. Coutts, *Bread for My Neighbour,* 55.

32. Ibid., 57.

33. Bramwell Booth, *Echoes and Memories,* 135.

34. Ibid., 137.

35. W. T. Stead, "Why I Went to Prison," *Penny Illustrated Paper* (November 19, 1910), 651, in The Salvation Army International Heritage Centre.

36. Ibid.

37. See for example "The Armstrong Case," *The War Cry* (September 16, 1885), 1; "Mrs. Josephine Butler on the Armstrong Trial," *The War Cry* (October 7, 1885), 1; "The Government Prosecution of Mr. Stead and Others," *The War Cry* (October 7, 1885), 1; and "The Armstrong Prosecution," *The War Cry* (October 17, 1885), 1.

38. "Letter from the Chief-of-Staff," *The War Cry* (October 7, 1885), 1.

39. Coutts, *Bread for My Neighbour,* 59–60.

40. Catherine Booth to Queen Victoria, in The Salvation Army International Heritage Centre.

41. The Salvation Army International Heritage Centre.

42. Booth-Tucker, *The Life of Catherine Booth,* 2:496.

43. Bramwell Booth, *Echoes and Memories,* 152.

44. Coutts, *No Discharge in This War,* 111.

45. Bramwell Booth, *Echoes and Memories,* 139–40.

46. "W. T. Stead at the Congress Hall," *The War Cry* (February 3, 1886), 2.

47. Jones, *Saint or Sensationalist?,* 34.

48. Ibid., 31.

49. Walker, "Pulling the Devil's Kingdom Down," 155.

50. Higginbotham, "Respectable Sinners," 217.

51. See the preface in William Booth, *In Darkest England and the Way Out* (London: International Headquarters, 1890). However, see also Stead's own words in "'In Darkest England' Entirely the General's Own," *The War Cry* (January 10, 1891), 7.

52. Ervine, *God's Soldier,* 2:657.

53. Raymond Caddy, "Co-Founder (Catherine Booth and The Salvation Army)" in Kew, ed., *Catherine Booth: Her Continuing Relevance,* 129.

54. William T. Stead, "The Late Mrs. Booth," *The War Cry* (October 11, 1890), 8.

55. Booth-Tucker, *The Life of Catherine Booth,* 2:489–90.

56. Ibid., 502.

57. William Booth, *In Darkest England and the Way Out,* preface, 4.

58. "'Mrs. Booth's Address' at the Anglo-Indian Wedding," *The War Cry* (April 21, 1888), 10.

59. See Watson, *Soldier Saint,* chap. 17.

60. "New General and His Plans," *Daily News and Leader,* September 2, 1912.

61. Barbara Bolton, "A Denouncer of Iniquity (Catherine Booth and Social Justice)," in Kew, ed. *Catherine Booth: Her Continuing Relevance,* 145.

62. "Mrs. Booth's Last Public Address (continued)," *The War Cry* (October 25, 1890), 9–10. See also "Mrs. Booth at the City Temple," *The War Cry* (June 30, 1888), 9.

63. Booth-Tucker, *The Life of Catherine Booth,* 1:232–33.

64. "'Mrs. Booth's Address' at the Anglo-Indian Wedding," 10.

65. Booth-Tucker, *The Life of Catherine Booth,* 2:546.

66. Ibid.

67. Ibid.

68. Ibid.

69. Ibid., 549.

Chapter 10: *On Dying and Death*

1. Booth-Tucker, *The Life of Catherine Booth,* 2:562–63. Ervine repeats this account, and largely quotes from this source in *God's Soldier,* 2:671–72. See also "The Army Mother: An Interview with the General," *The War Cry* (October 8, 1910), 9.

2. "'Mrs. Booth's Address' at the Anglo-Indian Wedding," 10. The heading to Catherine's speech read, "Mrs. Booth is presented and speaks with a power and vigor which astonishes all who know her present condition of health."

3. Booth-Tucker, *The Life of Catherine Booth,* 2:586.

4. Ibid., 588.

5. Wiggins, *The History of The Salvation Army,* 4:237.

6. "'Mrs. Booth to the Front Again' at Grand Celebration of the General's Sixtieth Birthday," *The War Cry* (April 20, 1889), 3.

7. Wiggins, *The History of The Salvation Army,* 4:302.

8. Ibid.

9. Booth-Tucker, *The Life of Catherine Booth,* 2:600.

10. Ibid., 607.

11. Stead, *Mrs. Booth,* 209.

12. Rack, *Reasonable Enthusiast,* 429.

13. Catherine always demonstrated great affection for her servants. She took Wesley's injunction seriously—"Your servants of whatever kind you are to look upon as a kind of secondary children" ("On Family Religion" in Baker, *The Works of John Wesley,* 3:338).

14. Booth-Tucker, *The Life of Catherine Booth,* 2:625.

15. Ibid., 633–34.

16. Stead, *Mrs. Booth,* 211–12.

17. "Mrs. Booth's Condition," *All The World* (January 1890), 46.

18. "Mrs. Booth's Latest Address," *All The World* (March 1890), 120.

19. Ibid.

20. "'Mrs. Booth's Address' at the Anglo-Indian Wedding," 10.

21. I am indebted to Mrs. Lt.-Colonel Roy M. Oldford for giving me a copy of this letter, as well as a copy of a letter from William Booth to Polly Ashton. The original letters were found by Mrs. Oldford at The Salvation Army U.S.A. Eastern Territorial School for Officers' Training while Colonel and Mrs. Oldford were stationed there.

22. "Have You Been a Self-Denier?" *The War Cry* (October 4, 1890), 1.

23. Catherine Baird, "Home to Thee," *Reflections* (London: Salvationist Publishing and Supplies, 1975), 28.

24. Booth-Tucker, *The Life of Catherine Booth,* 2:643.

25. William Booth, "Home at Last: To the Officers and Soldiers of The Salvation Army," *The War Cry* (October 11, 1890), 1.

26. Quoted in *The War Cry* (October 18, 1890), 4.

27. "The Mother of The Salvation Army," *The Methodist Times* (October 9, 1890), 1.

28. Dr. Joseph Parker, "A Tribute to Mrs. Booth," *The War Cry* (October 11, 1890), 8.

29. Booth-Tucker, *The Life of Catherine Booth,* 2:646. See also "Till the Resurrection Morning!" *The War Cry* (October 25, 1890), 1–2; and "Mrs. Booth's Funeral Services," *All The World* (November 1890), 538–40.

30. "Till the Resurrection Morning!" 1.

31. Booth-Tucker, *The Life of Catherine Booth,* 2:656–57.

32. "The Army's Warrior Mother," *The War Cry* (October 25, 1890), 5–6.

33. Ibid, 6.

34. Ibid.

35. Wiggins, *The History of The Salvation Army,* 4:306.

36. See the following articles about Catherine Booth: William Booth, "Mrs. Booth," 505–10; Bramwell Booth, "Mrs. Booth and Her Army Family," *All The World* (December 1890), 594–97; Bramwell Booth, "Catherine Booth: After Ten Years," *All The World* (October 1900), 563–69; Bramwell Booth, "Mrs. General Booth: A Retrospect," *All The World* (October 1910), 515–19; Mrs. Bramwell Booth, "Recollections of Mrs. General Booth," *All The World* (October 1910), 534–36; Consul Mrs. Booth-Tucker, "My Mother," *The Conqueror* (October 1896), 453–55; Evangeline Booth, "Memories," *Social News* (October 1915), 2; Evangeline Booth, "My Mother," *The Officer* (November-December, 1922), 404–5; Commissioner Mrs. Booth-Hellberg, "My Mother," *All The World* (October 1910), 549–52; T. H. Kitching, "William and Catherine Booth as I Knew Them," *The Officer* (February 1929), 141–45; David C. Lamb, "Catherine Booth" in R. S. Forman, ed., *Great Christians* (London: Ivor Nicholson and Watson, 1933), 53–66; George Scott Railton, "The Empty Chair," *All The World* (November 1890), 536–37; Mrs. Commissioner Railton, "A Personal Remembrance of Our Army Mother," *All The World* (October 1900), 594–96; Lt.-Commissioner Unsworth, "Our Army Mother," *The Officer* (May 1923), 385–88.

Bibliographic Essay

I hope that the works cited in the notes will lead the serious student to further studies in the life and ministry of Catherine Booth, as well as in the life and ministry of William Booth and the history of The Salvation Army. Those books and articles, both primary and secondary, will, I trust, bring light to the subject at hand and be useful for continued study. Many of those books and articles also provide helpful bibliographies or footnote references.

In addition to the notes, I am providing here some suggestions to both supplement and explain the references in the text. These may be found in The Salvation Army's International Heritage Centre in London, England, or in The Salvation Army's Archives and Research Center in Alexandria, Virginia. The Booth Papers referred to in this book are in the manuscripts room of the British Library.

Helpful as an overall source, although outdated now, is R. G. Moyles, *A Bibliography of Salvation Army Literature in English (1865–1987)* (Lewiston, N.Y.: Edwin Mellon Press, 1988). The best sources for a general history of The Salvation Army are the following: A seven-volume *History of The Salvation Army*, Sandall, vols. 1, 2, and 3; Wiggins, vols. 4, 5; Coutts, vols. 6, 7 (London: Nelson and Hodder and Stoughton, 1947–1986), begins with the founding of The Christian Mission in 1865 and continues through the 1970s; Frederick Coutts, *Bread for My Neighbour* (London: Hodder and Stoughton, 1978); Frederick Coutts,

No Discharge in This War (London: Hodder and Stoughton, 1974). Older, but interesting, works are George Scott Railton, *Heathen England* (London: S. and W. Partridge, 1877), and George Scott Railton, *Twenty-One Year's Salvation Army* (London: The Salvation Army, 1886). Helpful also are Bramwell Booth, *Echoes and Memories* (London: The Salvation Army, 1925), and Bramwell Booth, *These Fifty Years* (London: Cassell, 1929). Two excellent contemporary sources are Glenn K. Horridge, *The Salvation Army Origins and Early Days: 1865–1900* (Godalming, England: Ammonite Books, 1993), and Norman H. Murdoch, *Origins of The Salvation Army* (Knoxville: University of Tennessee Press, 1994), although some of Professor Murdoch's conclusions are debatable. See also the many references to The Salvation Army in K. S. Inglis, *Churches and the Working Classes in Victorian England* (Toronto: University of Toronto Press, 1963), and Norris Magnuson, *Salvation in the Slums: Evangelical Social Work 1865–1920* (Grand Rapids: Baker, 1990). *Christian History,* issue 26, vol. 9, no. 2, devoted the entire issue to The Salvation Army. The best source for the history of The Salvation Army in America is by Edward H. McKinley, *Marching to Glory: The History of The Salvation Army in the United States of America, 1880–1980* (San Francisco: Harper and Row, 1980). The many Salvation Army periodicals referred to in this work are helpful, but see especially *The East London Evangelist* (1868–1869); *The Christian Mission Magazine* (1870–1878); *The Salvationist* (1879); and *The War Cry* (published since December 27, 1879). Almost all references in this biography are to the English *War Cry,* although there are several national editions of this publication.

There has been considerable research on The Salvation Army since the 1960s, some of which has been produced in doctoral dissertations. Among these are Norman H. Murdoch, "The Salvation Army: An Anglo-American Revivalist Social Mission" (Ph.D. diss., University of Cincinnati, 1985), now published as *Origins of The Salvation Army,* and mentioned above; John R. Rhemick, "The Theology of a Movement: The Salvation Army in Its Formative Years" (Ph.D. diss., Northwestern University, 1984), now published as *A New People of God: A Study in Salvationism* (Chicago: The Salvation Army, 1994); R. David Rightmire, *Sacraments and The Salvation Army: Pneumatological Foundations* (Metuchen, N.J.: Scarecrow Press, 1990); and Pamela J. Walker, "Pulling the Devil's Kingdom Down: Gender and Popular Culture in The Salvation Army, 1865–1895" (Ph.D. diss., Rutgers, The State University of New Jersey, New Brunswick, 1992). Four books that are particularly helpful with background for The Salvation Army and the Booths are Richard Carwardine, *Transatlantic Revivalism: Popular Evangelicalism in Britain and America, 1790–1865* (Westport, Conn.: Greenwood Press, 1978); Owen Chadwick, *The Victorian Church*, 2 vols. (London: SCM Press Ltd., 1987); John Kent, *Holding the Fort: Studies in Victorian Revivalism* (London: Epworth Press, 1978); and Donald M. Lewis, *Lighten Their Darkness: The Evangelical Mission to Working-Class London, 1828–1860* (Westport, Conn.: Greenwood Press, 1986).

Many people influenced the thinking of both Catherine and William Booth, so to understand these people is to understand the Booths. For a biography of John Wesley, see Henry D. Rack, *Reasonable Enthusiast: John Wesley and the Rise of Methodism* (Philadelphia: Trinity Press International, 1989). For Charles Wesley, see Arnold A. Dallimore, *A Heart Set Free: The Life of Charles Wesley* (Westchester, Ill.: Crossway Books, 1988). For Charles Grandison Finney, see Keith J. Hardman, *Charles Grandison Finney, 1792–1875: Revivalist and Reformer* (Grand Rapids: Baker, 1990), and my article on Finney, "Charles Grandison Finney: The Social Implications of His Ministry," *The Asbury Theological Journal* 48:2 (Fall 1993): 5–26. For James Caughey, see the work mentioned previously by Richard Carwardine, *Transatlantic Revivalism: Popular Evangelicalism in Britain and America, 1790–1865*. For Phoebe Palmer, see Harold E. Raser, *Phoebe Palmer: Her Life and Thought* (Lewiston, N. Y.: Edwin Mellon Press, 1987). And for W. T. Stead, see Victor Pierce Jones, *Saint or Sensationalist? The Story of W. T. Stead* (East Wittering, West Sussex, England: Gooday Publishers, 1988).

There are several biographies of William Booth. Two earlier works are by George Scott Railton, *The Authoritative Life of General William Booth Founder of The Salvation Army* (New York: Reliance Trading Co., 1912); and W. T. Stead, *General Booth* (London: Isbister and Company Limited, 1891). Two of the standard, widely used biographies are Harold Begbie, *Life of General William Booth*, 2 vols. (New York: Macmillan, 1920), and St. John Ervine, *God's Soldier: General William Booth* (New York: Macmillan, 1934). Ervine is at times critical of Begbie as well as of one of Catherine Booth's biographers, Frederick Booth-Tucker. Ervine, generally, provides keener insight into the life and times of William Booth, although he can be jaundiced where Begbie and Booth-Tucker saw few faults in their subjects. William Booth wrote voluminously; here's a sampling of his writings: *How to Reach the Masses with the Gospel* (London: Marshall, Morgan, Chase, and Scott, 1872); *In Darkest England and the Way Out* (London: The Salvation Army, 1890); and his best work, *Purity of Heart* (London: Salvation Army Book Room, 1902). See also William Booth's article "What Is The Salvation Army?" *The Contemporary Review* 42 (August 1882): 175–82. From August to October 1882 that journal also published assessments of William Booth and The Salvation Army by Randall T. Davidson, Frances Power Cobb, and Cardinal Manning. For two divergent assessments of William Booth's social scheme, see my article "Theological Roots of *In Darkest England and the Way Out*" in *Wesleyan Theological Journal* 25:1 (Spring 1990): 83–105, and Norman H. Murdoch, "William Booth's *In Darkest England and the Way Out*: A Reappraisal" in the same issue of *Wesleyan Theological Journal*, 106–16. See also my article, "An Historical Salvation Army Perspective," in John D. Waldron, ed. *Creed and Deed: Toward a Christian Theology of Social Services in The Salvation Army* (Oakville, Ontario, Canada: Triumph Press, 1986). See also my book on the theology of William

Booth, *War on Two Fronts: The Redemptive Theology of William Booth* (Atlanta: The Salvation Army, 1989).

The best way to study the members of the Booth family is to read the many biographies that have been written about several of them. A partial list is provided here, which will also lead the reader to a study of the writings of this prolific family, should that be of interest. For Bramwell Booth (the eldest Booth son), see Catherine Bramwell-Booth, *Bramwell Booth* (London: Rich and Cowan, 1933); for Catherine Booth (the eldest Booth daughter), see Carolyn Scott, *The Heavenly Witch: The Story of the Maréchale* (London: Hamish Hamilton, 1981); and James Strahan, *The Maréchale* (New York: Doran and Co., 1914). For Emma Booth (the second Booth daughter), see Frederick de Latour Booth-Tucker, *The Consul* (London: Salvation Army Publishing Department, 1903). For Evangeline Booth (the fourth Booth daughter), see Margaret Troutt, *The General Was a Lady: The Story of Evangeline Booth* (Nashville: Holman, 1980); and Peter W. Wilson, *General Evangeline Booth of The Salvation Army* (New York: Scribner's, 1948). For Herbert Booth (the third Booth son), see Ford C. Ottman, *Herbert Booth* (New York: Doubleday, 1928). Helpful, also, may be the most recent biography of Frederick Booth-Tucker by Harry Williams, *Booth-Tucker: William Booth's First Gentleman* (London: Hodder and Stoughton, 1980). Finally, although not a member of the Booth family, George Scott Railton is critical to the theological development of The Christian Mission and The Salvation Army. Two biographies may prove helpful: Eileen Douglas and Mildred Duff, *Commissioner Railton* (London: Salvationist Publishing and Supplies, 1920); and Bernard Watson, *Soldier Saint* (London: Hodder and Stoughton, 1970).

This leads to an assessment of the voluminous material written by and about Catherine Mumford Booth, cofounder of The Salvation Army. Let's start with the three major biographies of Catherine Booth. The first deserving mention is that written by her son-in-law Frederick de Latour Booth-Tucker, *The Life of Catherine Booth: The Mother of The Salvation Army*, 2 vols.

(New York: Revell, 1892; London: The Salvation Army, 1893), and the abridged version, *The Short Life of Catherine Booth* (London: The Salvation Army, 1893; 1912). Booth-Tucker is needlessly wordy, and many of St. John Ervine's criticisms of this biography are deserved. Also, there are many inaccuracies in quoting from the original letters of Catherine Booth and from other sources in this biography. Its chief value is the chronology of Catherine's life. The second of the major biographies is Catherine Bramwell-Booth's *Catherine Booth: The Story of Her Loves* (London: Hodder and Stoughton, 1970), written by Catherine Booth's granddaughter. There are some good insights here, and this is a good supplement to the Booth-Tucker biography. Chronologically, however, this book is confusing. Also, like the Booth-Tucker biography, there is no critical analysis here, only praise. Third is W. T. Stead's *Mrs. Booth of The Salvation Army* (London: James Nisbet and Co., 1900). Although Stead admired Catherine greatly, he does not hesitate to criticize her. His last chapter, "Death and Afterward," is strange indeed, especially in his estimation of Catherine Booth as psychic.

There are many briefer biographies of Catherine Booth, such as Jennie Chappell, *Four Noble Women and Their Work* (London: S. and W. Partridge and Co., 1898); Mildred Duff, *Catherine Booth: A Sketch* (London: The Salvation Army Book Department, 1914); Jenty Fairbank, *William and Catherine Booth: God's Soldiers* (London: Salvationist Publishing and Supplies, 1974); Carvoso Gauntlett, *Queen of Protests: Catherine Booth* (London: Salvationist Publishing and Supplies, 1946); Joan Metcalf, *God Used a Woman* (London: Salvationist Publishing and Supplies, 1967); and Cyril H. Powell, *Catherine Booth* (London: Epworth Press, 1951). See also Bramwell Booth, *On the Banks of the River: Being a Brief History of the Last Days of Mrs. General Booth* (London: The Salvation Army, 1894).

See also articles on Catherine Booth, such as Carvoso Gauntlett, "The Army Mother in the Estimation of Outsiders," *The Staff Review* (January 1929): 5–12; "Catherine Booth: Cofounder of The Salvation Army," in Nancy Hardesty, *Great*

Women of Faith: The Strength and Influence of Christian Women (Grand Rapids: Baker, 1980), 103–7; Norman H. Murdoch, "Female Ministry in the Thought and Work of Catherine Booth," *Church History,* vol. 53 (Fall 1984): 348–62; "Catherine Booth and The Salvation Army," in Ruth A. Tucker and Walter Liefeld, *Daughters of the Church: Women and Ministry from New Testament Times to the Present* (Grand Rapids: Zondervan, 1987), 264–67; John Waldron, "Catherine Booth," *Holiness Digest* (Fall 1989): 10–11; and Pamela J. Walker, "Proclaiming Women's Right to Preach," *Harvard Divinity Bulletin,* vol. 23, no. 3/4 (1994): 20–23, 35. I have written many articles about Catherine Booth, but the most extensive one is "Settled Views: Catherine Booth and Female Ministry," *Methodist History,* vol. 31, no. 3 (April 1993): 131–47. Two other sources make frequent references to Catherine Booth: Donald W. Dayton, *Discovering an Evangelical Heritage* (New York: Harper and Row, 1976); and Nancy A. Hardesty, *Women Called to Witness: Evangelical Feminism in the 19th Century* (Nashville: Abingdon Press, 1984). For an excellent contemporary analysis of Catherine Booth by The Salvation Army, written on the hundredth anniversary of her promotion to glory, see Clifford W. Kew, ed., *Catherine Booth: Her Continuing Relevance* (London: The Salvation Army, 1990).

As one can see in this biography, Catherine Booth wrote voluminously for many Christian Mission and Salvation Army publications. These contained several of her speeches given on various occasions, usually either at Christian Mission or Salvation Army gatherings or at various places in the West End of London. I will mention first some of her published pamphlets and then her books. In terms of her pamphlets see, *Female Ministry; or Women's Right to Preach the Gospel* (London: The Salvation Army, 1909; New York: The Salvation Army, 1975); *Heart Backsliding* (London: The Salvation Army, n.d.); *Holiness, Being An Address Delivered in St. James's Hall, Piccadilly, London* (London: The Salvation Army, 1887); *The Mother of The Salvation Army* (two addresses published after her death): first, *An Address*

327

to the Society of Friends, 1882 (London: Edward Hicks, Bishopsgate, 1890), and Strong Drink Versus Christianity, 1874 (London: National Temperance Publications, 1891); Mrs. Booth on Recent Criticisms of The Salvation Army (London: The Salvation Army, 1882); Repentance: A Sermon Preached in St. Andrew's Hall, London (London: The Salvation Army, n.d.); The Training of Children, and Courtship and Marriage (London: Salvationist Publishing and Supplies, 1953, reprint of the original).

Catherine Booth's major books, often compilations of her articles and speeches, are as follows: Aggressive Christianity (London: The Salvation Army, 1880); Godliness (London: The Salvation Army, 1881); The Highway of Our God (London: Salvationist Publishing and Supplies, 1954); Life and Death (London: The Salvation Army, 1888); Popular Christianity (London: The Salvation Army, 1887); Practical Religion (London: The Salvation Army, 1884); and The Salvation Army in Relation to Church and State (London: The Salvation Army, 1889). The first edition only of these books has been mentioned. There were several subsequent editions of most of these works.

These sources, as well as others referred to in the bibliographies of many of the books mentioned here, are invaluable for those wishing to pursue further studies. May those who give themselves to such work discover the rewards in the research that this writer has found.

Index

Roger J. Green is professor and chair of biblical and theological studies at Gordon College in Wenham, Massachusetts. He also holds the Terrelle B. Crum Chair of Humanities at Gordon College. He is the son of Salvation Army officer parents and is active as a layperson in the ministry of The Salvation Army around the world. He has written *War on Two Fronts: The Redemptive Theology of William Booth* and several articles on the Booths and The Salvation Army.